Approaches to Healing in Roman Egypt

Jane Draycott

BAR International Series 2416
2012

Published in 2016 by
BAR Publishing, Oxford

BAR International Series 2416

Approaches to Healing in Roman Egypt

ISBN 978 1 4073 1014 5

COVER IMAGE *A lamp depicting a healing shrine, perhaps the Serapeum at Canopus.*
© British Museum Inv. 1893.1114.1

BAR Publishing is the trading name of British Archaeological Reports (Oxford) Ltd.
British Archaeological Reports was first incorporated in 1974 to publish the BAR
Series, International and British. In 1992 Hadrian Books Ltd became part of the BAR
group. This volume was originally published by Archaeopress in conjunction with
British Archaeological Reports (Oxford) Ltd / Hadrian Books Ltd, the Series principal
publisher, in 2012. This present volume is published by BAR Publishing, 2016.

Printed in England

BAR
PUBLISHING

BAR titles are available from:

       BAR Publishing
       122 Banbury Rd, Oxford, OX2 7BP, UK
EMAIL   info@barpublishing.com
PHONE +44 (0)1865 310431
  FAX   +44 (0)1865 316916
       www.barpublishing.com

CONTENTS

ACKNOWLEDGEMENTS

I would like to thank my doctoral supervisors Dr Mark Bradley and Dr Doug Lee for all the advice, help and support that they have both given me over the last three years, and my examiners Dr Patty Baker and Dr Andreas Kropp for their constructive criticism of my work.

I would like to thank the School of Humanities at the University of Nottingham for awarding me a Fees Bursary to assist with the cost of my second and third years of study, and also the Sir Richard Stapley Educational Trust, the Gilchrist Educational Trust, and the Access to Learning Fund for additional financial support, without which I would have been unable to complete my studies.

I would like to thank the Classical Association, the British Pharmacological Society's W. D. M. Paton Fund, the Society for the Promotion of Hellenic Studies, the University of Nottingham's Graduate School, the Fondation Hardt pour l'Étude de l'Antiquité Classique, the Scientific Instrument Society, the Association for the History of Glass, and the Wellcome Trust for the many research grants and bursaries that I have been awarded at various points over the last three years.

I would also like to thank the Faculty of Archaeology, History and Letters of the British School at Rome for awarding me a Rome Fellowship for the period 2011-12, during which time I was able to undertake the task of adapting my doctoral thesis into this monograph.

Finally - and most importantly - I would like to thank my partner Oliver Boyce, to whom this work is dedicated.

ABBREVIATIONS

Abbreviations of ancient literary texts follow those listed in the *Oxford Classical Dictionary* (third edition) (e.g. Plin. *HN*), and if an ancient literary text is not listed in the *OCD*, its author and title are given in full (e.g. Strabo, *Geographica*), with the exception of the many works of the Galenic corpus, where standard Galenic abbreviations are used (e.g. Gal. *SMT*).

Abbreviations of ancient documentary texts follow those listed in the *Checklist of Editions of Greek, Latin, Demotic, and Coptic Papyri, Ostraca and Tablets* (e.g. *P. Oxy.*). However, not all the papyri cited are included in the Checklist and for those that are missing, its format has been followed (e.g. *P. Vindob.* 6257, *A Medical Book from Crocodilopolis*). The magical papyri are an exception to this general rule. They are abbreviated as *PGM* (Greek magical papyri) and *PDM* (Demotic magical papyri) respectively, following the system used by H. D. Betz (ed.) (1997) *The Greek Magical Papyri in Translation, Including the Demotic Spells* (Chicago).

ILLUSTRATIONS

Not even the woods and wilder face of Nature are without medicines, for there is no place where that holy Mother of all things did not distribute remedies for the healing of mankind, so that even the very desert was made a drug store…Such things alone had Nature decreed should be our remedies, provided everywhere, easy to discover and costing nothing - the things in fact that support our life. Later on the deceit of men and cunning profiteering led to the invention of the quack laboratories, in which each customer is promised a new lease of his own life at a price. At once compound prescriptions and mysterious mixtures are glibly repeated, Arabia and India are judged to be storehouses of remedies, and a small sore is charged with the cost of medicine from the Red Sea, although the genuine remedies form the daily dinner of even the very poorest. But if remedies were to be sought in the kitchen-garden, or a plant or a shrub was to be procured from there, none of the arts would come cheaper than medicine.[1]

Pliny the Elder's *Natural History* has been described as both a cultural artefact and 'an unparalleled guide to the cultural systems which the ancient Romans used to understand their world'.[2] On display here are some (possibly even the most influential) of the discourses that informed ancient Roman approaches to medicine and medical practice, at least as far as members of the Roman political, social and intellectual elite were concerned.

One of these discourses was that Roman expansion and imperialism had a significant impact upon the *ars medicinae*. Simple medicaments and ingredients for more complicated preparations could be harvested at the furthest reaches of the Roman Empire or even beyond, and brought from this periphery to the centre where they were utilised enthusiastically by the inhabitants of the city of Rome. As Pliny eloquently demonstrates, this recognition of the exotic origins of much popular *materia medica* also formed part of the discourse against *luxuria* and the processes by which items became luxuries: when tracked down to their sources, luxury items like amber, frankincense and Tyrrhenian purple dye were found to have rather humble (even ignoble) origins, and it was only the vast distances that they had travelled to get to Rome that made them so very desirable.[3] However, also present is a succinct acknowledgement of the inherent

conflict between professionalised medical practice and alternative healing strategies.

These discourses are not unique to Pliny, but are found in the works of numerous other ancient writers.[4] They in turn have influenced the development of the study of ancient medicine and its division into the categories of 'high' and 'low' by scholars:

> 'High' medicine was the rational, theoretical approach to treating patients, the supreme example of which was Galen. 'Low' medicine, in contrast, was almost akin to folk medicine, of the sort found in abundance in Pliny's *Natural History*, and was characterised by a practical, cure-based approach to healing. This latter system was undoubtedly more commonly found among the lower classes, which had neither the means to contract and pay for a 'professional' doctor nor the education to practice 'high' medicine themselves.[5]

As a result, the discipline has tended (either purposefully or inadvertently) to focus on 'high' medicine and medical practice located primarily in the urban centres, as undertaken by 'professional' medical practitioners who either disregard or actively denigrate alternative healing strategies such as 'folk' medicine, magic or religion and those who practise them.[6] This has led to the assumption that medicine and medical practice were consistent throughout the Roman Empire.[7] Attempts to redress this imbalance were initially met with resistance, as exemplified by Plinio Prioreschi's identification of the 'clash between the more disciplined thinking and the less so':

> Some historians of medicine (usually among those who, not being physicians, are not familiar with medical science), in a desperate attempt to show that medicine played a secondary role in its own history, rehash vacuous concepts and doubts about medical progress and 'whiggish' historiography…In the field

---

[1] Plin. *HN* 24.1.1, 4-5.
[2] Murphy (2004) 2.
[3] Murphy (2004) 99; Bradley (2009), especially 87-110 and 113-17.

[4] For *luxuria* and luxury commodities, see Parker (2002). For conflict between dependence upon professional medical practitioners and self-sufficiency, see Beagon (1992) 208.
[5] Fagan (2002) 100. This distinction between 'high' and 'low' medicine and medical practitioners is also found in Riddle (1993) through his classification of Dioscorides and Galen as practitioners of 'high' medicine, and Marcellus Empiricus and the authors of the Egyptian papyri and the Hermetic works as practitioners of 'low' medicine, although he does acknowledge the importance of both types of medical practice for their respective influences on the history of medicine.
[6] For this approach to ancient medicine in general, see Scarborough (1969) and (1993), Jackson (1988) and (1993), and Prioreschi (1998). For the focus on elite, city-based physicians, see Mattern (1999).
[7] For the assumption of the consistency of medical practice throughout the Roman Empire with specific reference to medical and surgical instruments, see Jackson (1990) and (1993). For a critique of this entire approach to scholarship of Roman medicine, see Baker (2002).

of history of medicine, the elementary mistake of confusing medical science with health care delivery is repeatedly made and prominent members in the field, no longer interested in how medical science developed, would limit the history of medicine to the study of how social forces impinge on medicine.[8]

It is only in the last decade that there has been growing recognition of a valid alternative approach to the study of ancient medicine, exemplified by Vivian Nutton's observation that the most striking thing about ancient medicine was its diversity: 'More than in most societies, medicine in ancient Greece and Rome was open to influences of all kinds and could be studied, and indeed practised, by many who did not think of themselves as doctors'.[9]

An adherence to the former approach as advocated by Prioreschi serves to simplify an extremely complicated cultural system, employing arbitrary, artificial and even anachronistic distinctions between 'high' and 'low', 'professional' and 'amateur', 'rational' and 'irrational', and even 'natural' and 'supernatural', and placing them in binary opposition to each other.[10] It is only in recent years that the application of such a rigid approach to the study of ancient medicine has begun to be systematically challenged. Philip van der Eijk has dismissed the use of 'rational' versus 'irrational' and 'natural' versus 'supernatural' in particular as 'confusing rather than illuminating', and has stated that, in his opinion, it is not appropriate to apply the modern Western concept of 'rationality' to the medical beliefs and practices of ancient or even non-Western civilisations.[11] Rather, when studying these beliefs and practices, scholars should be aware of what he considers to be the 'plurality of rationalities', and search for the 'rationale' behind them.[12] Nutton likewise has argued against the 'neat distinction' between 'rational and irrational, proper and improper, formal and informal', criticising 'the further implication that anything not in the first categories is not medicine or not eligible to be studied as part of the history of medicine'.[13]

The employment of such a rigid approach to ancient medicine takes for granted that 'high'/'professional' medical practitioners are entirely different and separate from 'low'/'amateur' medical practitioners, and that 'high', 'rational' and 'natural' medical practice are entirely different and separate from 'low', 'irrational' and 'supernatural' medical practice; that mutually exclusive approaches are being undertaken by different individuals at different locations using different techniques.[14] This study aims to contribute to the ongoing and organic dialogue about the relationship between different approaches to healing by focusing on the edge of the Roman Empire as opposed to the centre, examining medicine and medical practice within the context of provincial culture and giving equal weighting to alternative healing strategies alongside what might be considered (by modern observers) more conventional medical practice. It is unfortunate that, for the sake of brevity and clarity, and in order to make sense of the vast amount of material that I have examined and discussed, I have been compelled to structure this study in such a way (that is, with so-called conventional medical practice and alternative healing strategies dealt with in separate chapters) that it could be said to support (even perpetuate) the aforementioned rigid approach. It is also unfortunate that I have found it impossible to avoid utilising terms such as 'professional' and 'amateur' and 'rational' and 'irrational' entirely. It is my hope that one of the outcomes of this study will be proof that this type of approach to ancient medicine, and even this sort of divisive terminology, can be dispensed with entirely, allowing scholars to refer simply to 'healing', 'healing strategies' and 'healers'.

Egypt is a particularly appropriate choice as a starting point for this type of study. The region was annexed by Rome comparatively late in the process of imperial expansion (in 30 BC) and, as well as being physically located at the juncture between the eastern and western halves of the empire, it also constituted the Roman Empire's southernmost extremity. Thus Egypt was in the unique situation of being simultaneously an ancient civilisation and a fledgling province, positioned at the geographical periphery of the Empire but serving as a crucial provider of both ordinary and luxury goods ranging from grain to olive oil to frankincense to pepper. The inhabitants of the region had long been renowned for possessing an expertise in healing that incorporated elements at once both 'high' and 'low', 'professional' and 'amateur', 'rational' and 'irrational', and 'natural' and 'supernatural'.[15] The underexploited evidence for healing in Roman Egypt means that it is possible to explore not only the distinctions and tensions present between the different types of healing as outlined by Pliny above, but also how this healing expertise was either adopted or

[8] Prioreschi (1998) xxi-xxiv. He also states at xxiv that 'for those who consider postmodernism a new and improved intellectual insight, science is culturally determined, that is to say, its discoveries do not reflect external reality but the prejudices, beliefs and biases of a given culture at a given time. As a consequence, the Second Law of Thermodynamics has no more cognitive value than the latest fashion in clothing and, in general, science is not more valid that any other construct, that is to say, astrology is as valid as astronomy, alchemy as chemistry, witchcraft as medicine'.
[9] Nutton (2004) 313.
[10] For criticism of these modern approaches, see von Staden (2003) 15-17.
[11] van der Eijk (2005) 49; van der Eijk (2004) 4. For an examination of the concepts of 'rationality' and 'irrationality' with regard to medicine and medical practice in a non-Western civilisation, see Horstmanshoff and Stol (2004).
[12] van der Eijk (2004) 4 and 7 respectively.
[13] Nutton (2004) 16.

[14] See for example the Greek and Demotic medico-magical papyri and the attempts made by scholars to separate the medical texts from the magical texts, and the Greek texts from the Demotic texts, despite the fact that they were all written on the same pieces of papyrus - Betz (1992) ix and xlv commented critically upon these attempts at segregation, but they continued with Brashear (1995) and Ritner (1995).
[15] Nunn (1996); Allen (2005).

adapted over the centuries during which the province was subject to Roman rule.

1. Egyptian Contexts

An understanding of healing in Roman Egypt presupposes awareness of the historical, cultural and social context of the region in antiquity, both prior to and during the period of Roman rule. This section presents, first, a brief overview of the history of medicine in Pharaonic, Persian and Ptolemaic Egypt: secondly, a survey of the climate, geography and environment of the region: thirdly, an outline of the social and political structures of the Roman province: and, finally, an introduction to the demography of the region during the Roman period. Each of these aspects provides important background for discussions in the body of the study.

Medical Practice in Pharaonic and Hellenistic Egypt

The development of medicine in the Pharaonic period (c. 2600-525 BC, encompassing the Old, Middle and New Kingdoms and twenty six separate ruling dynasties) is difficult to reconstruct precisely.[16] This is due to the sparse and fragmentary nature of evidence (a mere fourteen Egyptian medical papyri) spread unevenly across two millennia. A range of different healing strategies (both 'rational' and 'irrational') is attested by the handful of Egyptian medical papyri that survive from this period.[17] The papyri range from the Kahun Papyrus (dating to c. 1820 BC) which is concerned with gynaecology, to the Chester Beatty Papyri (dating to c. 1200 BC), which are concerned with conditions such as headaches, rectal diseases and scorpion stings, and were evidently part of a family archive. The Edwin Smith Papyrus (dating to c. 1550 BC) is mainly concerned with trauma surgery and contains very few magical spells, focusing instead on 'rational' methods of diagnosis and treatment, while conversely the London Medical Papyrus (dating from c. 1300 BC) consists mainly of magical incantations. Any attempt to reconstruct the entirety of Pharaonic medicine and medical practice using these few papyri is obviously extremely problematic; while there is a certain amount of repetition in the papyri that survive, there are references to other papyri that do not survive, such as a treatise on embalming cited by name in the Edwin Smith Papyrus.[18]

A certain amount of additional information can be gleaned by studying the epigraphic evidence for medical

practitioners in Pharaonic Egypt.[19] Although only 150 named physicians are known from 2500 years of ancient Egyptian history, the evidence for them primarily consists of honorific inscriptions or epitaphs in which the physicians or *swnw* are named, frequently listed as having religious or magical titles as well as medical ones, and even on occasion their duties are described. Thus, it is possible to gain an idea of the extent to which ancient Egyptian medicine involved a degree of specialisation (ophthalmologists, gastro-enterologists, proctologists and dentists are attested), treating the ailments of animals as well as humans (as evinced by physicians described as supervising butchery and overseeing herds and stables), and the possibility that women trained and practised as physicians just as men did (as indicated by the epigraphy in the tomb of the lady Peseshet, 'overseer of the female doctors' during the fifth and sixth dynasties of the Old Kingdom). The *Histories* of Herodotus, who visited Egypt during the Late Period, provide some information about medicine and medical practice in the years between the Pharaonic and Hellenistic periods that support the epigraphic evidence of these earlier periods:

> The practice of medicine they split up into separate parts, each doctor being responsible for the treatment of only one disease. There are, in consequence, innumerable doctors, some specialising in diseases of the eyes, others the head, others of the teeth, others of the stomach, and so on; while others, again, deal with the sort of troubles which cannot be exactly localised.[20]

The development of medicine during the Hellenistic period (332-30 BC) is much easier to follow due to the abundance of relevant literary evidence (written both contemporaneously and in subsequent centuries), although there is still a great deal of scholarly debate over the extent to which Egyptian medicine influenced Greek medicine and vice versa.[21] One particularly contentious issue is whether or not Greek anatomical studies were influenced by the Egyptian practice of mummification.[22] Ptolemy I Soter and Ptolemy II Philadelphus founded the Museion and Library of Alexandria and their royal patronage and that of their successors ensured that innovative medical research and scholarship could take place without interference, at least until the worsening political situation of the middle of the second century BC

---

[16] For an acknowledgement of the difficulties of reconstructing ancient Egyptian medicine and discussion of conservatism versus innovation during this period, see Ritner (2000).
[17] For the distinction between 'rational' and 'irrational' medicine in ancient Egypt, see David (2004).
[18] For a brief summary of the surviving Egyptian medical papyri and their contents, see Nunn (1996) 24-41. The naming conventions applied to ancient papyri are inconsistent; works can be named after the antiquarians who originally purchased them in Egypt (e.g. the Edwin Smith Papyrus), the geographical location at which they were found (e.g. the Kahun Papyrus), the institution that now owns them (e.g. the London and Brooklyn papyri) or even a generous benefactor (e.g. the Hearst Papyrus).

[19] For a concordance of Egyptian medical practitioners from the Old Kingdom to the Ptolemaic period, see Nunn (1996) 113-35, 211-14.
[20] Hdt. 2.84.
[21] See Littman (1996) for discussion of this issue. See Poole (2001) for discussion of a clay pot dating from between the fifth and the fourth centuries BC, labeled as being medicine for a cough and containing the same ingredients as a recipe for medicine for a cough found in the Berlin Papyrus, dating from around 1200 BC.
[22] See Hdt. 2.86-9 for the Greek understanding of the process of mummification. See Nutton (2004) 129-30 for discussion of this issue. See Nunn (1996) 42-56 for discussion of the evidence of Egyptian knowledge of anatomy and physiology.

and the decades following.[23] Scholars such as Herophilus and Erasistratus reportedly vivisected convicted criminals in order to further their research into the nervous and circulatory systems respectively.[24] Significant advances were also made in anatomy, care of wounds, pharmacology, ophthalmology and gynaecology.[25] This period also saw the development of the four main medical sects: the Dogmatists, the Methodists, the Empiricists and the Pneumatists respectively.[26]

By way of comparison with the literary evidence, papyrological evidence offers an insight into medicine and medical practice outside of Alexandria; Greek and Demotic tax returns from the Arsinoite nome explicitly list some physicians as Egyptian and others as Greek, indicating that there was at least some separation between Egyptian and Greek medical practices and their practitioners, and one of these papyri includes a reference to an oculist, indicating that a degree of specialisation in medical practice remained possible. In addition to this, some of the letters included in the Zenon archive demonstrate not only what a physician could be expected to do for the ill and infirm (including acting as personal physician to the members of the royal family) but also their more mundane concerns unrelated to medicine and medical practice such as the procurement of goods and livestock.[27] Thus it is possible to follow certain aspects of medical practice (and certain aspects of evidence for medical practice) from the Pharaonic period, through the Hellenistic period, and into the Roman period.

The Geography of Egypt
Throughout antiquity, the inhabitants of Egypt were thought to be extraordinarily healthy in comparison to other peoples, and the geography and climate of the region were frequently cited as the reason why this was thought to be the case.[28]

With regard to Egypt's geography, the region is essentially a long river valley cut into a limestone plateau with a desert on either side, and these deserts constitute over ninety five per cent of the land (see Figures 1 and 2).[29] The climate is more variable. In the far north, in

antiquity as today, Alexandria benefits from being a coastal city. It has a weather pattern with an average annual rainfall of around 190 mm, falling in the period between October and April. There is also less of a variation in temperature than in other parts of the country, with summer highs of around 30° C at noon and a winter night time low of around 10° C.[30] According to Strabo, 'the Etesian winds blow from the north and from a vast sea, so that the Alexandrians pass their time most pleasantly in summer'.[31] Further south, in Lower Egypt the annual rainfall is usually less than 24 mm, and this normally falls over a few days during winter. The temperature in summer ranges between a noon high of 35° C and a night time low of 22° C whilst in winter the corresponding range is 20° C to 10° C.[32] By contrast, in Upper Egypt there is very little rainfall. Of the deserts on either side of the Nile, the Western Desert is extremely arid while the Eastern Desert is slightly more habitable since moisture blown from the Red Sea and Indian Ocean can form storm clouds over the Eastern Desert mountain range.[33] However, the climate is still extremely harsh, with temperatures of up to 45.6° C recorded in the summer.[34] Rainfall is unpredictable and concentrated in the winter period. Short, heavy showers may produce huge quantities of water, but these occurrences are quite rare and tend to be localised.[35]

Such harsh climactic conditions ensured that during the Pharaonic, Hellenistic and Roman periods the vast majority of the region's settlements were located along the banks of the Nile. The Nile not only served as a constant supply of fresh water for drinking and washing, but also as a means of transport from Alexandria in the north to Philae in the south and back again.[36] As a consequence of the inundation of the Nile that occurred every summer, each autumn the agricultural land surrounding the river would be left covered with a layer of silt that rendered the soil much more agriculturally fertile and productive. There were also some agriculturally productive communities located in the oases of the Western Desert.

[23] For discussion of the foundation and development of the Museion and Library, see Fraser (1972) 305-36. For discussion of Herophilus and Erasistratus specifically, see Nutton (2004) 132-7.
[24] Celsus, *Med.* proem. 23.
[25] Littman (1996); Ritner (2000).
[26] See Littman (1996) 2698-2703 for a brief summary of the sects and their beliefs.
[27] See *Count P.* 3 (Arsinoite nome, June-July 229 BC) for 'Egyptian physicians'. See *Count P.* 2 (Arsinoite nome, June-July 229 BC) for 'Greek physicians'. See *Count P.* 9 (Arsinoite nome, mid third century BC) for *swnw-ir.t*: 'Simon the oculist'. With regard to physicians mentioned in the Zenon papyrus archive, see *P. Cair. Zen.* 3.59426.6 (mid third century BC) in which Attic honey is prescribed as a medicament for the treatment of an eye complaint. For regular correspondence between Zenon and Artemidoros the physician, see *P. Cair. Zen.* 1.59044 (257 BC, Alexandria); 2.59190 (255 BC, Alexandria); 2.59225 (253 BC, Alexandria); 2.59251 (252 BC, Syrien); 3.59310 (250 BC, Alexandria); 3.59311 (255-50 BC, Alexandria); 4.59555 (255 BC, Alexandria); and 4.59571 (243-2 BC, Alexandria).
[28] See for example Hdt. 2.77; Diod. Sic. 1.34.3-5 and 1.82.1; Strabo, *Geographica* 17.1.7; Lucr. 6.1103; Amm. Marc. 22.16.8.
[29] Kuhrt (1995) 118 and 120; Jackson (2002) xx.

[30] Alston (1995) 13.
[31] Strabo, *Geographica* 17.1.7.
[32] Alston (1995) 13.
[33] Alston (1995) 13.
[34] Peacock and Maxfield (1997) 9; Maxfield and Peacock (2001) 2.
[35] Cappers (2006) 21.
[36] Rufus of Ephesus praised the Nile as a source of drinking water, cited at Oribasius, *Collectiones* 5.3.6.

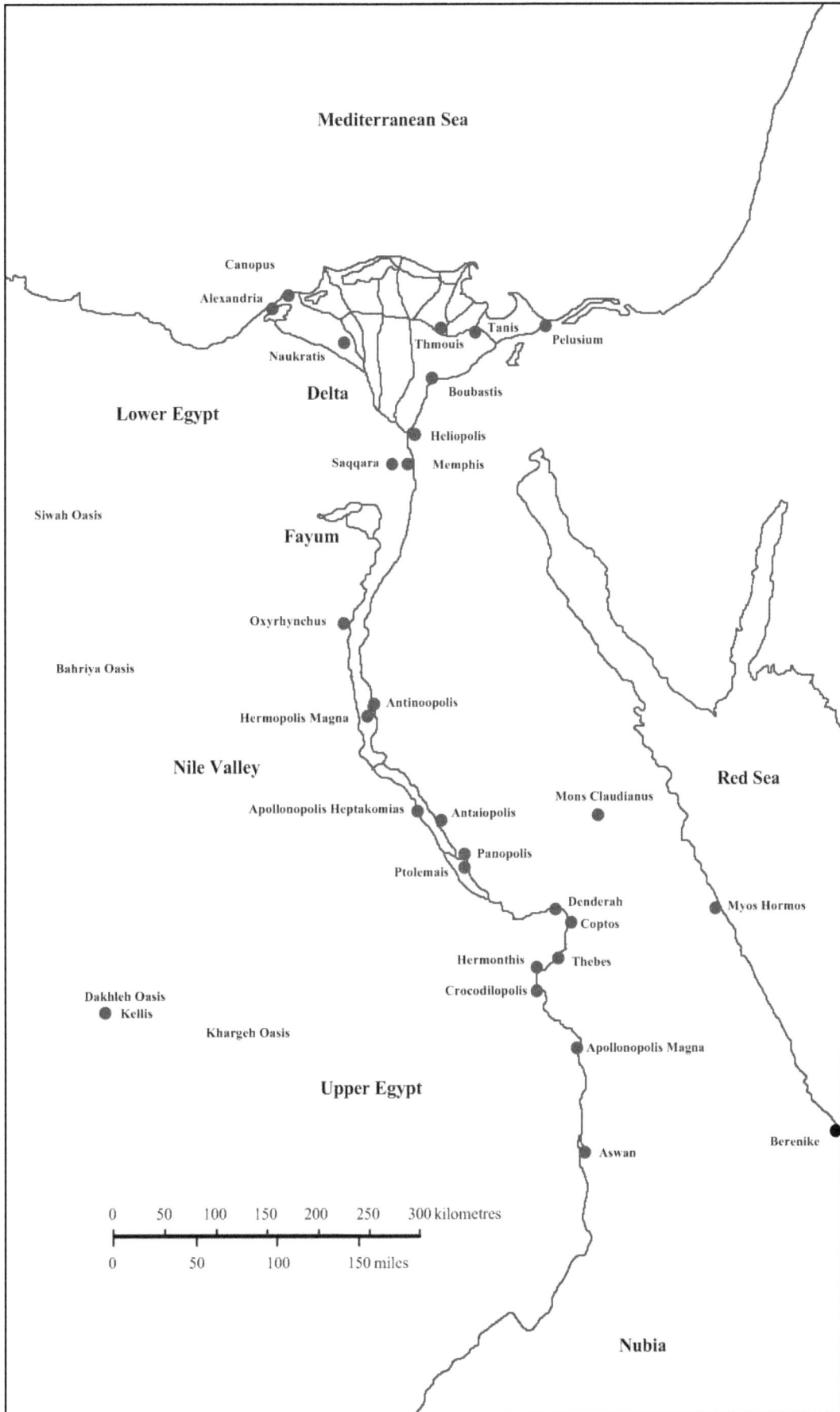

Figure 1: Map of Graeco-Roman Egypt (map drawn by author)

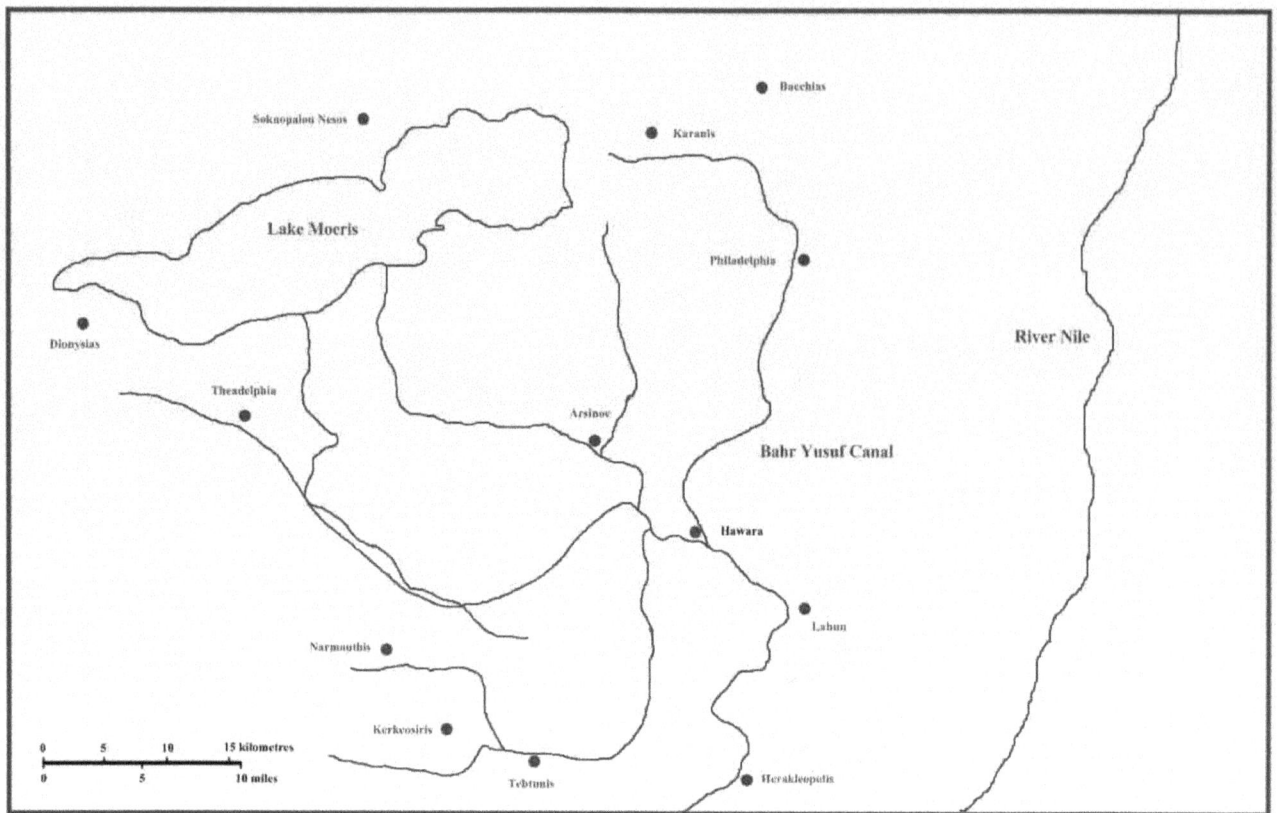

Figure 2: Map of the Graeco-Roman Fayum (map drawn by author)

However, agriculture was not Egypt's only natural resource: settlements such as Mons Claudianus and Mons Porphyrites were established in the Eastern Desert in order to quarry stone and minerals, while ports such as Myos Hormos and Berenike were founded on the Red Sea coast in order to facilitate trade with the Far East and the Orient.

It is important to note that the communities situated along the length of the Nile had to deal with very different terrains and microclimates to those communities located in the desert oases or quarries, or those on the Mediterranean or Red Sea coasts. These settlements also had very different purposes, ranging from agricultural production in the Nile Valley, to quarrying in the Eastern Desert, to trading on the Red Sea coast. They in turn had very different populations, some remaining static while others were constantly in flux due to seasonal migration. All of these factors are significant if the disease environments of these communities are to be reconstructed as accurately as possible in order to provide an historical, social and cultural context for a study of healing in Roman Egypt. For example, those communities living in proximity to the Nile or its canals and irrigation works would be more likely to encounter water-borne diseases and the associated health problems, while those living out in the deserts and working in the quarries would be more likely to suffer from respiratory disorders, while those living on the coast would be more likely to encounter new pathogens brought into Egypt

from abroad.[37] Consequently, a certain amount of regional variation, not only in the health problems suffered, but also the healing strategies utilised to deal with them, is to be anticipated.

Despite the fact that Alexandria was the most heavily populated urban centre in Egypt, comparatively little papyrological or archaeological evidence has been recovered from the site of the ancient city due to a combination of the damp climate and terrestrial subsidence into the Mediterranean.[38] On the contrary, the vast majority of the papyrological and archaeological evidence for the inhabitants of the province comes from the Nile Valley and thus these communities are rather disproportionately represented in modern scholarship. The Fayum, the area around Lake Moeris just to the south of the Nile Delta, contains a number of towns and villages that have been excavated either for papyri (such as Arsinoe and Soknopaiou Nesos) or for papyri and archaeological artefacts (such as Karanis and Tebtunis). By far the most papyri have been recovered from the rubbish dumps of Oxyrhynchus, further south, although hardly anything else remains of what would have been a

---

[37] On the Nile: according to Theophrastus' treatise *On Waters*, 'A drought once having been produced in the region of the Nile, the water of the stream became poisonous and killed off many Egyptians', cited at Ath. 2.15.41 E-F.

[38] For a summary of recent archaeological excavation in and around Alexandria, see Bagnall (2001), and Bagnall and Davoli (2011) 103-8.

heavily populated ancient city.[39] Sites on the periphery of Egypt such as the Dakhleh Oasis in the Western Desert, Mons Claudianus in the Eastern Desert, and Berenike on the Red Sea coast would have housed much smaller numbers of inhabitants but have produced useful combinations of papyrological and archaeological evidence.[40]

It is thus crucial to take into account external factors such as climate, geography, and the nature and size of specific communities as these all impact heavily upon the nature of medicine and medical practice within the province.

Social and Political Structures, Administration and Interaction

The prefect of Roman Egypt was based primarily at the Brucheion in Alexandria and was supported by a series of other government officials appointed by the imperial administration. These included a *iuridicus*, or legal adviser, a *dioiketes*, or finance officer, a chief priest and a number of procurators and military commanders (in the early years of Roman rule, three legions were posted in Egypt and this was later reduced to two, and then one).[41] These government officials were assisted by four *epistrategoi*, or regional administrators (the four regions were the Thebaid, the Heptanomia, the East Delta and the West Delta), and each nome had its own royal scribe, *strategos* or administrator, and accountant. There were also district and village scribes, and local magistrates and town councillors were elected while liturgists were compulsorily appointed.[42] At least some provincial administrators held positions associated with medicine and medical practice, as the reports of the public physicians addressed to the *strategoi*, *epistrategoi* and on occasion the prefect make clear.

There were four Greek metropoleis in Egypt: Alexandria (founded by Alexander the Great in 331 BC), Naukratis (a trading colony founded in the seventh century BC), Ptolemais (founded by Ptolemy I Soter in the fourth century BC), and Antinoopolis (founded by Hadrian in AD 130). The inhabitants of these metropoleis were especially privileged, possessing Greek (and in some cases Roman) citizenship and being entitled to hold citizen assemblies, councils, magistracies and membership of the gymnasia. Each nome, or administrative region of Egypt, had a capital such as Arsinoe (of the Arsinoite nome) and Oxyrhynchus (of the Oxyrhynchite nome), and their inhabitants were also allowed magistracies and gymnasia. While the metropoleis and nome capitals accounted for a significant proportion of the total population of Egypt, the majority of the inhabitants of the province seem to have lived in villages such as Kellis or Karanis, where the number of

occupants varied over time from several hundred to several thousand, depending upon a range of factors such as the standard of the irrigation system or outbreaks of plague.

The population of Egypt was ethnically diverse, consisting of Romans, Greeks, Egyptians, Jews and even individuals originally from outside of the Roman Empire.[43] However, it is difficult to say for certain which of these categories an individual considered him or herself to belong to. Since most of the Greeks and Romans who ultimately chose to settle in Egypt had originally entered the region for political, military, or economic reasons and were thus male, a certain amount of cohabitation and/or marriage between Greek and Roman men and Egyptian women inevitably occurred.[44] However, relying upon classifying an individual's name as Egyptian, Greek or Roman and thus identifying their ethnicity is problematic; numerous papyri attest to individuals having had both Egyptian and Greek (and sometimes even Roman) names, or Egyptianised Greek names, or Hellenised Egyptian names. Then there is the question of citizenship: in the years immediately following the Roman annexation of Egypt, anyone who was not a citizen of Alexandria, Naukratis and/or Ptolemais was classed as an Egyptian, no matter when their ancestors had originally settled in the region, what language they could speak and/or write in, or which pantheon they worshipped. Until the *Constitutio Antoniniana* was declared in AD 212, an individual had to obtain Alexandrian citizenship before they could obtain Roman citizenship, and since Alexandrian citizenship was extremely difficult to obtain, Roman citizenship was rare indeed. Consequently, the Romans and the Greeks (the former primarily the imperial administrators, soldiers and army veterans, the latter the descendents of the Hellenistic army veterans and those who had settled in Egypt under the Ptolemies) were comparatively privileged, forming part of the local elite in areas where they settled, while the Egyptians were less fortunate and many learned Greek and changed their names in order to access these higher levels of privilege.[45] Although Latin was frequently used in military contexts and Demotic in private, Greek remained the official language of government, law and education.[46] Thus, the extent to which Egyptians, Greeks and Romans interacted with each other on a daily basis seems to have been extremely variable and it is difficult to establish a consistent pattern.[47] While the inhabitants of Alexandria and the metropoleis would theoretically have had more opportunities for social and cultural interaction due to the sheer size and diversity of each city's population, the highly stratified social, cultural and religious hierarchies

---

[39] See Bagnall and Rathbone (2004) 158-61 for discussion of the remains of Oxyrhynchus, including evidence of what could have been the largest theatre in Roman North Africa.
[40] Bingen *et al.* (1992); Peacock and Maxfield (1997); Maxfield and Peacock (2001); Wendrich *et al.* (2003); Cappers (2006); Sidebotham (2011).
[41] Alston (1995) 32.
[42] Bowman (1986) 66-9; Capponi (2005) 25-51.

[43] Thompson (2009); Fournet (2009).
[44] For discussion of a range of different aspects of the 'multi-cultural' society of Egypt during the Late, Ptolemaic and Roman periods, see Johnson (1992).
[45] See for example the case of Gemellus Horion from Karanis, who used his Roman citizenship to have a neighbour prosecuted under Roman law for casting a magical spell on him, Frankfurter (2006).
[46] Fewster (2002); Adams *et al.* (2002).
[47] Thompson (2009) 400-6.

of those cities might well have discouraged such contact. Likewise, although the towns and villages of the *chora*, and the oases, mining and quarry settlements of the Western and Eastern Deserts had much smaller and often much less diverse populations, their economies and institutions would have been much more interdependent.

Native Egyptian religious practice was permitted to continue after the Roman annexation, although Egyptian temples were subject to certain restrictions and their sources of revenue were severely curtailed.[48] The appointment of a Roman government official as Chief Priest of Alexandria and Egypt ensured that all aspects of public religious life came under the remit of the imperial administration, and a code of conduct known as the *Gnomon of the Idios Logos* was produced. However, traditional Greek and (less frequently) Roman religion was also practised in the province and certain Greek and (again less frequently) Roman deities (particularly those that could undergo syncretism or be associated with Egyptian gods and goddesses) were extremely popular; for example, the healing deity Asclepius came to be associated with Imhotep, the fabled ancient Egyptian physician and architect of the Great Pyramid at Giza. Likewise, Greek and Roman religious healing practices such as incubation were adopted. As in other Roman provinces, the imperial cult was promoted and temples were dedicated to members of the imperial family throughout the region, although one development specific to Egypt was the fact that the Roman emperors were worshipped as kings, pharaohs and gods during their lifetimes as well as after their deaths.[49] All of these factors (the Egyptian provincial government, the extent of urbanisation, and the ethnic and religious diversity of the population) influenced medical practice.

Demography

Over three hundred census returns survive from Roman Egypt, spanning the period AD 11/12 to AD 257/258. They have been comprehensively examined in an attempt to establish the size and structure of Egyptian households, age and sex distribution, and patterns of mortality, marriage, fertility, and migration.[50] Analysis of these census returns has resulted in the suggestion that life expectancy at birth in Roman Egypt in this period would have been in the early to mid twenties, with male life expectancy slightly more favourable than female; male life expectancy at birth would have been at least twenty-five years, while female life expectancy at birth would probably have been twenty-two and a half years, increasing at age ten to between thirty-four and a half and thirty-seven and a half years.[51] Consequently it appears

that the population of Roman Egypt would have been a comparatively young one, with individuals aged sixty-five and over accounting for only 3% of the population while individuals under fifteen accounted for 35%.[52] These conclusions are broadly consistent with the generally accepted parameters for the demography of the Roman World, based on Model Life Tables.[53]

A number of the mummy labels that were put on mummified corpses also survive and analysis of these sheds light on patterns of mortality during the course of the year. This evidence suggests that in Roman Egypt, about half of a year's deaths occurred during the four month period between May and August.[54] The use of funerary inscriptions in addition to mummy labels has suggested that seasonal mortality in Roman Egypt varied with age; during the first twenty years of life, 40.5% of all deaths fell into the same four month period previously identified, May to August. However, only 18.9% of adult deaths occurred in this period. On the contrary, 63.5% of all adult deaths took place in the period from September to February.[55] These studies of the demography of Roman Egypt indicate that the inhabitants of the province had a low life expectancy and consequently the population was, on average, a young one. However, according to patterns of seasonal mortality, being younger, the members of the population seem to have been more likely to die during the hotter months of May to August, possibly due to increased exposure to infectious diseases.

One unusual demographic feature of society in Roman Egypt revealed by the census evidence is the practice of brother-sister marriage. It has been calculated that this practice accounts for between 15 and 20% of all ongoing marriages in the first three centuries AD.[56] In total, 121 brother-sister marriages are attested in the census returns and forty-three of these couples reside in metropoleis while seventy-eight reside in villages.[57] Brother-sister marriage is particularly well-attested in the census returns from the Arsinoite nome and here at least marriages between siblings are characterised by the husband being older than the wife.[58] Due to the high mortality prevalent in Roman Egypt during this period, only about 40% of families had both a son and a daughter or both sons and daughters that survived to a marriageable age.[59] Of these, only around 20% would be likely to have an older son and younger daughter.[60]

---

[48] Frankfurter (1998) 27 and 198.

[49] Glare (1994).

[50] Bagnall and Frier (1994) 1: unfortunately, analysis of this evidence does not provide anything like a complete picture of the population of Roman Egypt as the vast majority of the census returns come from three nomes out of fifty (the Arsinoite, the Oxyrhynchite and the Prosopite) and date from the second century AD. However, the limitations of the material are made perfectly clear and are taken into account throughout the analysis.

[51] Bagnall and Frier (1994) female at 90; male at 100.

[52] Bagnall and Frier (1994) 104.

[53] Scheidel (2007).

[54] Scheidel (1996b) 153.

[55] Scheidel (2001a) 26-7: however, the selection of material used here is questionable - 542 out of 938 funerary inscriptions (58%) dating from the first to the tenth centuries AD.

[56] Hopkins (1980) 304.

[57] Bagnall and Frier (1994) 129: the incidence of brother-sister marriage in Alexandria (excluding the royal family) is, unfortunately, completely unknown.

[58] Scheidel (1995).

[59] Hopkins (1980) 327; for archaeological evidence of high infant mortality, see Kellis 2.

[60] Scheidel (1995) 149.

The majority of brother-sister marriages attested in the census returns resulted in offspring; the most fertile of these matches had eight surviving children between the ages of twenty-nine and seven.[61] However, there are substantial negative genetic consequences to inbreeding at such an intimate level, particularly if inbreeding continues over successive generations. Inherited conditions such as mental retardation and congenital deformities, in addition to sterility, are attested for incestuous and inbred offspring.[62] Not all of these defects would be immediately apparent at birth. Despite claims to the contrary by ancient writers such as Strabo, during the Roman period the inhabitants of Egypt did expose unwanted children, although this may have been a Greek rather than Egyptian practice.[63] It seems likely that any children who were obviously deformed or disabled in some way were exposed at birth, particularly if exposure was primarily practised by the Greek population and, as Shaw argues, brother-sister marriage was practised primarily among the Greek municipal elite.[64] However, many congenital disabilities are not immediately apparent and might only become evident if an individual survived beyond infancy. Considering the frequency with which full and half brothers and sisters seem to have married and produced offspring, it seems probable that at least some of these offspring would have survived to adulthood while suffering ill health as a result of their parents' inbreeding and consequently would have utilised a range of healing strategies out of necessity.

The history, geography, social and political structures and demography of Egypt are all highly significant factors for this study; as has been made clear, Egypt was unusual in many respects and it is necessary for these distinctive features to be both acknowledged and taken into account when considering not only the general state of health and health problems of the inhabitants of the province, but also the healing strategies utilised to combat them, alleviate symptoms and possibly even develop cures.

2. Scholarly Contexts
In addition to the Egyptian contexts outlined in previous sections, it is important to have an understanding of scholarly contexts relevant to the subject of this study. This section presents, first, a brief overview of recent issues in scholarship on the status of Egypt as a Roman province; secondly, a summary of the 'Black Athena' controversy and its relevance to healing in Roman Egypt; and thirdly, a survey of the most important trends in the

study of ancient medicine, and of work on medicine and healing in Roman Egypt.

Roman Egypt
For a long time Egypt was viewed by scholars as an atypical Roman province. This view derived in part from a description of the region found in Tacitus' *Histories*:

> Egypt, with the troops to keep it in order, has been managed from the time of the deified Augustus by Roman knights in place of their former kings. It had seemed wise to keep thus under the direct control of the imperial house a province which is difficult of access, productive of great harvests, but given to civil strife and sudden disturbances because of the fanaticism and superstition of its inhabitants, ignorant as they are of laws and unacquainted with civil magistrates.[65]

Subsequently reinforced by Tacitus elsewhere, these claims were written with the benefit of hindsight in the early second century AD. This was not only after the disgrace of Cornelius Gallus (the first senator appointed prefect of Egypt by Augustus) in 26 BC and the unauthorised tour of the province by Germanicus in AD 19, but also after Vespasian had seemingly realised Augustus and Tiberius' fears and effectively utilised the province and its resources in his campaign to become emperor during the latter stages of the civil war in AD 68-9.[66] Consequently, the province came to be considered by scholars as something akin to the emperor's private property.[67]

Consequently, emphasis has frequently been placed upon the idea of Egypt as politically separate, geographically and geophysically distinct, and culturally dissimilar from the rest of the Roman Empire.[68] However, papyrological discoveries have increasingly given reason to question aspects of this picture. For example, while members of the imperial family, senators and prominent equestrians may have been forbidden entry to Egypt, they were not necessarily restricted from owning property or having business interests there; there is evidence to suggest that certain members of the imperial family such as Livia and Germanicus owned private estates in Egypt, which gives reason to doubt Tacitus' claim that the province was the property of the emperor alone.[69] More recently, the traditional view has been challenged by Naphtali Lewis in a series of influential papers. He argued that once Egypt had been annexed by Rome, the region underwent such fundamental political and social changes that the

---

[61] Scheidel (1996a) 323.

[62] Scheidel (1996a) 328. Huebner (2007) has argued that brother-sister marriage took place between adopted siblings and was, therefore, not incestuous and would not result in inbred offspring. However, this has subsequently been challenged by Remijsen and Clarysse (2008), and by Rowlandson and Takahashi (2009).

[63] Strabo, *Geographica* 17.2.5: 'One of the customs most zealously observed among the Egyptians is this, that they rear every child that is born'; see *BGU* 4.1104 (9-8 BC, Alexandria): 'Since Dionysarion is also pregnant, she shall not bring action about the expenses of the child's because of being compliant about these matters; and she is allowed to expose her infant'; *P. Oxy.* 744 (1 BC, Alexandria): 'If it is a male, let it be, but if it is a female, cast it out'.

[64] Shaw (1992).

[65] Tac. *Hist.* 1.11.

[66] Suet. *Aug.* 66; Dio Cass. 53.23.

[67] Tac. *Ann.* 2.59.

[68] Rathbone (2007) 698.

[69] For imperial estates in Egypt owned by Livia, later Julia Augusta, see *P. Col.* 8.211 (AD 10, Philadelphia) and *SB* 16.12835 (AD 6, Philadelphia). For an imperial estate in Egypt jointly owned by Livia and Germanicus, see *SB* 6.9150 (AD 5, Karanis) and *P. Lond.* 2.445 (AD 14-19, Bakchias). See also Bowman (1976) 160-1.

traditional moniker of 'Graeco-Roman Egypt' is entirely unsuitable. He considered a clear distinction between 'Hellenistic Egypt' and 'Roman Egypt' more appropriate, suggesting that Egypt under the Romans was very different to the way Egypt had been under the Pharaohs and the Ptolemies, and thus was much more like the other provinces of the Roman Empire than had previously been acknowledged.[70] Awareness of the extent to which different aspects of life in Egypt during the Roman period were influenced by 'Egyptian', 'Greek' and/or 'Roman' practices and traditions is of crucial import if a study of healing is to be attempted, so it is necessary to survey briefly the relationship between the Egyptian, Greek and Roman elements.

Dominic Rathbone has argued that as far as the province's finances were concerned, Egypt was by no means exceptional, but rather a prototype for fiscal systems subsequently introduced throughout the Roman Empire.[71] The administration of the province during the earliest years of Roman rule has recently been examined by Livia Capponi in order to study the transition from Hellenistic kingdom to Roman province, and she concluded that the typical view of Egypt as a country of unchanging continuity is incorrect, and that the early Principate was a decisive turning point in many respects.[72] While these more recent studies have confirmed Lewis' work with regard to taxation and provincial administration (both particularly well-represented through documentary papyri) there are still some areas in which Egypt remained distinctive from the rest of the Roman Empire. Interestingly, despite the alterations made to the fiscal and administration systems of the province, the Egyptian system of currency remained closed and the exchange of foreign currency mandatory until AD 296.[73] There are also clear differences with regard to Egypt's complex cultural background. The calendar adhered to within the province was the traditional Egyptian one consisting of three seasons that corresponded to the agricultural cycle and the inundation of the Nile.[74] Despite the introduction of the imperial cult to the province in conjunction with measures to curb the power of the native Egyptian temples and priests, Greek and Roman settlers consistently adopted Egyptian religious beliefs and practices.[75] These religious beliefs and practices ranged from worshipping Egyptian deities and participating in Egyptian religious cultic activity such as the dedication of animal mummies, to undergoing mummification after death.[76] As already noted, Egypt also remained unique in

the Roman Empire in its practice of brother-sister marriage.

Just how 'Roman', then, was Roman Egypt? Unlike in Gaul, for example, no member of the provincial elite in Egypt ever became a Roman senator.[77] Social mobility within the province was extremely difficult and Egyptians were not permitted to join the army or serve in the provincial administration, although admittedly some did rise to political prominence.[78] Until Caracalla's decree in AD 212, it remained very difficult for an Egyptian to become a Roman citizen; as Pliny the Younger's letters to Trajan make clear, before an Egyptian could become a citizen of Rome, he had to become a citizen of Alexandria, and this privilege was generally hereditary.[79]

Did Egypt undergo 'Romanisation' and was the population 'Romanised' after the initial conquest and annexation? According to John Barrett, the term 'Romanisation' 'is applied generally to all those processes whereby diverse indigenous peoples were incorporated in or aligned themselves with the Roman Empire'.[80] However, this approach to the study of provincial culture has been subject to much criticism in recent years. According to David Mattingly, 'cosy and uncritical views about the civilising benefits of Roman rule still abound'.[81] As discussed above, Egypt arguably experienced 'Romanisation' with regard to the ways in which the province was administered by its prefect and other Roman officials, its position within the economy of the Roman Empire and the application of Roman law and order, but whether the population was 'Romanised' or not is difficult to answer.[82] While the members of the urban elites living in Alexandria or Antinoopolis, the soldiers of the Roman army posted in Alexandria, Babylon and on the desert frontiers, and even the military veterans who settled in the Fayum could arguably be described as 'Romanised', the vast proportion of the population, living in rural areas, speaking Demotic and worshipping native Egyptian deities, probably were not. According to Naphtali Lewis, the transition from Ptolemaic to Roman rule made little difference to the traditional Egyptian way of life.[83] As discussed previously, there is a range of both physical and anecdotal evidence for medical practice in the Pharaonic and Hellenistic periods, so understanding the extent to which Egypt and its population were 'Romanised' and consequently how this 'Romanisation' did or did not affect medical practice is crucial.

[70] Lewis (1970); Lewis (1984).
[71] Rathbone (1993) 111-12. See also Bowman and Rathbone (1992); Rathbone (1991).
[72] Capponi (2005) 170.
[73] On the currency, see Bowman (1986) 92-3.
[74] On the calendar, see Bagnall (1993) 20-2 and Ritner (1998) 3-4.
[75] On the imperial cult in Egypt, see Glare (1994). On Egyptian religion during the Roman period, see Evans (1961); Frankfurter (1998). On Egyptian funerary practices, see Corcoran (1995); Walker (2000).
[76] On the worship of Isis and Sarapis, see Wild (1981). On mummification and mummy portraits, see Corcoran (1995); Walker and Bierbrier (2000); Aufderheide *et al.* (2004).

[77] For the extension of membership of the Senate to the provinces, see Tac. *Ann.* 11.23-5. See also Bowersock (1984).
[78] See for example Tiberius Julius Alexander, born in Alexandria to an equestrian Jewish family, who served as procurator of Judea (AD 46-8) and prefect of Egypt (AD 66 onwards).
[79] Plin. *Ep.* 10.5-10. See also Sherwin-White (1966) 566-71 and 575-6 for discussion of Pliny's attempts to gain Roman citizenship for a medical practitioner.
[80] Barrett (1997) 51.
[81] Mattingly (1997a) 7.
[82] On the issue of language, Greek and Latin, see Fewster (2002). On bilingualism in Roman Egypt, see Adams (2003) 527-641.
[83] Lewis (1984) 1080.

Perhaps if the provincial culture of Egypt is examined, the extent to which the province was 'Romanised' or not will become clearer. There have been a number of important attempts to deal with the challenge of understanding various aspects of life in Egypt during the Hellenistic and Roman periods respectively, all of which are relevant for the study of provincial culture and thus healing strategies in Roman Egypt. Raffaella Cribiore has produced two important studies on education in Egypt, *Writing, Teachers and Students in Graeco-Roman Egypt* (1996) and *Gymnastics of the Mind: Greek Education in Hellenistic and Roman Egypt* (2001), which are relevant due to their discussion of the issue of medical education, particularly in Alexandria. David Frankfurter's *Religion in Roman Egypt* (1998) approaches religion in Egypt in the period AD 100-600, focusing on rural contexts and what he describes as the 'progressive centrifugal tendency from regional centres toward local and domestic practice during the Roman period'.[84] He examines the role that local temples and their cults played in healing, recognising the integrated nature of medicine, magic and religion in Roman Egypt.[85] Important sources relating to the lives of women in Graeco-Roman Egypt have been collated in Jane Rowlandson's *Women and Society in Greek and Roman Egypt* (1998) and Roger Bagnall and Raffaella Cribiore's *Women's Letters from Ancient Egypt 300 BC-AD 800* (2006), each of which contain sections specifically devoted to health and healthcare. General studies of Roman Egypt, then, typically integrate some consideration of medical practice into their surveys, but there is still work to be done on healing as a subject and an issue in its own right.

Black Athena
The relationship between the history, society and culture of Egypt and its healing strategies has often been contentious in modern scholarship. Almost twenty five years ago, Martin Bernal published the first volume of his controversial study *Black Athena: the Afroasiatic Roots of Classical Civilization* (1987), in which he argued that over the last two centuries classicists have been responsible for deliberately either suppressing or ignoring the weight of overwhelming evidence for Egyptian and Semitic contributions to the origins of ancient Greek civilisation.[86] He suggested an alternative model for the study of the history and culture of the ancient Mediterranean that he designated the 'Revised Ancient Model', which accepted a basis in reality for the stories of Egyptian and Phoenician colonisation of Greece but saw them as beginning earlier, in the first half of the second millennium BC. This 'Revised Ancient Model' also argued that Greek civilisation was the result of the cultural mixtures created by these colonisations and subsequent borrowings from across the eastern Mediterranean.[87]

One of the responses to this study was Robert Palter's article 'Black Athena, Afro-centrism, and the History of Science' (1993), in which he took exception to claims made in both *Black Athena* and Bernal's subsequent article 'Animadversions on the Origins of Western Science' (1992) that there were not only scientific elements in Egyptian medicine, mathematics and astronomy, but that these had a critical influence upon the development of the corresponding Greek scientific disciplines.[88] In his subsequent discussion of the native Egyptian medical tradition, Palter acknowledged the difficulties of formulating any kind of general characterisation regarding it:

> It is perfectly clear that no single, homogeneous medical tradition exists; and if, for example, a tradition of 'scientific' or 'rational' medicine could somehow be identified, it would quite arbitrarily exclude many nosological, diagnostic, and therapeutic considerations of central importance in the ancient historical context just because they involve folklorical, magical and religious elements.[89]

However, considering that Bernal's scholarship was concerned with the prehistory of the Mediterranean, it seems somewhat arbitrary (and perhaps counter-productive) that Palter focused his subsequent attempts to prove or disprove the possibility of any native Egyptian influences on Greek medicine on medical practice in Alexandria during the Hellenistic period, relying primarily upon the work of Heinrich von Staden to justify this approach.[90] In his response to Palter's article, Bernal also questioned Palter's utilisation of von Staden's scholarship, although his criticism arose primarily from the fact that Palter was citing an older work. However, Bernal also criticised the fact that Palter cited Ann Ellis Hanson's argument that broadly similar drugs, techniques and remedies can be documented widely among societies at similar stages of development, in preference to the variety of ancient authors from Homer onwards who commented on Egypt's extensive pharmacology.[91] On the contrary, according to Bernal, 'Hanson's attempt - supported by Palter - to claim that the Greeks living in Egypt did not derive their use of particular drugs and treatments from Egyptian healers is still more preposterous'.[92]

Palter is certainly correct in claiming that, at the time that he was writing, there was a scholarly consensus as to the apparent lack of progress and change in native Egyptian medicine. According to Robert Ritner, ancient Egypt was commonly viewed by scholars as having been an extremely conservative culture, dedicated to the preservation of traditional concepts and techniques that

[84] Frankfurter (1998) 6.
[85] Frankfurter (1998) 46-52.
[86] Bernal (1987); Levine (1992) 441.
[87] Bernal (1987) 1.

[88] Palter (1993) 227-8; Bernal (1992).
[89] Palter (1993) 265.
[90] von Staden (1989) 4.
[91] Hanson (1985) 27.
[92] Bernal (1994) 458.

were scrupulously maintained through the centuries with barely any modification. However, Ritner sought to challenge this assumption with his article 'Innovations and Adaptations in Ancient Egyptian Medicine' (2000). He pointed out that any attempts made by modern scholars to trace change in ancient Egyptian medical practice were hindered by the lack of consistent evidence to support them: only fourteen medical papyri survive from a period of over two thousand years, during which Egypt itself saw a huge amount of change which included the end of the Pharaonic period and invasion, conquest and subsequent annexations by the Persians, Macedonians and Romans respectively. He noted the range of new plant and mineral ingredients that appear in the later Egyptian medical texts, the result of unprecedented international trade that resulted from Egypt's inclusion within the Persian, Ptolemaic and Roman empires. His conclusion was that Egyptian conservatism should be recognised as reluctance to discard society's traditions rather than being resistant to new or different ideas.[93]

Egypt was unquestionably shaped by the political, cultural and social influences of the Persian, Ptolemaic and Roman empires. It is inevitable, then, that native Egyptian medicine was influenced by Persian, Greek and Roman medicine. Why do studies on medicine and medical practice during the Ptolemaic and Roman periods focus on Greek and Roman medicine and medical practice, but very rarely on native Egyptian? The paucity of evidence for native Egyptian medicine and medical practice is an excuse which, particularly given recent developments in the study of papyrology, is now increasingly less justified.[94] The modern understanding of ancient Greek and Roman medicine has been transformed over the last century by the accession of this new material, which takes the form of medical papyri written not only in Greek and to a lesser extent Latin, but also Demotic. Admittedly, the Demotic texts are being translated and published at a much slower rate than the Greek or Latin ones, but there are still a comparatively high number available for discussion and these provide evidence for the co-existence of Graeco-Roman medicine with older forms of healing.[95] Perhaps following Ritner,

Isabella Andorlini has observed that medical practitioners drew upon a store of knowledge which consisted both of Greek medical writings and of Egyptian traditions, while medical recipes relied on a pharmacopoeia that was an amalgamation of the two.[96] Consequently, this study will build on the work of Bernal and, to a lesser extent, Ritner and Andorlini, by taking care to examine Egyptian healing strategies in conjunction with those of the Greeks and Romans.

Ancient Medicine

The final and most important scholarly context requiring comment is recent work in the field of ancient medicine. Particularly worthy of discussion is the extent to which there has been a willingness (or unwillingness) to use a broad definition of healing. Vivian Nutton's *Ancient Medicine* (2004) is the most up to date and wide-ranging study of the history of medicine in antiquity, covering over one thousand years from the eighth century BC to the seventh century AD while focusing primarily upon medical practice in the territories occupied first by the Greeks and then by the Romans. Nutton examines a range of healing strategies, 'not all of which would be universally accepted, either then or now, as falling within medicine proper'.[97] He emphasises the sheer diversity of healing practices available in the ancient world, asserting that 'in the absence of any formal, legal and enforceable definitions of what medicine was, it is hardly surprising that ancient medicine operated in an open market'.[98] Although he does not focus upon medicine in Egypt specifically, there are several lengthy sections on Alexandria, Hellenistic medicine and the medical papyri, and perhaps more importantly for this study, he frequently considers medicine and the role of medical practitioners within rural and domestic environments, at least in passing.[99] Ultimately, his stated aim is to 'give an appropriate weight to the three elements involved in any medical practice, the healer, the patient and the illness'.[100] With regard to Roman medicine, several scholars have examined medicine during the Roman Republic and Empire, with varying degrees of success: John Scarborough's *Roman Medicine* (1969) is now dated, having been superseded by more recent research (not least his own on ancient pharmacy) while Audrey Cruse's *Roman Medicine* (2004) provides only a very general overview and is focused primarily on medicine and medical practice in Roman Britain.

Specific studies of medicine (or healing) in Roman Egypt are thin on the ground. While John Nunn's *Ancient Egyptian Medicine* (1996) focuses solely upon Egypt, the majority of the study is concerned with medicine and medical practice in the Predynastic and Pharaonic periods

---

[93] Ritner (2000) 107-10. Consequently, it would appear that certain medical practices can be identified as having been either Egyptian or Graeco-Roman in origin through an examination of the historical, geographical and cultural context in which they appear, e.g. the medical practices referred to in the Pharaonic medical papyri that involve the use of ingredients that were only found in Egypt (e.g. crocodile fat and excrement), or medicaments used to treat injuries or illnesses that could (usually) only be experienced in Egypt (e.g. the use of meat to bind wounds inflicted by animals such as lions and crocodiles), or techniques inspired by something peculiarly Egyptian (e.g. the ibis performing an enema on itself with Nile water) are in all probability Egyptian in origin, and the medical practices referred to in the Graeco-Roman medical papyri that redeploy these strategies were influenced by them, as opposed to the Graeco-Roman medical papyri that refer to ingredients and techniques only available in Egypt after the Roman annexation (e.g. aloe, measuring quantities according to weight rather than volume).

[94] For a recent tentative attempt to broach the subject and address this very issue, see Andorlini (2007) 23-34.

[95] Nutton (2007) 6-12.

[96] Andorlini (2007) 24.

[97] Nutton (2004) 12.

[98] Nutton (2004) 313.

[99] For work focusing specifically upon Egypt see Nutton (1972); Nutton (1977) specifically 212-15; Nutton (1993).

[100] Nutton (2004) 316.

from 2600 to 525 BC.[101] Nunn provides a synthesis of Egyptian medicine, systematically discussing the different branches of Egyptian medical specialisation, using palaeopathological evidence to illustrate examples of health problems that the ancient Egyptians experienced, and emphasises the crucial role that the unique natural environment and agricultural productivity of Egypt played in the development of medicine and medical practice.[102] Marie-Hélène Marganne's survey article on 'La médecine dans l'Égypte romaine: les sources et les méthodes' (1996) gives an overview of the literary, papyrological, epigraphic and archaeological sources for medicine and medical practice in Roman Egypt, but does not undertake any kind of detailed examination due to the summary nature and purpose of the piece. She has, however, also published a number of works on the Greek medical papyri. The first of these was *Inventaire analytique des papyrus grecs de médecine* (1981), which contains an inventory, general overview and bibliographic information for all known medical literary papyri, but excludes magical medical papyri and documentary papyri that provide evidence for the actual practice of medicine in Graeco-Roman Egypt.[103] This was subsequently supplemented by *L'Ophtalmologie dans l'Egypte greco-romaine d'après les papyrus litteraires grecs* (1994) and *La Chirurgie dans l'Egypte greco-romaine d'après les papyrus grecs* (1998), which contained translations and detailed discussions of the medical papyri dealing with ophthalmology and surgery respectively, but still excluded magical or documentary papyri.[104] Ultimately, Marganne's papyrological concordances serve as an extremely useful resource for research into certain aspects of healing practice in Graeco-Roman Egypt and provide an excellent starting point for those wishing to undertake more detailed and integrated analyses, particularly those that also take into account the Egyptian historical, social and cultural context in which these Greek papyri were written.

More recently, Marguerite Hirt Raj's *Médecins et malades de l'Égypte romaine* (2006) focused specifically upon medicine and medical practice in Roman Egypt, and she identified three main areas of medical activity: the public sector (medical practitioners such as *demosioi iatroi* that reported to those in positions of authority and were part of the imperial administration), the private sector (medical practitioners who operated out of surgeries and hospitals), and the army.[105] Her assessment of the medical profession, ranging from medical education and specialisms to social status and legal privileges was primarily confined to what is attested by documentary papyrological evidence, although some

examples of epigraphic evidence and graffiti were utilised as well. In addition to her examination of the practical aspects of medicine and medical practice in Egypt during the Roman period, she also made some tentative suggestions as to the extent to which aspects of folk medicine, rational medicine, religious beliefs and superstitious beliefs contributed to the medicine that was practised by these individuals.[106] However, this section of the study relied upon the information contained in works of ancient literature of writers such as Pliny, Celsus, Galen, Aelius Aristides and Philo as opposed to that which can be found in documentary papyri, particularly private letters, and other material from Roman Egypt. The work of Marganne and Hirt Raj, therefore, has set out some important groundwork for approaching medicine via papyrological evidence but still leaves ample scope for a study of healing in Roman Egypt that integrates literary evidence with papyrological, archaeological, bioarchaeological and archaeobotanical evidence.

The question of the extent to which the inhabitants of Egypt were 'Romanised' is particularly relevant with regard to the study of approaches to healing in Egypt. Previous scholarship of healing strategies has tended to focus on 'rational' medicine and practitioners thereof such as Galen, while in turn previous scholarship on 'rational' medicine in the Roman period has tended to treat the subject as a standardised discipline throughout the Empire, a major component in the dissemination of imperial knowledge and authority from the elite centres to the colonial periphery.[107] Even those studies specific to Egypt have suffered from this tendency: the most recent, by Hirt Raj, focuses on the status and practice of medicine in Egypt primarily but not exclusively during the Roman period, but her work has been criticised for misunderstanding the subject by projecting questions relating to Greek and Roman medicine in general onto Egypt instead of exploring the complex cultural background of the province.[108]

Over the last decade Patricia Baker has made a number of important attempts to argue that healing strategies were not standardised throughout the Roman Empire, but varied significantly according to the history and culture of the province in question. This issue was given focused attention at a Cambridge conference in 2000 on 'New Approaches in Medical Archaeology and Anthropology: Practitioners, Practices and Patients'. The subsequent edited volume, *Practitioners, Practices and Patients* (2002) confronted the presumption that medical treatment was homogenous throughout the ancient world, and that medical practitioners undertook medical practices as laid down in the works of medical writers.[109] In her individual contribution to the volume ('Diagnosing Some Ills: the Archaeology, Literature and History of Roman Medicine') Baker proceeded to elaborate on what she

---

[101] For discussion of how Egyptian medicine changed after the Pharaonic period as a result of increased contact with Greece, Rome and the East, see Ritner (2000).
[102] Nunn (1996) 23.
[103] For inventories of the magical medical spells see Ritner (1995) and Brashear (1995). For discussion of irrationality and rationality in Egyptian medicine see David (2004).
[104] For the practice of ophthalmology in the Roman Empire at large, see Jackson (1996).
[105] Hirt Raj (2006) 102-62.

[106] Hirt Raj (2006) 278-304.
[107] See for example Scarborough (1969); Jackson (1988) and (1993).
[108] For reviews, see Charlier (2007) 1 and Dasen (2008) 554.
[109] Baker and Carr (2002) vii.

considered to be the fundamental flaws with this approach - that what was written in the Mediterranean about medicine, whether by professional physicians such as Galen or educated laymen such as Celsus, was not necessarily read, understood or agreed upon in other areas of the Roman Empire, particularly where people may have had contact with the Romans, but were not necessarily adopting Roman lifestyles.[110] Her subsequent study *Medical Care for the Roman Army on the Rhine, Danube and British Frontiers from the First through Third Centuries AD* (2004) dealt specifically with healing strategies in the Roman army in the northern provinces, while recent work has focused on the Spanish provinces, with similar results.[111]

While Baker's methodology sets an important basic benchmark for approaching healing in provincial cultures, the effects of variations in natural environment (which in turn influence disease environment and consequently have a significant impact upon healing strategies) must be considered in addition to the effects of variations in local history and culture. Walter Scheidel produced a study combining research on the disease environment of Roman Egypt with the province's demography, *Death on the Nile: Disease and Demography of Roman Egypt* (2001), in which he initially attempted to acknowledge this.[112] However, it has been argued that the data that he used for this study was flawed and consequently his conclusions were open to serious doubt.[113] Thus, if an integrated examination of the healing strategies employed by the inhabitants of Egypt during the Roman period is to be attempted, it is necessary to consider the history, society and culture of Egypt in the Roman period, in conjunction with the province's unique natural environment and its concordant disease environment. This is particularly important for an exploration of how Egyptian, Greek and Roman elements interacted, and assessing the extent to which the provincial culture of Egypt was usual, unusual or even unique in the Roman Empire in its approach to healing.

3. Source Material
There is a wide range of source material that can be drawn on to elucidate a study of healing in Roman Egypt. This source material includes Greek and Roman literature from a variety of genres, documentary papyri, ostraca and epigraphy, artefacts recovered through archaeological excavation, and human mummified and skeletal remains.

Literary Evidence
The earliest extant classical writer to describe Egyptian health and medicine in any depth was Herodotus, writing the *Histories* in the middle of the fifth century BC, who claimed that 'every month for three successive days [the Egyptians] purge themselves, for their health's sake, with emetics and clysters, in the belief that all diseases come

from the food a man eats'.[114] A version of this claim was repeated by Diodorus Siculus in the *Historical Library* during the middle of the first century BC, indicating that the practices described were either entirely genuine, or at least firmly believed to be so, unless Diodorus was simply drawing on Herodotus.[115] As discussed earlier, Herodotus claimed that Egyptian medical practitioners specialised to an extreme degree. Diodorus did not repeat this claim, but he did describe the nature of the medical profession in Egypt in the mid first century BC:

> On their military campaigns and their journeys in the country they all receive treatment without the payment of any private fee; for the physicians draw their support from public funds and administer their treatments in accordance with a written law which was composed in ancient times by many famous physicians. If they follow the rules of this law as they read them in the sacred book and yet are unable to save their patient, they are absolved from any charge and go unpunished; but if they go contrary to the law's prescriptions in any respect, they must submit to a trial with death as the penalty, the lawgiver holding that but few physicians would ever show themselves wiser than the mode of treatment which had been closely followed for a long period and had been originally prescribed by the ablest practitioners.[116]

This description implies a state-sponsored and rather egalitarian approach to healing in Egypt during the Hellenistic period but its simultaneous recording of the punitive measures taken against innovative physicians and experimental medical practice have often been used by scholars to support claims that native Egyptian medicine was conservative and essentially static.[117] It also contradicts at least some of what is recorded regarding medical research and experimentation at the Museion in Alexandria by individuals such as Herophilus and Eristratus. However, the reference to the role of the sacred texts in Egyptian medicine is interesting in light of the claims made by Clement of Alexandria, writing the *Miscellanies* in the late second century AD:

> There are forty-two books of Hermes that are indispensable and necessary; of these, the thirty-six containing the whole philosophy of the Egyptians are learned by the aforementioned personages; and the other six, which are medical, are learned by the

---

[110] Baker (2002) 19-22.
[111] Baker (2004a); (2009); (2010)
[112] Scheidel (2001).
[113] Rathbone (2003) 115-16.

[114] Hdt. 2.77.
[115] Diod. Sic. 1.82.1. It is worth noting that some private letters dating from the Hellenistic and Roman periods mention the use of purgatives and emetics.
[116] Diod. Sic. 1.82.2-3.
[117] For discussion of the extent to which Egyptian medicine was conservative, see Ritner (2000).

pastophoroi, treating of the structure of the body, and of diseases, and instruments, and medicines, and about the eyes, and the last about women. These are the customs of the Egyptians.[118]

It would appear from the claims made by Diodorus, Plutarch and Clement of Alexandria that there were significant traditional and religious components to Egyptian medical practice.[119]

However, none of these writers were primarily concerned with medicine and medical practice; rather, their works are specifically religious and historical. With regard to those professional physicians such as Soranus, Galen, Rufus and Oribasius or even educated laymen such as Celsus who wrote medical treatises, they do not discuss medicine and medical practices in Egypt specifically; rather they mention Egypt and Egyptian practices as and when it is appropriate to do so, such as Soranus advocating the use of sheets of papyrus in which to wrap newborn babies, or Galen remembering the medical training he undertook in Alexandria, or Celsus recommending the Canopus salve for eye infections.[120] Likewise, those writers who compiled botanical information or wrote pharmacological treatises such as Pliny the Elder, Dioscorides and Gargilius Martialis, mentioned individual plants, spices, and ingredients harvested from animals that originated in Egypt but did not necessarily dwell on Egypt itself. Therefore, while this literature does not offer any sustained or detailed evidence for the subject of healing in Roman Egypt, it offers a number of important, if isolated, windows on to individual customs and traditions, as well as broader Mediterranean perceptions of the role of healing in Egyptian culture.

The literary papyri recovered from Egypt indicate that during the Roman period some individuals within the province (possibly medical practitioners but not necessarily so) were in possession of medical literature originally written outside of Egypt, texts from the Hippocratic corpus, and works by Galen, Dioscorides and numerous other less well-known writers.[121] Thus, comparisons between healing strategies as explored by ancient medical literature and healing strategies as detailed by documentary papyri such as letters or archaeological artefacts such as medical instruments, or even works of art recovered from the province are not necessarily inappropriate. Likewise, this study utilises the works of ancient writers when they refer specifically to practices undertaken in Egypt, such as Celsus, Pliny the Elder or Pliny the Younger. One of the aims of this study is to integrate appropriate literary evidence alongside

archaeological, artistic, demographic and papyrological evidence.

Documentary Evidence

Thousands of papyri and ostraca and hundreds of inscriptions dating from the Roman period have been recovered from Egypt. While the vast majority of these were written in Greek, many examples of Demotic and Latin writing and inscriptions survive too. Papyri and ostraca had a variety of uses: official documents such as edicts issued by the emperor and the imperial government; documents related to the complex administration of the province such as tax rolls and census returns; legal documents such as wills, contracts, sales and leases; and private letters written by the inhabitants of the province to members of their family and their friends. Inscriptions were used for commemorative purposes such as the founding of forts, quarries, towns and cities, as well as for more personal matters such as religious dedications and epitaphs.

The hundreds of personal letters that survive from Roman Egypt are particularly informative with regard to healing strategies. These letters, written to family members and friends, are an extremely useful source of information about the health of the inhabitants of the province in addition to their attitudes towards health and healing. It is apparent that there was not only an understanding of good health and ill health, but an active interest in both states in a variety of different social contexts throughout the province for the duration of the Roman period. This interest is not so surprising when considered in conjunction with the low life expectancy and high mortality of the inhabitants of Roman Egypt; the health of a family member or friend was of paramount importance because an illness could so easily prove fatal.

The expression 'I pray for your health' (*opto te bene valere* / ἐρρῶσθαί σε εὔχομαι) appears frequently, usually towards the end of a letter.[122] This positioning could support the idea that the prayer for health was an afterthought, merely a social or literary convention and the ancient equivalent of the modern 'best wishes'. However, the sheer frequency with which health is mentioned before being elaborated upon in private letters belies this, as do the specific ways in which the expression is personalised and elaborated upon.[123] Writers frequently exhort their letters' recipients to tell them about their present state of health, praising them when they do and criticising them when they do not.[124] If the writer is sick or injured, they give details. If the recipient was sick or injured the last time the writer heard from them, they ask for an update on their condition. The writer often informs the recipient that they have made obeisance before a certain god or goddess for them; letters sent from Alexandria often specifically state that

---

[118] Clem. Al. *Strom.* 6.4.
[119] See also Diodorus' discussion of Isis and healing at 1:25.1-6
[120] Sor. *Gyn.* 2.6; Gal. *SMT* 9.1.2; Celsus, *Med.* 6.6.
[121] See Marganne (1981), (1994), (1998); Andorlini (1993) 458-562; and Hirt Raj (2006) for inventories of the Greek medical papyri.

[122] For example *P. Oxy.* 2782 (AD 217, Oxyrhynchus).
[123] For example *P. Mert.* 2.82 (late second century, unprovenanced); *BGU* 2.423 (AD 139-40, Karanis); *P. Mich.* 8.478 (early second century AD, Alexandria).
[124] For example *BGU* 2.423; *P. Oxy.* 3356 (AD 76, Oxyrhynchus).

the writer has been to the Serapeum to make obeisance before Sarapis.[125] One writer even states his belief that his prayers will be more effective coming from the Serapeum.[126] Furthermore, letter writers often even offer to send the recipients items that will help them get well, such as medicine or ingredients for medicinal remedies. Healing and medicine, then, constitute a recurring motif in Egyptian epistolary communication and as such are important evidence for actual healing strategies and practice within communities throughout the province.

Using papyrological evidence can be problematic. Collections of papyrus documents have been recovered from many but by no means all sites in Egypt. For example, because of the damp conditions arising from its position between the Delta and the sea, no papyri have been recovered from Alexandria, the largest and most heavily populated city of Roman Egypt with in all probability the highest number of literate individuals. However, some papyri that were written in Alexandria and sent to recipients living in towns such as Oxyrhynchus in the Nile Valley have survived there, while mummy cartonnage from Heracleopolis has been found to contain administrative documents from Alexandria dating from the very beginning of the Augustan Principate, so information contained within a papyrus does not always relate to where it was eventually found.

Not all papyri have been recovered properly, using modern standards of archaeological excavation; the original provenance of many is unknown because they were found and then sold illegally.[127] Of those papyri that have been properly recovered through archaeological excavation, they have generally been found on village and town rubbish dumps, thought to have been discarded by their owners; this begs the question, were they thrown away because they were considered unimportant or concluded, and if so, what was considered important and kept? Also, while thousands of papyri have been published, translated and even republished and translated if new evidence comes to light in the interim, many thousands more remain in storage. Of those papyri that have been translated, most were written in Greek or Latin, as there are more scholars able to work on them than those written in Hieratic, Demotic or even Coptic.

For the purposes of this study, I have relied upon previously published papyri, ostraca, and inscriptions readily available through academic libraries and digital and internet resources. The majority of the papyri, ostraca and inscriptions I have discussed were written in Greek, although some notable examples were written in Latin and Demotic. I have included papyri, ostraca and inscriptions ranging in date from the first century BC to the fourth century AD and in provenance from the Fayum

in the north down to Philae in the south, from Kellis in the west to Berenike in the east; Tebtunis, Oxyrhynchus and Mons Claudianus feature particularly heavily as a result of the systematic archaeological excavation that has taken place at those sites, resulting in the discovery of extensive collections of papyri and ostraca. Although on numerous occasions I have used available translations as starting points, the close analysis of the texts and terminologies utilised within them, and the accompanying discussions are mine throughout unless stated otherwise.

Archaeological Evidence

According to Ernst Künzl, the advantage of the discipline of archaeology is the 'genuineness of the source material' in comparison to literary texts that are not themselves original.[128] Since this study is concerned with examining the full range of healing strategies utilised by the inhabitants of Egypt during the Roman period, I have utilised a wide variety of 'source material': different types of archaeological evidence ranging from artefacts to works of art to botanical remains.

Archaeologists interested in Roman medicine tend to focus their scholarship on either the premises where medical activity is thought to have taken place, such as the houses and surgeries of physicians or the *valetudinaria* of the Roman army, or those items that have been identified as being medical or surgical instruments.[129] No *valetudinaria* and very few medical or surgical instruments have been recovered through archaeological excavation of sites dated to the Roman period in Egypt.[130] However, in addition to documentary papyri and medical and surgical tools, artefacts such as metal instruments, clay and glass vessels, kohl sticks, amulets and charms can be equally as informative about healing strategies, although the interpretation of what precisely their presence signifies can be problematic, particularly when they lack a secure provenance and detailed excavation report. I have also utilised works of art that provide an alternative perspective on certain aspects of health and healing. These include mummy portraits and masks, terracotta figurines and models, and stelae and statues where it has been suggested that the individuals depicted were suffering from identifiable medical conditions, or are otherwise informative about aspects of health and healing strategies. Likewise, interpretation of these items can be problematic and modern approaches such as retrospective diagnosis should only be used with extreme caution.[131] In addition to material culture, the development of the archaeological sub-discipline archaeobotany has enabled the analysis and identification of plant remains which have the potential to clarify many issues regarding the use of medicinal plants, although it is not always easy to infer from the archaeological context in which plant remains

---

[125] For example *P. Oxy.* 3992 (second century AD, Alexandria); *P. Oxy.* 2984 (second-third century AD, Oxyrhynchus).

[126] *P. Oxy.* 1070 (third century AD, Alexandria).

[127] For discussion of the illegal recovery of papyri, see Cuvigny (2009) and Fearn (2010).

[128] Künzl (1988) 27.

[129] Baker (2002) 16.

[130] For the publication of some of the few that have, see Arnst (1990).

[131] See for example Grmek and Gourevitch (1998). For a critique, see Leven (2004).

are found whether they are being utilised for medicinal purposes, or as food or for the production of garlands or aromatics.[132]

The excavations that have been undertaken in Egypt have been done so under the auspices of numerous international institutions and the artefacts recovered have been divided up accordingly.[133] For example, Karanis was excavated by the University of Michigan and the finds are currently housed in the University of Michigan's Kelsey Museum of Archaeology, while parts of Tebtunis were excavated by the University of California at Berkeley and these finds are currently housed in the Centre for the Tebtunis Papyri at the Bancroft Library. Unfortunately, it has not been possible for me to travel abroad to institutions such as these. However, I have made full use of the collections exhibited in British institutions such as the British Museum, the Wellcome Library, the National Museums of Scotland, and those collections that are either available online or have been fully photographed and published.

Evidence from Forensic Anthropology
Palaeopathology can be defined as 'the study of disease in ancient populations by the examination of human remains'.[134] Egypt is an excellent source of material for such studies for several reasons. The first reason is the hot, dry climate which naturally aids the preservation of human remains while the second is the endurance of the practice of mummification, which serves to preserve human remains artificially.

There are limitations to using palaeopathology as a means of ascertaining the health of the population of Roman Egypt; whether skeletal or mummified, the inhabitants of a cemetery are only one small fraction of any given population at any given time. As far as skeletal human remains are concerned, not all medical conditions are evident from an individual's bones. However, skeletal remains offer an excellent opportunity to examine injuries caused by accident or assault. As far as mummified human remains are concerned, certain illnesses, both congenital (such as diabetes) and contracted (such as parasitic infestations) only affect soft tissue. Due to the adoption of traditional Egyptian burial practices, skeletal and mummified human remains from Roman Egypt can be used in conjunction with each other to provide information on health and ill health that is simply not available from cemeteries located in other provinces of the Roman Empire.

The primary source for studies in the palaeopathology of the inhabitants of Roman Egypt is the work of the Dakhleh Oasis Project, a long-term regional study of environmental changes and human activity in the Western Desert, spanning the centuries from the Middle

Pleistocene to the present day. Included in the extensive archaeological excavations that have been undertaken in the area were Kellis, an ancient town occupied during the Late Ptolemaic and Roman Periods, and an associated cemetery, the East Cemetery or Kellis 2, which was in use between AD 100 and AD 450. Due to the arid conditions of the Western Desert, the human skeletal remains recovered from Kellis 2 were in an excellent state of preservation, allowing the palaeopathology of the inhabitants of Kellis to be comprehensively studied. Kellis 2 is the only Roman cemetery in Egypt that has been systematically excavated during the latter part of the twentieth century; the human remains have been comprehensively recorded, examined and analysed with the findings published.

There is other archaeological evidence that can be employed to the same ends as palaeopathological examination of skeletal and mummified human remains, at least speculatively. The corpus of mummy portraits recovered from the Roman cemetery at Hawara in the Fayum, produced from the first to the third centuries AD, comprises primarily encaustic or tempera portraits painted onto wooden panels that covered the head of a mummified individual and were then buried with him or her. One purpose of the portraits is thought to have been to serve as a record of how the individual had appeared during life. To that end, the portraits can be seen to be highly detailed, extremely varied and perhaps as a result realistic, so much so that it might be possible to identify certain medical conditions from them.[135]

4. Research Aims and Methodology
The purpose of this study is to examine the healing strategies employed by the inhabitants of Egypt during the Roman period, from the late first century BC to the fourth century AD, in order to explore how Egyptian, Greek and Roman customs and traditions interacted within the province. Thus this study aims to make an original contribution to the history of medicine, by offering a detailed examination of the healing strategies (of which 'rational' medicine was only one) utilised by the inhabitants of one particular region of the Mediterranean during a key phase in its history, a region, moreover, which by virtue of the survival of papyrological evidence offers a unique opportunity for study. Its interdisciplinary approach, which integrates ancient literary, documentary, archaeological and scientific evidence, presents a new approach to understanding healing strategies in Roman provincial culture. It refines the study of healing within Roman provincial culture, identifies diagnostic features of healing in material culture and offers a more contextualised reading of ancient medical literary and documentary papyri and archaeological evidence.

This study differs from previous attempts to examine healing in Roman Egypt in that it tries, as far as possible,

[132] Ciaraldi (2002) 81.
[133] For surveys of the archaeological excavations and publications that have taken place over the last fifteen years, see Bagnall (2001) and Bagnall and Davoli (2011).
[134] Aufderheide (1998) xv.

[135] For the mummy portraits see Corcoran (1995); Doxiadis (1995); Walker (2000). For the possibility of identifying medical conditions from them, see Appenzeller (2001); Ikram (2003); Johnson (2005).

to encompass the full spectrum of healing strategies available to the inhabitants of the province. It addresses the extent to which both 'rational' means of healing (such as those practices instantly recognisable to a modern scholar, e.g. pharmacology or surgery) and 'irrational' means of healing (such as magical incantations, amulets and divine intervention) were utilised. It assesses the presence of and demand for 'professional' practitioners (such as individuals who called themselves physicians or midwives, had undergone some form of training and charged a fee for their services) and 'amateur' practitioners (such as well-meaning family members, friends, and those individuals whose services were employed on an ad hoc basis). It examines the role of both secular organisations (such as the provincial government or army and their members who operated under the auspices of imperial authority) and religious institutions (such as Egyptian, Greek and Roman temples and their priests, priestesses and other staff, both officially sanctioned and independent). It focuses on a variety of different types of community in a range of geographical locations, not just the city of Alexandria but also the villages of the Fayum, the towns and cities of the Nile Valley, the oases of the Western Desert, the quarry settlements in the Eastern Desert and the ports on the Red Sea coast. In this way I aim to compare and contrast healing strategies throughout the province, and in a range of natural and social environments.

The first stage towards achieving these goals is to undertake a systematic and comprehensive survey of evidence for centralised, professional medical practice in Roman Egypt, an approach that is representative of most existing scholarly approaches to medicine in Roman provincial cultures. However, in addition to this I also survey and analyse the evidence (largely neglected by scholars of Roman Egypt) for healing carried out on a localised or domestic basis and the integration of family traditions, religious structures, magical practices and acquired knowledge of the medicinal properties of native Egyptian plant and animal species. These two surveys are then complemented by three distinct case studies identifying ailments that were prevalent in Egypt during the Roman period and examining the range of ways in which they were approached and treated by the inhabitants of the province. These case studies not only provide an opportunity to examine some of the ideas explored in the first two chapters in more specific contexts, but they also allow a more detailed and nuanced study of particular conditions that were characteristic of the natural environment of Roman Egypt.

5. Structure
The first part of this study comprises two chapters and focuses on the practitioners of healing strategies, both 'professional' and 'amateur'. Chapter 1 ('Identifying Medical Practitioners in Roman Egypt') examines the different types of 'professional' or even 'official' medical practitioners, individuals whose position was formalised through membership of the provincial administration, the army or a religious institution, and who could be classified by others as an *iatros* or *medicus*. This chapter

first approaches the issue of the 'professional' medical practitioner from the top down, utilising primarily papyrological but also epigraphic evidence, as these are the means by which 'official' medical practitioners are attested, beginning with medical practitioners in Alexandria before moving on to the different categories of 'official' medical practitioners and the hierarchy of the 'official' medical profession as reflected in references to *archiatroi, demosioi iatroi*, and military physicians in the epigraphic record. Then it approaches the issue of the 'professional' medical practitioner from the bottom up, utilising the archaeological evidence such as the remains of architecture, equipment and literature to examine evidence for those medical practitioners operating independently, outside of provincial administration and the army, figures who have been attested in other provinces such as Britain and Italy. Finally, it examines the evidence for medical practitioners in both the Graeco-Roman and native Egyptian religious institutions of Roman Egypt, utilising different types of religious institutions such as the Graeco-Roman temple of Sarapis and Isis at Canopus and the Graeco-Egyptian temple of Soknebtunis at Tebtunis.

Chapter 2 ('Identifying Alternative Healing Strategies') examines those areas of ancient medicine that have traditionally been neglected or summarily dismissed by scholars: 'domestic' and 'folk' medicine (these terms are themselves evidence of scholarly prejudice) with particular emphasis on the extent to which the specific natural environment of any given location affects healing strategies. First, this chapter addresses the reasons why the inhabitants of Roman Egypt might have preferred alternative healing strategies to those espoused by 'professional' or 'official' medical practitioners. These reasons could have been positive and active (such as a desire to perpetuate what they considered to be natural or even traditional practices) or negative and passive (such as fear of incompetent or dishonest medical practitioners, lack of availability or the prohibitive cost of treatment). Then it examines the papyrological and archaeological evidence for the inhabitants of Roman Egypt providing each other with medicine and medicinal ingredients, ranging from private letters in which these subjects are discussed to botanical and pharmacological remains recovered through excavation to chemical analysis of mummified and skeletal remains. The unique natural environment of Egypt, the utilisation of its natural resources such as Nile water, riverbank clay, fish and animal species, and the harnessing of this natural environment in order to cultivate and produce fruit, vegetables, herbs and oils with medicinal properties is scrutinised. The alternative healing strategies employed in order to deal with a universal health condition, pregnancy and childbirth, are examined. Finally, it examines the evidence for the employment of alternative healing strategies in four different communities: Kellis in the Dakhleh Oasis of the Western Desert; Oxyrhynchus in the Nile Valley; Mons Claudianus in the Eastern Desert; and Berenike on the Red Sea coast.

The second part of this study (consisting of three individual case studies) provides an opportunity to explore in greater detail the approaches and ideas examined in the first two chapters. This approach ensures a more detailed and nuanced study of the specific ways in which the natural environment of Egypt impacted upon certain aspects of health by contributing to eye disease, fever and injuries inflicted during attacks by wild animals, in addition to demonstrating the significance of specific historical, cultural and environmental factors in the development of healing strategies within a specific province.

Chapter Three ('Eye Complaints in Roman Egypt') examines the nature and frequency of eye diseases and injuries suffered by the inhabitants of Roman Egypt. This chapter scrutinises the experiences of two victims of eye complaints that are particularly well represented in papyrological archives (Tryphon from Oxyrhynchus and Gemellus Horion from Karanis), then examines the range of healing strategies available to those suffering from a range of different eye complaints. These include both 'rational' healing strategies such as eye salves and surgery and 'irrational' healing strategies such as magical incantations and divine intervention, particularly that of the Graeco-Egyptian god Sarapis.

Chapter Four ('Fever in Roman Egypt') examines the nature and frequency of the fevers suffered by the inhabitants of Roman Egypt, focusing first on the disease malaria, which is attested by papyrological, archaeological and palaeopathological evidence as having been suffered throughout Egypt, both in the communities located adjacent to the Nile and those out on the desert oases, then other types of fever, before examining the range of healing strategies available to those suffering from fevers. These include both 'rational' healing strategies as recommended by Latin, Greek and Demotic medical treatises and 'irrational' healing strategies such as magical amulets and divine intervention, particularly that of the syncretised god Imhotep-Asclepius.

Chapter Five ('Wild Animals in Roman Egypt') examines the dangers that the animal species of Egypt could pose to the inhabitants of the province, focusing particularly upon snakes, scorpions, crocodiles and lions, as attested by papyrological and epigraphic evidence such as private letters, mummy labels and epitaph inscriptions. It scrutinises cases in which individuals were bitten, stung or scratched by these animals and the healing strategies utilised to treat these injuries, examines the ways in which ingredients harvested from these creatures were either used as or incorporated into medicinal remedies to treat these and other medical conditions, and examines the ways in which these creatures were associated with Egyptian, Greek and Roman healing deities such as Serket, Sekhmet, Sobek, Sarapis, Isis and Asclepius, cults that played a regular role in the practice of healing and medicine in the province.

Finally, the conclusion underlines the importance for a study of the healing strategies utilised in any province of the Roman Empire (or indeed any region in the ancient world) of taking into account the historical, geographical, cultural and social context of the location in question. In the case of Egypt during the Roman period, the healing strategies of the Pharaonic period and the Hellenistic period remained extremely influential. The hot and dry climate, the proximity of most human settlements to the river Nile, and the local wildlife all impacted upon the disease environment. The living conditions in built-up areas, in which extended families and their livestock shared extremely small spaces without fresh running water or appropriate and hygienic waste disposal, all impacted upon health. It is apparent that, in addition to a centralised medical doctrine espoused by 'official' and 'professional' medical practitioners (in part an inevitable consequence of Roman colonisation and Romanisation), there existed in Roman Egypt extremely well-established localised traditions of alternative healing strategies oriented around domestic and folk medicine. I argue that healing in Egypt during the Roman period, far from being merely one part of a discipline that was homogenous throughout the Roman Empire over the course of nearly five centuries, consisted of a multiplicity of complex approaches to healing that originated and developed over time according to the specific nature of the individual province and its unique provincial culture.

CHAPTER ONE

IDENTIFYING MEDICAL PRACTITIONERS IN ROMAN EGYPT

1. Introduction

In the Roman Empire no formal training or educational qualifications were necessary for an individual to be able to call himself an *iatros* or *medicus* (or herself an *iatrinē* or *medica*).[136] Such titles appear in the epigraphic record in the epitaphs of numerous extremely young people, for example two *medici ocularii* named Primitivus and Phasis, who died at ages nineteen and seventeen respectively.[137] Individuals who wished to become physicians could undertake formal training in the form of an apprenticeship of some sort, but the duration of such an apprenticeship was not regulated, so was by no means uniform throughout the empire.

There was no formal assessment and no certification or qualification was required before an individual could begin to practise medicine - either for free or for payment. Consequently, the extent to which an individual received any training and was actually competent seems to have varied dramatically; physicians were commonly characterised as being incompetent to the point of endangering the life of the patient in all genres of ancient literature.[138] However, there is evidence to suggest that some medical practitioners took and considered themselves to be bound by the 'Hippocratic Oath'.[139] One papyrus dating to the early third century AD and clearly not written by a professional scribe contains an extract from the 'Hippocratic Oath' that seemed to have been adapted for a particular purpose, and it is possible that it was copied out for use in some sort of oath-taking ceremony. Also, a recently published papyrus which appears to have derived from the *proem* of a medical treatise, perhaps some kind of introductory manual, states

'for those young men who are being introduced in a systematic way to medicine…it is proper, as *I* see it at least, in the first place to make the beginning of learning from the Hippocratic Oath'.[140]

The most recent study of physicians in Roman Egypt is Marguerite Hirt Raj's *Médicins et malades de l'Égypte romaine*, which focused on the status and practice of medicine in Egypt primarily but not exclusively during the Roman period. However, it is a study with certain limitations.[141] In particular, the study is concerned only with what might be described as the secular, 'professional' medical practitioner, essentially the Greek *iatros*, as attested by the documentary papyri. In this chapter, I will examine evidence not only for the Greek *iatros* and the Roman *medicus* but also for the Egyptian *swnw* and practitioners of temple medicine in both the city of Alexandria and throughout the *chora* of Egypt from the late first century BC to the end of the fourth century AD. I will not only incorporate documentary evidence such as papyri, ostraca and epigraphy, but will also utilise archaeological evidence such as artefacts and works of art.

The first part of this chapter will focus on the medical profession in Roman Egypt from the top down, identifying those medical practitioners with official status who were engaging in medical practice that was formally recognised and even subsidised by the imperial administration. The evidence for these individuals is primarily papyrological and epigraphic; documentary papyri such as legal documents, formal petitions and medical reports in conjunction with honorific inscriptions and epitaphs. The second part will focus on the medical profession in Roman Egypt from the ground up, examining the literary and archaeological evidence for the day to day activities of medical practitioners in Roman Egypt who do not otherwise appear in the historical record. This will include coverage of locations where medical practice took place, medical equipment and medical literature, as has been done for other provinces in the Roman Empire such as Britain, Gaul and Italy. The third part will examine the evidence for medical practitioners within temple complexes in Roman Egypt; it is clear that it was not only laymen who undertook medical training and then practised medicine for payment in the Roman Empire. Since Augustus designated a Roman official as the High Priest of Alexandria and Egypt and consolidated priestly authority, tradition, lifestyle and economic activities according to the *Gnomon of the Idios Logos*, in one sense medical

---

[136] One medical apprenticeship contract written on papyrus and dating to the Hellenistic period stipulates a six year training period; *P. Heid.* 3.226 (215-13 BC, unprovenanced). There is also evidence which suggests the passing down of medical knowledge within a family. See the epitaph of the child Machaon, son of Sabbataios, at *CIJ* II: 1539, dating to 14th March AD 8. Machaon is an extremely unusual name that was used predominantly by physicians and members of medical families, perhaps indicating that his parents intended him to follow in his father's footsteps and thus may well have started his medical education and training while he was still very young. See also the dedicatory inscription of the physician brothers Horos and Papsos, whose father Paos and grandfather Kollouthos were possibly also physicians, at *IGRom.* I:1289, dating to AD 88 and set up at Elephantine, and the family of physicians from Oxyrhynchus at *P. Oxy.* 4001, dating to the fourth century AD. For discussion of medical families, see Samama (2003) 19-20.

[137] Jackson (1996) 2233.

[138] For the issue of payment of physicians generally, see Kudlien (1976); for the issue of payment of physicians for forensic and expert witness services rendered, see Amundsen and Ferngren (1978) 338-9; for a list of ancient references portraying physicians in a negative light, see Amundsen (1974) 320 n1 and n2. For a graffito in which an individual refers to himself as 'Dadouxios, learned physician' (Δαδούχιος σχολαστικὸς ἰατ[ρικὸς]), see *CIG* 4781c (second century AD, Thebes).

[139] For discussion of the 'Hippocratic Oath' in the ancient and modern world, see Miles (2005). See also *P. Oxy.* 2547 (early third century AD, Oxyrhynchus).

[140] *P. Oxy.* 4970 (second century AD, Oxyrhynchus). See also Scribonius Largus, *Compositiones* pref. 5.

[141] For reviews of this work, see Charlier (2007) 1; Dasen (2008) 554.

practitioners practising in the native Egyptian temples were officially recognised and sanctioned too.[142]

Categorisation and Classification

There are numerous different literary and archaeological contexts in which individuals record themselves as being either an *iatros* or a *medicus*. Inhabitants of Egypt during the Roman period wrote private letters to members of their families and their friends that incidentally happened to state their professions, in addition to producing official documents by submitting census returns, entering into legal contracts and paying taxes, all of which included their line of work as a matter of course.[143] Alternatively, tourists scratched their names and occupations as graffiti on ancient monuments such as the royal tombs in the Valley of the Kings and the Colossi of Memnon, and these include many references to medical practitioners.[144] However, it is important to remember that this is self-definition; while there were restrictions placed upon the number of physicians exempt from taxation or participation in liturgies in any given administrative area, there were no restrictions placed upon who could call themselves a physician.[145] All that can be inferred from this self-definition is that being known as a physician does not seem to have been considered detrimental in Egypt, although this certainly seems to have been the case in other parts of the Roman Empire such as Italy.[146]

Despite the range of contexts, both informal and formal, public and private, in which these statements of profession were made, the vast majority of these individuals simply describe themselves as being either an *iatros* or a *medicus*, meaning 'one who heals', 'physician', 'surgeon' or 'doctor', rather than as a more specialist medical practitioner, like those attested in the epigraphic evidence from other provinces such as the *medicus ocularius*.[147] The lack of specialisation apparent from the documentary papyri contrasts with the claims of earlier writers such as Herodotus that 'the practice of medicine they split up into separate parts, each doctor being responsible for the treatment of only one disease'.[148] There is also no evidence that the *swnw*, so

frequently attested in Pharaonic Egypt, the Late Period, and even the Ptolemaic period, was known as such during the Roman period, although there are some disparate references to practitioners of native Egyptian medicine.[149]

Medical Practitioners in Roman Alexandria

Long after Galen had left Egypt, he commented that Alexandria and Rome were the only two cities in the ancient world that had populations large enough to support numerous different kinds of medical specialists: 'The number of their inhabitants ensures a livelihood for those who practise any single branch of medicine in those cities, not to mention a livelihood for those who have a broader medical competence than that'.[150] Certainly, following the foundation of the Museion and Library of Alexandria by Ptolemy II Philadelphus, Alexandria came to be renowned throughout the ancient world as a centre of learning and culture. Scholars and intellectuals were recruited from all over the Mediterranean, paid generous stipends, provided with free accommodation and subsequently referred to as 'one of those receiving sustenance in the Museion and not subject to taxes'.[151] The majority of works of modern scholarship that discuss the Museion and Library are concerned with these institutions during the Hellenistic period, as this is the period best attested by ancient literary evidence.[152] However, Alexandria appears to have continued to play an important part in intellectual life and scholarship during the Roman period too.

However, there is some contention amongst modern scholars regarding the presence of medical practitioners at the Museion and Library and the extent to which they practised medicine, if they practised it at all. According to Peter Fraser, the practice of medicine in the Museion and Library at Alexandria consisted of 'scientific or academic medical work carried out by highly skilled specialists'. He states that the members of the Museion 'were no doubt primarily concerned with the advancement of their subject by investigation, but it is natural to suppose that they also taught and gave lectures'.[153] Certainly, individuals who would later go on to become prominent physicians such as Rufus of Ephesus, Soranus of Ephesus, Galen of Pergamum and Oribasius are known to have travelled to Alexandria specifically to study medicine there.[154] However, John Vallance takes a different view. While observing that modern scholars tend to assume that the Library *must* have contained the

---

[142] Frankfurter (1998) 27.

[143] For an example of a census return of a physician, see *P. Hamb.* 60 (AD 90, Hermopolis). For an example of an estate account making a payment to a physician, see *P. Mich.* 620 (AD 239-40, Theadelphia). For an example of a tax roll recording the payments of five doctors from one village, see *P. Mich.* 4.1 (AD 172-3, Karanis).

[144] For the Valley of the Kings, see *Syringes* 11, 15, 53, 114, 120, 130, 142, 160, 658, 663, 805, 930, 1009, 1081, 1136, 1144, 1167, 1194, 1256, 1272, 1402, 1525, 1575, 1617, 1801, 1847, 1911 and 2053. For the Colossi of Memnon, see *IGA* III: 24, 256, 278, 354, 439, 473, 498 and 591. Of course, it is impossible to tell whether these graffiti were the work of the residents of Egypt, or of tourists from outside the province.

[145] For the restrictions placed upon the number of physicians in a given administrative area and the consequent two-tiered system of medical practitioners - those who were exempt and those who were not - see Horsley (1982) 12; for self-definition of physicians extending to membership of medical sects, see von Staden (1983), particularly 83.

[146] Mattern (2008) 22.

[147] Jackson (1996) 2233; for collections of artefacts and inscriptions organised according to province see also Künzl (1983); Rémy (1984); Rémy (1987a); Rémy (1987b).

[148] Hdt. 2.84.

[149] Six *swnw* from *Count P.* 2 (229 BC), three *swnw* from *Count P.* 4 (254-31 BC), five *swnw* from *Count P.* 8 (243-17 BC) and one *swnw-ir.t*, an oculist, from *Count P.* 9 (251-0 BC), and *P. Lond.* 1.43, for this translation of this papyrus with commentary, see Bagnall *et al.* (2006) 113.

[150] Gal. *Ars med.* 2.3.

[151] *OGI* 714; *SB* 6012.

[152] Fraser (1972) 305-35; Delia (1992) 1449-61; Littman (1996) 2678-97; Nutton (2004) 128-39.

[153] Fraser (1972) 338.

[154] On Galen's reasons for travelling to Alexandria and his expectations of what he would find there, see von Staden (2004) 181-5. On Soranus in Alexandria see *Suda* S851; on Galen in Alexandria see *Trem. Palp.* 7, *Alim. Fac.* 1.25.2, *MM* 1.7; on Oribasius in Alexandria see Philostr. *V S* 530-7.

important, canonical works of Greek philosophy and medicine, and that local and visiting scholars *must* have had access to them, he suggests that this assumption be subject to qualification.[155] There do appear to have been a substantial number of medical treatises within the Library; Galen records that customs officials were instructed to confiscate any medical books brought to Alexandria by travellers, copy them and then return the copies to the travellers before depositing the originals in the Library.[156] However, although there were apparently medical treatises within the Library, it is important to remember that the Museion and Library were not public buildings to which anyone could gain access.[157]

Although there is substantial evidence (and numerous examples) of individuals from outside Egypt travelling to Alexandria in order to study medicine there, the extent to which individuals already living in Egypt travelled to Alexandria to study medicine is less well known. In his discussion of the extent to which the native Egyptian scientific disciplines influenced the development of those of Greece, Palter suggested a possible explanation for why, as far as he could see, Egyptian medicine did not influence Greek medicine. He surmised that since the ways in which the Egyptian and Greek medical professions were organised differed quite substantially in the Hellenistic and Imperial periods, there was little opportunity for social and professional contact between their respective members: 'Egyptian physicians were public officials, working for the state and providing free care to their patients while Greek physicians were, so to speak, in private practice collecting fees from both their patients and apprentices; and Egyptian physicians tended to be specialists, Greek physicians general practitioners', and opined that native Egyptians do not seem to have participated in the work of the Museion and Library.[158] Considering that the Egyptian inhabitants of Alexandria reportedly segregated themselves and resided in one particular area of the city where the settlement of Rhakotis had originally been, this is not surprising.[159] However, there is evidence for knowledge regarding the type of innovative medical practice that was taking place at Alexandria spreading from there to the *chora* in the form of works authored by Galen that were being copied and read in the Nile valley soon after his death.[160] Exactly how much of this transmission was the result of physicians trained in Alexandria going to towns and villages in the *chora* to practise medicine there is uncertain.[161]

In addition to those medical practitioners who appear to have been living and working at the Museion and Library, there were also medical practitioners in

Alexandria who did not. Their presence in the city was presumably only tangentially related to those institutions, perhaps a result of the belief that residence in Alexandria automatically elevated a medical practitioner, but equally perhaps also due to the size of the city's population.[162] One example of an individual claiming a link with Alexandria, perhaps in order to elevate his own professional standing, was the itinerant physician 'prudent' Dorotheos (Δωρόθεος σαόφρονα), who according to the epitaph set up for him on Ios was born and trained in Alexandria where 'he grasped all his skill'.[163]

Categories of Physician and the Medical Hierarchy in Roman Egypt

Once Octavian had annexed Egypt, direct rule over the province was undertaken by a series of provincial governors or prefects who were based primarily in Alexandria in the Brucheion, the former royal quarter, and at Memphis. The provincial governor would have been ultimately responsible for all the administrative appointments made within his province. In turn, the *strategoi* and *logistes* whom he appointed oversaw the members of the medical hierarchy associated with imperial administration on a local level such as the *demosioi iatroi* and the military officials that he commanded oversaw the physicians that served the army and navy.

Archiatroi

During the Ptolemaic period, the title *archiatros* denoted a physician at the royal court.[164] However, over the course of the Roman period the definition changed until an *archiatros* was recognised as being essentially a civic or public physician.[165] Four *archiatroi* are known by name from various dates in Egypt across the Roman period: Gaius Proculeius Themison, Ammonius, Porphyrius and Zeno.[166]

Gaius Proculeius Themison is known from an inscription that would have been attached to an honorific statue dating to AD 7: 'The body (πλῆθος) of physicians [...] in Alexandria [honours] Gaius Proculeius Themison the *archiatros*, on account of his beneficence'.[167] Despite its brevity, this inscription poses significant interpretive

[155] Vallance (2004) 95.
[156] Gal. *Hipp. Epid.* 3.17A.
[157] Delia (1992) 1452.
[158] Palter (1993) 273.
[159] Strabo, *Geographica* 17.1.6; Plin. *HN* 5.11.62; for the Jews of Alexandria reportedly doing the same and living in the Delta district see Joseph. *BJ* 494-8.
[160] Nutton (2007) 8; see *P. Berol.* Inv. 21141.
[161] Marganne (2002) 1-16.
[162] On claiming an education in Alexandria in order to improve one's prospects, see Amm. Marc. 22.17. Diod. Sic. 17.52.6 claims that the ἐλεύθεροι population of Alexandria was over 300,000 during the Ptolemaic period, presumably referring to citizens of both genders and all ages; Delia (1988) 290 gives an estimated total population of 500-600,000 during the Roman period.
[163] *GVI* 1.766: ὅμ ποτ' Ἀλεξάνδρεια λοχεύσατο πατρὶς ἀγ[ητή] νειλόρυτος, πάσης ἀψάμενον σοφιη[ς]. See Horsley (1982) 20 for translation and brief discussion.
[164] Nutton (1977) 194, 214.
[165] Nutton (1977) 214.
[166] Additionally, three *archiatroi* are known by name from the Ptolemaic period: Nicanor from Alexandria (*Aristeas ad Philocratem Epistula* 182 (late second-early first century BC)), Phalous from the Arsinoite nome (*SB* 15.12375 (180 BC)), and Athenagoras from the Fayum (*SB* 1.5216 (middle of the first century BC)).
[167] Römer (1990) 81. Γάιον Προκλήιον Θεμίσωνα ἀρχιατρὸν τὸ πλῆθος τῶν ἐν Ἀλεξανδρείαι [...] μένων ἰατρῶν εὐνοίας χάριν.

problems. One of those problems is the meaning of the word πλῆθος: does it refer to a formal body, or does it simply mean 'the majority'? Understanding its significance is not helped by damage to the inscription after the word 'Alexandria', where scholars have proposed restorations varying from 'the physicians assembled in Alexandria' to 'the physicians residing in Alexandria', to 'the physicians practising in Alexandria'. How one deals with these issues not only has implications for the existence or otherwise of a recognised guild of physicians in the city, but also for the extent of Themison's authority. Cornelia Römer's reconstruction of the inscription favours 'the physicians assembled in Alexandria' (Ἀλεξανδρείαι [συνηγ]μένων), implying that some of these physicians may have come from outside of the city, and has led her to believe that while Themison was probably not responsible for the physicians of Alexandria, he did hold the office of *archiatros* in Alexandria (perhaps even in association with the Museion) and so it was for that reason that the other physicians chose to honour him there.[168] However, François Kayser prefers a reconstruction of the inscription that reads 'the physicians residing in Alexandria' (Ἀλεξανδρείαι [καθη]μένων), while Évelyne Samama and Marguerite Hirt Raj both suggest 'the physicians practising in Alexandria' (Ἀλεξανδρείαι [ἐργαζο]μένων).[169] Additionally, Hirt Raj has suggested that, on the basis of his name, Themison received Roman citizenship from Gaius Proculeius, one of Octavian's most trusted aides - in point of fact, the man who was responsible for arranging the surrender of Cleopatra VII in 30 BC. If so, this would mean that he was already moving in the highest circles of Alexandrian society decades before he was honoured there by his peers.[170]

Ammonius is known from one papyrus letter dating to the second century AD, in which the writer addresses him as *archeiatros*. However, this letter reveals nothing about his professional role beyond the fact that he appears to have been reasonably affluent.[171] Nutton has suggested that Ammonius might have been a member of the Museion like Lucius Gellius Maximus, although there is no evidence of this.[172] Interestingly, evidence of another, unnamed *archiatros* survives in the form of an order for food dating from between the third and fourth centuries AD, indicating that the individual in question was also reasonably affluent.[173]

Porphyrius is known from an estate account from Hermonthis, dating to 25th April, AD 338, in which he is referred to as *archiatros*, without any further detail.[174] Zeno is known from the letters of the emperor Julian. He was banished from Alexandria by Bishop George in AD

360, but recalled at the insistence of the Alexandrians upon Julian's accession in AD 361. Julian's letter to Zeno provides some information regarding Zeno's role as *archiatros*:

> There is indeed abundant evidence of other kinds that you have attained to the first rank in the art of medicine and that your morals, uprightness and temperate life are in harmony with your professional skill...For I think that Homer was right when he said "One physician is worth many other men". And you are not simply a physician, but also a teacher of that art for those who desire to learn, so that I might almost say that what physicians are compared with the mass of men, you are, compared with other physicians.[175]

Like Themison, he appears to have been well-regarded by other members of the medical profession resident in Alexandria, but whereas Themison's connection with the emperor Augustus is pure conjecture, Zeno's is confirmed by the writings of the emperor Julian himself. The fact that Zeno was acquainted with the emperor of the Roman Empire at all (perhaps they were introduced by Oribasius) indicates that he was an exceptional individual and does not provide us with much information about the typical *archiatros*.

Henri Pleket has argued that *archiatroi* were not members of the urban elite, since they do not appear to have held the magistracies or other positions of civic responsibility that were the privilege of the social elite, going so far as to state that this is the case for around 60% of all recorded cases of *archiatroi*.[176] However, his argument encompasses *archiatroi* known throughout the entire Roman Empire, rather than those in Egypt specifically. On the other hand, Nutton has examined the role of the *archiatroi* in the medical profession from province to province, concluding that Egypt resembles Africa and the Western provinces, rather than the empire as a whole.[177] What can be inferred from these four examples is that these individual *archiatroi* seem to have been well-regarded by their peers, were reasonably affluent and could be acquainted with high status individuals. However, no information is provided about their duties and responsibilities, medical or administrative.

Demosioi Iatroi

The title *demosios iatros*, signifying some form of public physician, does not seem to have occurred in Egypt before the middle of the second century AD and its appearance was perhaps related to the legislation of Antoninus Pius restricting the number of physicians

---

[168] Römer (1990) 87.
[169] Kayser (1994) 283-5; Samama (2003) 474-5; Hirt Raj (2006) 41.
[170] Hirt Raj (2006) 63, 167-8.
[171] *P. Oslo* 53 (second century AD, unprovenanced).
[172] Nutton (1977) 215.
[173] *O. Ashm. Shelt.* 75 (third-fourth century AD, Oxyrhynchus).
[174] *P. Lips.* 97 (AD 338, Hermonthis).

[175] Julian. *Ep*.17.
[176] Pleket (1995) 31.
[177] Nutton (1977) 215.

entitled to exemptions.[178] Such public physicians are subsequently attested frequently in the documentary papyri (although not in the surviving epigraphic evidence from Egypt during the Roman period), as one of their duties involved documenting forensic medical investigations and examinations.[179] According to Darrel Amundsen and Gary Ferngren, these documents can be classified as belonging to four different categories: a request to an official (a *strategos* prior to the middle of the third century AD and a *logistes* or *curator civitatis* from the late third century AD onwards) for an examination or an investigation; an order from an official to his assistant to take a physician with him and then submit a written report of their findings; a *prosphonesis* or medical report; and a record of a *prosphonesis* being used as evidence in a trial.[180] Such documents were important pieces of evidence in the legal cases pursued by inhabitants of Egypt during the Roman period, serving a means of establishing responsibility, apportioning blame, ensuring prosecution and facilitating financial compensation. Currently thirty nine such documents have been edited, translated and published.[181]

One such report submitted by a public physician, dated to AD 96, details how he was called to examine a slave who had received an injury to her finger, an injury which he then proceeded to treat.[182] However, this explicit statement of the public physician providing treatment himself is an isolated case. A second document, a request for the attention of a public physician, dating from 9th February, AD 246, concludes with the following statement: 'I submit this petition requesting you to dispatch an assistant to inspect their condition so that they may be able to receive the necessary treatment".[183] Whether it would have been the public physician providing the 'necessary treatment', or whether the afflicted individual would have received it after their examination from someone else entirely is uncertain. If an individual was seriously injured to the point where their future health and well-being, or even their life, was

threatened, it would not be practical to wait too long before allowing them to receive some kind of medical attention, no matter who was responsible for providing it; in this particular instance, the petitioner writes that a gang of criminals had broken into her home, wounded her husband in the arm and hand with a sword and struck her son in the head, their injuries likely to be severe.

The main function of the public physician in instances where they were sent to examine sick or injured individuals appears to have been solely bureaucratic (either certifying death or making a record of the petitioner's injuries or illness that could be used in any forthcoming legal proceedings) as the vast majority of these reports do not give any indication of any treatment having occurred at all. However, considering the administrative and legal uses to which these reports were ultimately intended to be put, if medical treatment had been provided by the public physician, it would surely have been useful to include a record of the severity of the injuries or illnesses experienced by the petitioners *and* details of exactly what treatment was necessary, for the purposes of ensuring a prosecution and/or determining the degree of financial compensation to be awarded.

It is possible that an examination of the terminology used within these reports might indicate the extent of the medical training that public physicians had undertaken. In one case dating to the 13th June, AD 331, the public physicians of Oxyrhynchus use a combination of simple and complicated medical terminology.[184] While the victim's wounds are simply described as τραύματα, with οἴδημα and πελιώμα, there is also mention of ὑμενος (membrane) and this is the only occasion upon which this term appears in a documentary papyrus. Precisely which membrane is designated by this term varies according to context.[185] Considering that the victim has suffered head wounds, it could be the membrane around the brain or the eye. However, what is apparent from the rest of these records is that the language and terminology used by the *demosioi iatroi* in most surviving reports was relatively unsophisticated compared to that used in ancient medical treatises. The descriptions of the wounds inflicted are for the most part extremely basic, consisting of terms such as τραύμα, 'wound' or 'hurt'; τύμμα, 'blow' or 'wound'; οἴδημα, 'swelling'; ἀμυχάς, 'scratch' or 'skin wound'; πελιώματος, 'bruise'.[186] Of course, such limited

---

[178] Amundsen and Ferngren (1978) 350. On Antoninus Pius' restrictions, see Nutton (1971). A similar position to that of the δημόσιος ἰατρος, that of the δημόσιος γραμματικός, is recorded in *P. Coll. Youtie* 2.66 (AD 258, Oxyrhynchus).
[179] See Samama (2003) and Hirt Raj (2006) for the lack of inscriptions attesting the presence of public physicians in Egypt during the Roman period.
[180] Amundsen and Ferngren (1978) 343.
[181] The CEDOPAL database lists thirty-nine in its current collation of petitions and medical reports, at http://promethee.philo.ulg.ac.be/cedopal/Bibliographies/Petitions.htm, accessed 1st January 2012, three more than Hirt Raj (2006) 316-17 included in her collation (Table III).
[182] *P. Oslo* 95 (AD 96, Oxyrhynchus): ἐπιδὼν οὖν ταύτην ἐπακολουθοῦντος τοῦ ὑπηρέτου εὗρον ἐπὶ τῷ μέσῳ δακτύλῳ τραῦμασυβστ, ὃ καὶ θεραπεύω. Although the medical practitioner is fulfilling the role of a *demosios iatros*, he simply calls himself an *iatros*. However, Amundsen and Ferngren (1978) 350 summarises the discussion as to whether this can be classed as evidence of a public physician.
[183] *P. Oxy.* 3926 (Oxyrhynchus): ἐπιδίδωμι τάδε τὰ βιβλίδια ἀξιοῦσα ἀποτάξαι σε ὑπηρέτην τὸν ἐποψόμενον τὴν περὶ αὐτοὺς διάθεσιν πρὸς τὸ νασθαι αὐτοὺς τῆς δεούσης θεραπείας τυχεῖν.

[184] *P. Oxy.* 3195 (AD 331, Oxyrhynchus): ὅθ[εν] τοῦτον ἐπείδομεν ἐπὶ γρ[αβά]του ἐν τῷ δημοσίῳ λογιστηρί[ῳ] ἔχοντα ἐπὶ τοῦ δεξιοῦ μ[έρους] τῆς κορυφῆς τραύματ[α] ... ὑ μένος κ[α]ὶ ἐπὶ τοῦ δεξιοῦ μέρο[υς τοῦ] μετώπου οἴδημα κ[αὶ] ἐ[π]ὶ [τοῦ] πήχυος τῆς ἀριστερᾶς χειρὸ[ς] πελίωμα μετὰ ἀμυχῆς καὶ ἐπ[ὶ] τοῦ πήχυος τῆς δεξιᾶς χειρὸ[ς] πελιωμάτιον, ἄπερ προσφων[οῦ]μεν.
[185] For example Sor. *Gyn.* 1.57 and Porphyry, *Ad Gaurum* 10.3 use it to refer to a foetus, while Sor. *Gyn.* 1.103 and Gal. *UP* 10.7, 9 both use it to refer to an eye.
[186] See for example *P. Oslo* 3.95 (AD 96, Oxyrhynchus); *BGU* 2.647 (AD 130, Karanis); *PSI* 5.455 (AD 178, Oxyrhynchus); *BGU* 3.928 (AD 307, Herakleopolis).

medical vocabulary could simply be the result of the ordinary nature of the conditions assessed in the surviving medical reports; the purpose of these medical reports seems to have been a primarily forensic one, providing written evidence that could be used in legal proceedings in which the plaintiff demands some kind of legal redress or financial compensation after being assaulted by the defendant. In most cases, a physical assault would simply result in minor injuries such as wounds, swellings, scratches or bruises. Equally, it could be the result of the *demosios iatros* deliberately simplifying his medical vocabulary for the purpose of clarity, so that the laymen reading his reports and subsequently incorporating them into legal proceedings would comprehend them. Nonetheless, the available evidence does not for the most part indicate more than a basic level of medical knowledge on the part of the *demosioi iatroi*.

Army Physicians
While the general and other elite members of a Roman legion could ensure they received medical treatment from personal physicians, the rank and file legionaries were generally left to the *medicus ordinarius* in the army and the *medicus duplicarius* in the navy, and the extent of their medical competence has been debated; Scarborough suggested that there were no professional army physicians in the Roman legions during the Republic and early Empire and that the Roman legionaries treated themselves, a theory that Nutton disputed.[187]

As the *praefectus Alexandriae et Aegypti*, a member of the equestrian order with *imperium ad similitudinem proconsulis*, was primarily based in Alexandria, there was a strong military presence there, as well as a fleet docked in the harbour.[188] There is certainly papyrological evidence to suggest that there were army physicians practising in Alexandria. In AD 52, the prefect Gaius Vergilius Capito was informed that a man named Tryphon had been declared exempt from military service after undergoing an eye examination within the city.[189] In AD 270, an army physician named Marcus who was based in Alexandria wrote to his family describing hostilities between the Roman army and a tribe called the Anoteritae and their consequences: 'Fifteen soldiers of the *singulares* have died, not to count the legionaries, the *evocati*, and those exhausted'.[190] As an army physician, he was so busy dealing with casualties that he could not come home to visit. Guido Majno includes Alexandria in his list of possible *valetudinaria* located in the Roman frontier provinces. This location makes sense, considering the continuing military presence in Egypt, the

volatile situation in the Levant during the first and second centuries AD and the campaigns in the East in the third and fourth centuries AD.[191] There is also a papyrological reference to a *valetudinarium*, and it is posited that this refers to a *valetudinarium* located in Alexandria. Dating from the first century AD, during the reign of either Augustus or Tiberius, it states that a *signifer* named Domitius was assigned to or sent to the *valetudinarium*.[192]

A papyrus dating to 3rd September AD 117 refers to an individual named Longinus Titouleios who bears the otherwise unattested title of ἰατρὸς ἑκατόνταρχος ('centurion physician').[193] Graffiti were carved by individuals serving as ἰατρὸς λεγιῶνος, one by a soldier of the legion II Traiana Fortis named Asclepiades in the Valley of the Kings on 27th January AD 147, and a second by a soldier named Auphidios Klemes at Pselkis and after AD 132.[194] An inscription found near a disused quarry at Wadi Fakhari in Upper Egypt and provisionally dated to either the first or second century AD recorded an act of worship undertaken by a member of a cavalry detachment who was also a physician (or possibly even a veterinarian) called Longinus: Τὸ προσκύνημα Λονγίνου ἱππέ[ω]ς καὶ τοῦ ἱππ[ικοῦ] ἰατ[ροῦ].[195] Another inscription, recovered from the Temple of Ammon at Luxor and provisionally dated to the third century AD, attests to the presence of an army physician at the fort there: Πτολλίων ἰατρὸς δὶς τῆς σπειρης εὐχαριτῶ τῷ Ἄμμωνι.[196]

If the evidence for army physicians from Alexandria and the Nile Valley is limited, that recovered from the quarry settlements at Mons Claudianus and Mons Porphyrites in the Eastern Desert is more informative.[197] Several unpublished ostraca imply the presence of physicians although hardly any information is given about their duties.[198] However, one ostracon from the period AD 137-47 attests to the fact that not only was there at least one *iatros* in residence at Mons Claudianus, but that this individual was responsible for supplying saffron,

[187] Scarborough (1968); disputed by Nutton (1969). For more recent studies, see Webster (1998) 257-64 and Southern (2006) 233-7. For a study of Roman army medicine in the northern provinces, see Baker (2004).
[188] Devijver (1974) 459; Alston (1995) 163-4. However, see Epplett (2001) for members of the Roman army hunting animals throughout the province.
[189] *P. Oxy.* 39 (AD 52, Oxyrhynchus).
[190] *P. Ross. Georg.* 3.1 (AD 270, Alexandria); for discussion of the identity of the Anoteritae, see Roberts (1950); for translation (into French) and discussion of this papyrus, see Raj (2006) 335-6.

[191] Majno (1975) 383. See also Zos. 2.34 and John Malalas, *Chronographia* 12.138 for the emperor Diocletian building forts along the *limes* in Egypt.
[192] *PSI* 13.1307 (early first century AD, possibly Alexandria): *Domitius signif ad ualetudinari[um]*.
[193] *PSI* 9.1063 (AD 117, unprovenanced).
[194] *GRR* I: 1212 (AD 147, Valley of the Kings) and *GRR* I: 1361 (after AD 132, Pselkis).
[195] *IGRom* I: 1252 (first-second century AD, Wadi Fakhari). Samama (2003) 483 describes Longinus as an army physician rather than a veterinarian: 'Médecin militaire affecté aux soins des cavaliers, Longinus était cavalier lui-même'.
[196] El-Saghir *et al.* (1986) 115 n37. Samama (2003) 486 also includes this inscription, but she records it as coming from Thebes and dates it to the fourth century AD.
[197] For a list of Roman roads and stations in the Eastern Desert, including Mons Claudianus and Mons Porphyrites, as well as an analysis of their relationship with the ports in the area, see Murray (1925) 138-50.
[198] *O. Claud.* Inv. 2055; 3260; 2795; 3739; 1538; 2921. The latter two mention ἱππιατροί, horse doctors or veterinarians, who might also have treated humans.

κρόκος, and sticks of salve that could have been intended to treat eye conditions or more general aches and pains, κολλύρια.[199] However, archaeological excavation of the site provided no evidence that the fort contained a *valetudinarium*.[200] Despite this apparent lack of a location for it, some sort of organised medical care was clearly going on at Mons Claudianus; a number of lists of sick or injured military personnel, known as a *pridianum* and recording accessions to the unit, losses and absentees in order to give an indication of the unit's military strength on any given day, have been recovered. Although other military strength reports survive from Egypt, these lists from Mons Claudianus are particularly interesting because three of them state exactly what sort of medical conditions the sick or injured personnel are suffering from.[201] This not only provides an insight into the disease environment of the Eastern Desert, but also, when viewed in conjunction with the letters recovered from this site, the sort of treatment available.[202] These are similar to the military strength reports recovered from other locations such as the fort and settlement at Vindolanda in Britain.[203]

The first of these lists dates to between the 2nd and 14th July AD 137 to 145:

σκλη[ρουργὸς] μαθητής
      Ἑρμαίσκο[ς] ὀφθαλμ[ιῶν]
λιθοφό[ρος]
      Μοσχίων ἀναλαμβ[άνων]
παρασφη[νάριος]
      Ἀγρίππας τραυμ[ατισθείς]
φαρμαξάρις
      Ῥωμέων τραυμ[ατισθείς]
ἀκουάρις
      Καλπῆνο[ς] σκορπιόπ[ληκτος]
ἐργ[άται]
      Σπὴς πυρεκ[τικός]
      Μηνοφάνης
      Σιλας καυσάρις
ἀκισκ[λάριοι]
      Τερέντις τραυμ[ατισθείς]
      Ἀφροδ[...] τραυμ[ατισθείς]
      Δημήτρις Σίκυς[204]

Apprentice mason
      Hermaiskos ophthalmia
Stone-carrier
      Moschion convalescing
Stone-splitter
      Agrippas injured
Metallurgist
      Romeon injured
Water-carrier
      Kalpenos stung by a scorpion
Workmen
      Spes feverish
      Menophanes
      Silas recovered
Chisellers
      Terentis injured
      Aphro[...] injured
      Demetris Sikus

The term ὀφθαλμία was used indiscriminately to refer to any disease of the eyes that was accompanied by a discharge of humours, with the verb ὀφθαλμιάω used to refer to suffering from the condition.[205] The term πυρεκτικός, 'feverish', was likewise used to refer to any type of fever, no matter what the underlying cause.[206] The other words used to describe the conditions suffered by the individuals unfit for duty (ἀναλαμβάνω, 'convalescing', τραυματίζω, 'injured', σκορπιόπληκτος, 'stung by a scorpion', and καυσάρις, 'recovered') are relatively unsophisticated. The second and third lists are contemporary with the first and consist of five and three individuals respectively, seven of whom are suffering from the same illnesses or injuries as those in the first list.[207] However, one man included in the second list whose name is not entirely preserved is listed as suffering from κιονίς, which is thought to relate to κίων, referring to either the uvula, the interior of the nose, possibly the division of the nostrils or the cartilage, or a type of wart.[208]

The relatively unsophisticated terminology employed in these lists is reminiscent of that used in the reports of the public physicians examined previously. While the simple language could indicate that the medical practitioners of Mons Claudianus were relatively unsophisticated and not versed in complicated medical terminology, it could equally be the case that they were, but simply did not see the point in using it. Considering the primarily pragmatic purpose of a military strength report, it is possible, if not plausible, that these lists were written to be read and

[199] *O. Claud.* 220 (AD 137-47, Mons Claudianus).
[200] See Baker (2002) 69-80 for the extent to which it is possible to identify *valetudinaria* in the archaeological record.
[201] For a *pridianum* from Egypt, see *P. Brookl.* 24 (undated and unprovenanced). The lists that contain information about illnesses are *O. Claud.* 212 (AD 137-45, Mons Claudianus), 213 (AD 137-45, Mons Claudianus) and 217 (AD 137-45, Mons Claudianus).
[202] Cuvigny (1992) 75-110; thirty-five so-called ἄρρωστοι are published. Cuvigny (1997) twenty-three ἄρρωστοι, here referred to as *aegri*, are published.
[203] *O. Claud.* 100-6; see also *T. Vindol.* Inv. 88, translated and discussed in Bowman and Thomas (1991) 62-73, particularly 69: this text is unique in dividing the members of the unit who are unfit for duty into categories according to their affliction; 'sick', *aegri*, 'wounded', *uolnerati*, and 'suffering from inflammation of the eyes', *lippientes*.
[204] *O. Claud.* 212 (AD 137-45, Mons Claudianus); for translation (into French) and discussion, see Cuvigny (1997) 31-3.

[205] Hippoc. *Aer.*10.
[206] Gal. *Hipp. Prorrh.* 1; Paul of Aegina, *De Re Medica Libri Septem* 3.43.
[207] *O. Claud.* 213 (AD 137-45, Mons Claudianus); translated (into French) and discussed in Cuvigny (1997) 33-4. *O. Claud.* 217 (AD 137-45, Mons Claudianus); translated (into French) and discussed in Cuvigny (1997) 36-7.
[208] Uvula: Hippoc. *Epid.* 1.26; Arist. *Hist. an.* 493a3. Nose: Rufus of Ephesus, *Onomasticon* 37, Poll. *Onom.* 2.79, 80. Wart: Hippoc. *Nat. mul.* 65; *Mul.* 2.212.

subsequently utilised by individuals without medical training, such as military or administrative personnel, and thus the language used to describe the afflictions is no reflection upon the capabilities of the medical practitioners who wrote them.

Conclusion

It is to be expected that during the periods when Egypt was under the control of the Ptolemaic and Roman Empires respectively, a number of medical practitioners would have been employed, or at least appointed, by the government in order to fulfil certain requirements and undertake specific duties, as is the case with the *archiatros*, the *demosios iatros* and the army physician.[209] However, these positions seem to have been comparatively few.

It is important to remember that the evidence for medical practitioners in Roman Egypt is primarily papyrological, and is consequently subject to significant limitations: a disproportionately large number of papyri have been recovered from the villages of the Fayum and Oxyrhynchus, as opposed to other areas of Egypt; the vast majority of the papyri are written in Greek, as opposed to Latin or Demotic; and those documentary papyri that mention the *iatros* or the *medicus* generally do so in passing without elaborating on the extent to which the individual in question actually practised medicine, or even what type of medicine was being practised.

2. Reconstructing the *iatros* / *medicus*

Diagnostic Features

Having examined the evidence for medical practitioners from the top down, the aim of this section is to reverse the enquiry and examine the evidence for medical practitioners from the bottom up. A combination of the sporadic nature of archaeological investigation of Graeco-Roman sites in Egypt, the lack of comprehensive record-keeping and infrequent publication of excavation reports over the last two centuries has ensured that there is comparatively little securely provenanced physical evidence for the daily lives of the inhabitants of Graeco-Roman Egypt at all, let alone for the practice of medicine in Egypt during the Roman period. This not only contrasts sharply with the wealth of material evidence for the practice of medicine in Egypt during the Pharaonic period, but also for other provinces of the Roman Empire such as Britain, Gaul and Italy, in which archaeological excavations have revealed physicians' houses, graves and tombs.[210] The most recently discovered, excavated and comprehensively published physician's house is that of Eutyches of Rimini (the *House of the Surgeon* at Rimini) so I propose to use this site as a point of comparison for

the examination of diagnostic features of the practice of medicine in Egypt during the Roman period.[211]

Although an equivalent site has not yet been identified or excavated in Egypt, there are numerous references to different aspects of the practice of medicine on the ground, so to speak, in the documentary papyri. Thus it is theoretically possible to reconstruct a variety of different aspects of the practice of medicine in Roman Egypt from these texts, which can be supplemented in places by findings from the meagre archaeological record. These reconstructions can then be used in conjunction with the information already gathered and previously discussed regarding medical practitioners with official status, the nature of such officially sanctioned medical practice and the medical hierarchy in Roman Egypt.

Medical Premises and Surgeries

Archaeological excavations of sites that have subsequently been identified as doctors' houses elsewhere in the Roman Empire such as the *House of the Surgeon* at Rimini have suggested that medical practitioners practised primarily from their houses, or perhaps from a separate surgery that was nonetheless attached to their home.[212] There would be a small room specifically set aside for this, a *taberna medica*, perhaps even with an independent entrance. There is some evidence for similar practices in Roman Egypt, although this evidence comes in the form of references in documentary papyri rather than artefacts recovered through archaeological excavation.

In a report from Karanis dating to AD 130, an unnamed physician described himself as 'having a surgery in the village' (ἔχων τὸ ἰατρεῖον ἐν κώμῃ Καρανίδι).[213] A government worker named Serenus wrote a letter to his mother Antonia in AD 268-70, explaining that his brother Marcus was unable to come home to visit her because his surgery was so busy.[214] A report from the guild of masons, stone-cutters and carpenters of Oxyrhynchus dating to AD 315-16 lists work to be done at 'the surgery of Dioscorus' (ἰατριω Διοσκορ[ου]), seemingly a rather grand building as twelve columns required replacement bases.[215] In a letter recovered from Oxyrhynchus and dating to the fourth century AD, Eudaimon wrote to his family and addressed the missive to 'the surgery' (ἀπόδος εἰς τὸ ἰατρεῖον).[216]

---

[209] This recalls the claims made by Diodorus Siculus about Egypt having a rudimentary health service during the late Hellenistic period, Diod. Sic. 1.82.2-3.

[210] See Nunn (1996) for medicine in Pharaonic Egypt; see Künzl (1983) for graves and tombs of physicians in the Roman Empire.

[211] See De Carolis (2009) for comprehensive publication and discussion of all aspects of the *House of the Surgeon* at Rimini. See also Jackson (2003) for an account of the medical assemblage.

[212] Jackson (2003) 313; these identifications are subject to the discovery of artefacts that can be associated with the practice of medicine. The *House of the Surgeon* at Rimini contained 150 medical and surgical instruments primarily for the treatment of bone trauma and wounds.

[213] *BGU* 647 (AD 130, Karanis).

[214] *P. Ross. Georg.* 3.2 (AD 270, Alexandria): ὁ ἀδελφός μου Μάρκος ἐν προλήμψει ἐστὶν πολλῇ τῇ περὶ τοὺς κ[ά]μνοντας καὶ τὸ ἰατρεῖον.

[215] *P. Oxy.* 4441 (AD 315-6, Oxyrhynchus).

[216] *P. Oxy.* 4001 (fourth century AD, Oxyrhynchus).

So although no firm trace of a physician's surgery dating to the Roman period has yet been found in Egypt, it is clear that during the Roman period, there were specific locations from which medical practitioners, generally designated as ἰατροί, were known to practise, leading to these places being described accordingly as ἰατρεῖα.

Medical Equipment

It is no easy task to establish the precise nature of an ancient medical practitioner's expertise; in the case of Eutyches in Rimini, the predominance of medical and surgical instruments associated with the treatment of bone trauma and wounds, including a 'Dioclean spoon' for the removal of arrow-heads, the only one of its kind in the world, has led to the assumption that he originally served as a military physician.[217] The distribution of medical instruments recovered from secure archaeological contexts across the Roman Empire is uneven, favouring the northern provinces. Like physicians' houses and surgeries, evidence for medical instruments in Roman Egypt comes primarily from references to such items in the documentary papyri and even this is not ideal as the terminology used to refer to them varies.[218] This is unsurprising, as Roman medical instruments were multifunctional; they could be utilised for cosmetic and toiletry purposes, as craft tools and they could also be employed for veterinary surgery.[219] Such is the case with a set of bronze spoons recovered during excavations for papyrus at Dime, or a metal ring from which a pair of tweezers and a needle were strung recovered from Abusir el-Meleq, both provisionally dated to the Graeco-Roman period, or four pairs of shears and one pair of scissors, all lacking an exact provenance but known to have been recovered from Egypt and dated to the Roman period. All these items have been classed as surgical instruments by the museums that own them despite their possible cosmetic, toiletry or even craft applications.[220]

The term σκεῦος is a case in point with regards to the unreliability of terminology. Its meanings range from 'vessel', to 'implement', to 'utensil'. It is often employed in the documentary papyri and it can be difficult to say for certain whether the objects so referred to are being used as household implements or medical apparatus, a problem that is also encountered when such items are excavated from isolated archaeological contexts.[221] For example, in a will dating to 19th December, AD 123, Thaesis bequeathed to her daughter 'the house, yard, and all effects belonging to Thaesis...and the furniture, utensils, household stock and apparel left by Thaesis', the context making it clear that in this case, σκεῦος refers to

domestic utensils rather than medical ones.[222] In a private letter dating to the third century AD, Copres requests that his father Hermes 'come out and bring me resin and a blade to work with and a basket'.[223] The word used for blade is σπάθε, which indicates that Copres was a weaver and that these utensils were being utilised for a specific professional purpose, albeit not for medical practice. However, the diminutive σπαθίον is frequently used in medical texts, and probably refers to a kind of scalpel that was similar to a weaver's knife.[224]

In a list of items consisting of substances such as saffron, realgar and orpiment which were commonly utilised for therapeutic purposes, the words πῖλος and γλωσσόκομον, although commonly used in contexts unrelated to medical practice, could in this instance be intended to refer to a type of bandage and a medicine chest, particularly one made of wood, respectively.[225] In a private letter dating to between the second and third centuries AD the medical context is clearer, as Horieon asks his father Apollonius to send him two different types of medicine as well as a φάρμακοθος, clearly a medicine chest.[226] Likewise, in an acknowledgement of receipt of a dowry, dating to AD 54-5, the groom, Chrates, and his parents record that amongst the bride Kroniana's possessions were a set of 'bronze utensils...and a box for ointment', χαλκώμα[τα] ἰδον καὶ σμηματοδοκίδα, in addition to a set of 'women's utensils of tin', γυναικεῖα σκεύη κασσιτέρινα.[227]

With the exception of the Cairo Museum, the Kelsey Museum of Archaeology at the University of Michigan houses the world's largest collection of material recovered from a Graeco-Roman town, comprising some 45,000 items recovered during archaeological excavations undertaken by the University at Karanis in the period 1926-35. Amongst the items recovered from within domestic contexts were one bronze knife blade and two iron knives.[228] However, there were also numerous bronze and bone needles, clay and glass vessels, oil flasks, wooden boxes and chests, all of which could have been used for purposes relating to medical practice. During the excavations of the *House of the Surgeon* at Rimini, containers used for the preparation and storage of medicine were recovered, their purpose indicated by the words inscribed in Greek upon them.[229]

---

[217] Jackson (2003). For Diocles of Carystos, see Plin. *HN* 26.6; for his invention of the 'Dioclean Spoon', see Celsus, *Med.* 7.5.3.

[218] For an inscription found in Rome mentioning an ὀργανοποιός, possibly a medical instrument maker, see *IG* XIV: 1717.

[219] Baker (2004) 4-5.

[220] Arnst (1990): bronze spoons 28; ring with tweezers and needle 31. Notis and Shugar (2003): shears and scissors 13.

[221] Nunn (1996) 164.

[222] *P. Tebt.* 381 (AD 123, Tebtunis); for an example of σκεῦος referring to a druggist's stores, see Thphr. *HP* 9.17.3.

[223] *SB* 18.13613 (third century AD, unprovenanced): διὸ οὖν ἐξερχόμενος ἔνε[γ]κέ μοι ῥητίνην καὶ σπάθιά εἰς ἐργάζειν καὶ τὸ ταλάριον, ὃ εἶπέν σοί.

[224] Paul of Aegina, *De Re Medica Libri Septem* 6.78 and 45.73. On the σπαθίον, see Milne (1907) 88-9.

[225] *P. Oxy.* 4979. On medicine chests and ointment boxes, see Milne (1907) 168-73.

[226] *P. Oslo* 54 (second-third century AD, unprovenanced).

[227] *P. Mich.* 343 (AD 54-5, Tebtunis); for an example of σκεύη referring to sacred vessels and implements, see *IG* XII: 313.20.

[228] Kelsey Museum of Archaeology Inv. 0000.02.3117; 0000.00.7598; and 0000.00.7704.

[229] Jackson (2003) 321.

According to Jackson, the majority of the largest and seemingly most complete sets of medical *instrumentaria* comprise three types of material: pharmaceutical implements and remains; a basic surgical kit; and a number of more specialised instruments.[230] Nothing even remotely comparable to these large and seemingly mostly complete sets of medical instruments recovered primarily from the northern provinces has ever been recovered from Egypt. However, it would be absurd to surmise that because no complete sets of medical instruments have been recovered from Egypt, there were no professional medical practitioners in the province.[231]

Hippocrates defined the components of a basic surgical kit as a scalpel (σμίλη / *scalpellus*)[232], hook (τυφλάγκιστρον / *hamus acutus* and *hamus retusus*), forceps (σαρκολάβος / *forfex*)[233], cautery (καυτήριον / *ferrum candens*)[234], needle (ῥαφις / *acus*) and probes (σπαθομέλε / *specillum*).[235] However, these basic instruments could be utilised to perform a wide variety of simple surgical procedures, even ones that required a comparatively skilled or a specialist practitioner. It is unlikely to be a coincidence that all of these appear carved in relief on one of the walls of the Temple of Sobek and Horus at Kom Ombo, dating from the Roman period, which also depicts knives, a saw, two tri-valve specula (διόπτριον / *dioptra*), a male catheter (αὐλίσκος / *anea fistula*)[236], a bowl or mortar, a set of scales, a sponge (σπόγγος), shears (κουρίδες / *forfex*), cupping vessels (σικυώνη / *cucurbitulae*), tooth forceps (ὀδοντάγρα / *forfex rhizagra*)[237], flasks, and an instrument case (see Figure 3). That the majority of these instruments are recognisable indicates that no matter who commissioned the relief and what their reasons for doing so might have been, whoever carved it had access to a comprehensive *instrumentaria*.

However, although the subject of the relief is easily recognisable as a medical *instrumentaria*, its reason for being there is less apparent. There are a number of different interpretations of certain aspects of the relief, as scholars tend to approach it in isolation, even to the extent of focusing upon specific sections of it to the exclusion of the rest; for example, Mary Knight views some of the instruments as confirmation that female circumcision and genital mutilation was practised in Egypt during the Roman period, while M. A. Dollfus views others as confirmation that ophthalmological procedures were particularly associated with Horus and perhaps even took place within the temple precinct.[238] It has also been suggested that the relief is simply a cryptogram, or is intended either to be or to represent a votive offering made to the gods of the temple.[239] If the panel upon which the medical instruments are depicted is considered in conjunction with the rest of the relief covering the temple wall, which depicts the Pharaoh sacrificing to the god Horus and two goddesses, a different meaning can be inferred; A. Stettler has done this, and as a result suggested that the decoration was intended as a prayer for the health and wellbeing of the emperor.[240] However, Paul Ghaliangui went further, and suggested that the relief should be viewed in conjunction with numerous others from elsewhere in the temple precinct; these show Ptolemy VI pouring sand into a foundation trench and taking part in the inauguration ceremony, Ptolemy XIII presenting the temple to the god Sobek and the goddess Hathor, and the goddess Seshat (the patron of architects) pitching stakes around future precincts. He believed that the medical instruments represented a foundation deposit.[241]

Of this wide variety of instruments, cupping vessels and folding instrument boxes containing scalpel blades were often carved onto the tombstones of physicians in other parts of the Roman Empire, just as tools appeared on the tombs of craftsmen and ironmongers.[242] There is also documentary evidence for their use in Roman Egypt; when Eudaimon wrote to his mother and grandmothers, he requested that they send him a folding bronze case, χα[λ]κοῦν δελτάριόν, and cupping vessels, τὰς σικύας.[243] From the context of the letter, it is clear that Eudaimon was a medical practitioner and it is possible that his brother Theodorus was as well. In a letter recovered from Mons Claudianus and dating to the early second century AD, the author demands a διαστολεύς, a surgical instrument used as a retractor in order allow a physician or dentist to examine cavities (πέμψεις τὸ τραῦμα διαστολείδειν).[244]

---

[230] Jackson (1995) 193.

[231] The only feasible means of addressing this apparent disparity and establishing the extent to which it is an accurate representation of the reality of the situation would be to undertake a comprehensive study of all the utensils (including those not currently classed as medical) housed in museums that possess collections known to have come from secure contexts dating to the Roman period from sites within Egypt.

[232] The term σπάθη can also be used to refer to a scalpel or the blade of a scalpel, see Sor. *Gyn.* 2.63.

[233] Oribasius, *Collectiones* 45.10.2.

[234] Gal. *Hipp. Art.* 42-3.

[235] Hippocrates, *De decenti habitu* 8.10-13; of these constituents, hooks and needles have been recovered from Karanis.

[236] Oribasius, *Collectiones* 8.38.3.

[237] Sor. *Gyn.* 2.63, Gal. *Hipp. Epid.* 6.9.

[238] Knight (2001) 329; Dollfus (1967) 15.

[239] Marganne (1987) 404. Votive offerings in the form of stone carved reliefs are found elsewhere in the Roman Empire; examples include one marble relief depicting a box of scalpels and two cupping vessels from the Temple of Asclepius on the Athenian Acropolis, and another in the St John Lateran Museum in Rome.

[240] Stettler (1982) 53.

[241] Ghaliangui (1963) 103.

[242] Jackson (1995) 191. See also Cassar (1974) for an example of a tomb slab from a Roman catacomb in Malta, dating to between the second and fifth centuries AD, which depicts a case containing a range of surgical instruments.

[243] *P. Oxy.* 4001 (fourth century AD, Oxyrhynchus).

[244] *O. Claud.* 120 (AD 100-20, Mons Claudianus); see also Gal. *Gloss.* K, Paul of Aegina, *De Re Medica Libri Septem* 6.78.

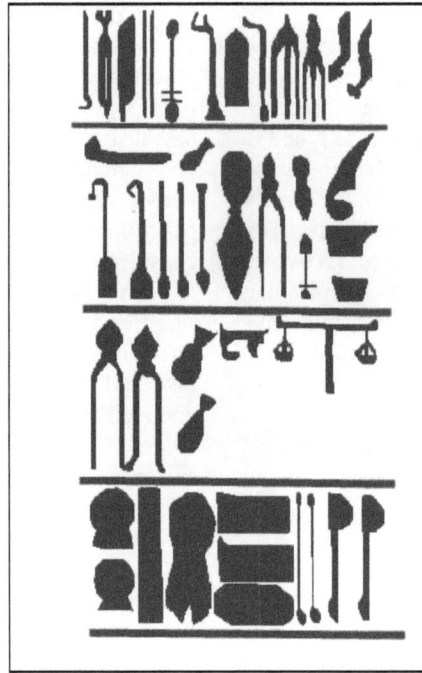

Figure 3: Relief, Temple of Sobek and Horus at Kom Ombo, second century AD, Egypt (drawn by author)

Although the majority of attention paid to the Kom Ombo relief tends to concentrate upon the items identifiable as medical instruments (and thus indicative of 'rational' medical practices, attributed to Roman influence due to the presence of the weighing scales), there are other objects included here too.[245] In the top left hand corner of the second panel is an incense burner, while in the centre of the third panel are two Eye of Horus symbols (perhaps amulets), and in the bottom right hand corner of the third panel (which is, admittedly, damaged) there appears to be a pot containing flowers, perhaps even those emblematic of Upper and Lower Egypt.[246] This could indicate that the owners of the *instrumentaria* used in Egypt during the Roman period incorporated elements of magical or religious ritual into their healing practices, just as the inclusion of a sponge indicates a more intimate level of physical care such as washing the patient.

Although the documentary papyri provide ample evidence for the existence of individuals who called themselves *iatros* or *medicus* in addition to evidence for surgeries from which these medical practitioners worked, there is far less evidence for specific medical apparatus and instruments.[247] However, perhaps it is unreasonable to expect that such items would be regularly mentioned in documentary papyri. The one particularly good papyrological source for medical instruments is Eudaimon's letter to his family, and these are mentioned

because he is specifically writing to request them by name.

Medical Literature

In addition to cupping vessels and folding instrument boxes, papyrus scrolls and codices were also frequently carved onto the tombstones of physicians, although according to Galen medical practitioners were by no means always literate: 'Many of those who embark on a career in medicine or philosophy these days cannot even read properly, yet they frequent lectures on the greatest and most beautiful field of human endeavour, that is, the knowledge provided by philosophy and medicine. This kind of laziness existed many years ago too, but it had not yet reached the extreme state it is now'.[248] Nonetheless, a significant amount of medical literature survives from Roman Egypt.[249] In some cases, the amount of medical literature recovered through archaeological excavation of ancient settlements has even seemed disproportionately high; Antinoopolis and Oxyrhynchus are particularly well represented.[250] These medical works can be classified as falling into two categories: literary papyri in the form of works or extracts of works of medical literature, such as specialist treatises and illustrated herbals; and sub-literary

---

[245] For the Egyptian method of dispensing medicines by volume, not involving the use of weights, and thus the *instrumentaria* being Roman, see Nunn (1996) 140 and 164.

[246] Ghaliangui (1963) 101.

[247] See Marganne (1987) 406-10 for discussion of Greek literary papyri that contain references to medical and surgical instruments. These include hooks, needles, cauteries and saws. However, it is to be expected that medical treatises would contain references to medical instruments, so these will not be considered here.

[248] Gal. *Libr. Prop.* 9. For a painting of a togate man, seated in a high backed chair in front of a cabinet of scrolls and holding a pair of shears or scissors, recovered from a grave deposit at Hawara and dating to the second century AD, see Petrie (1911) 20. For the identification of this man as a physician, possibly an obstetrician, see Walker and Bierbrier (1997) 82 and Rowlandson (1998) 336.

[249] For an inventory of all known Greek medical literature recovered from Graeco-Roman Egypt as of 1981, see Marganne (1981). For inventories of medical literature recovered from Graeco-Roman Egypt dealing specifically with ophthalmology and surgery respectively, see Marganne (1994) and (1996). According to Andorlini (2007) 23, around 260 papyri of medical content written in Greek have been found to date. For a comprehensive list of all known Greek medical literature from Graeco-Roman Egypt as of 1993, see Andorlini (1993) 458-562.

[250] Andorlini (1993) 549.

papyri in the form of collections of recipes or prescriptions.

Regarding the former category, it is debatable as to whether these literary papyri belonged to individual medical practitioners. Raffaella Cribiore has observed that books were not necessarily a feature of specialised education in areas such as medicine.[251] Instead, she posited that students received instruction directly from their teachers, apprentices from their masters. Hanson has in turn suggested that rural medical practitioners such as temple priests were supplied with medical treatises by their wealthy patrons, who directly contributed to their own healthcare.[252] However, some private letters from Roman Egypt indicate that medical practitioners could own and did use medical treatises. In his letter to his family, Eudaimon acknowledged receipt of some books in conjunction with other things his family had sent to him, 'I found only four books in the baggage, but you wrote "We have sent off five"' (μόνα δ βιβλία εὗρον ἐν τῇ δισακκίᾳ, ὑμεῖς δὲ ἐγράψατε ὅτι, ε ἀπεστείλαμεν) - although it is important to note that these books were not necessarily medical treatises.[253] The fact that Eudaimon seems to have been a member of a family of physicians could account for his possession of so many books. In a letter sent from Alexandria and dating to AD 268-70, Marcus wrote to his mother Antonia, requesting that she dust his shelf of medical treatises (ἐκτινάξαι μου τὰ ἰατρικὰ βυβλία) although clearly these books were not in his possession and being used by him at the time.[254]

Of the documentary papyri that attest the presence of book collections in Roman Egypt, two contained medical literature.[255] The first, a list of fourteen authors and twenty two works of literature written by them, found at Memphis and dating to the third century AD, includes one medical writer, Theodas of Laodicea, who was active during the second century AD.[256] The second, a list of thirteen authors and the number of rolls of papyrus present in the collection, was found in the Arsinoite nome and also dates to the third century AD.[257] The authors consisted of six philosophers and seven medical writers: Glaucon, Xenophon, Chrysippus, Thessalus, Erasistratus, Themison and Harpocration. While the works of the philosophers consisted of 142 rolls of papyrus, the works of the medical writers consisted of either 296 rolls of papyrus in themselves, or 154 rolls of papyrus in addition to the 142 rolls of philosophical treatises, making 296 rolls in total. It is impossible to tell whether each of these lists detailed an entire collection or simply part of a larger collection; in the case of the list from Memphis, the papyrus was torn both above and below the text that

survives, so it could feasibly have been much longer and included works from other literary genres besides philosophy and medicine.

The sheer range of the literary papyri is very informative about the depth and breadth of medical education available and presumably undertaken to varying degrees by individuals who aspired to be medical practitioners as well as members of the social elite with an interest in the subject. The simplest texts, which perhaps served as an introduction to the subject for students, consist of lists of body parts.[258] Others are more complicated, consisting of prognostics of medical conditions, or medical catechisms on subjects such as the medicinal properties of olive oil or even tumours.[259] One of these medical catechisms, dating from the late second century AD, is written in a hand that is almost identical to that of a fragment of Dioscorides' *On Medical Materials* that has also been dated to the late second century AD.[260] The fact that the catechism is written on the *recto* side of the papyrus, with a letter later in the third century being written on the unused *verso* side, is very significant, particularly when it is considered in conjunction with the fact that it was probably written by the same person as a copy of Dioscorides' treatise on pharmacology. It is feasible that if the writer was a scribe, he was commissioned by a medical practitioner to copy both texts. In view of the link with Dioscorides, the fact that the catechism contains a section on the medicinal properties and applications of olive oil is particularly interesting:

> [... But when the fruit is still unripe, the] oil pressed from the olive is able to produce the contrary effect. For it yields *omphakinon*, an astringent. It draws together and constricts the bodily organs, for it holds in check those that are being dispersed. But sweet oil loses astringent power with the ripening of the fruit, and it has a suppling effect. For we use *omphakinon* oil on the parts that are inflamed when we desire to inhibit the immoderate activity of the ailment in the constricted areas, so that the lowered tension may relax the organs. And it is necessary that these be scanned to determine the virulence of the condition, so that one neither employs embrocation at a late stage, for such treatment is of no avail, nor too often, for that provokes the ripening of the disease.[261]

---

[251] Cribiore (2001) 145.

[252] Hanson (2005) 400-1.

[253] *P. Oxy.* 4001 (fourth century AD, Oxyrhynchus).

[254] *P. Ross. Georg.* 3.1 (AD 268-70, Alexandria).

[255] Houston (2009) 233-67.

[256] *P. Ross. Georg.* 1.22 (third century AD, Memphis); for Theodas of Laodicia, see Gal. *MM* 2.7; Diog. Laert. 9.116; Andromachus cited at Gal. *Comp. Med. Gen.* 6.14.

[257] *P. Vars.* 5 Verso (third century AD, Arsinoite nome).

[258] *P. Mich.* 762 (second century AD, Karanis). See also *PSI* 12.1275 (second century, Oxyrhynchus) for an excerpt from the proem of a medical manual addressed to a student named Demosthenes, which emphasises the necessity of learning the names of the parts of the body from the outset of medical education. See also Rufus of Ephesus, *De Corporis Humani Appellationibus* pref. 6-7.

[259] *P. Mich.* 766 (fourth century AD, Karanis); *P. Turner* 14 (late second century AD, unprovenanced); *P. Oslo* Inv. 1576 (third century AD, Oxyrhynchite nome).

[260] *P. Turner* 14 / *P. Mich.* Inv. 6657 (late second century AD, unprovenanced).

[261] *P. Turner* 14 (late second century AD, unprovenanced).

The term ὀμφακίνος, means 'made from unripe grapes', and the oil made from unripe grapes, ἔλαιον, is included in Dioscorides' *On Medical Materials* .[262] Dioscorides' treatise was the pre-eminent pharmacological work during the Roman period. Three fragments of it have been recovered from Egypt and considering that Dioscorides had firsthand experience of Egypt's fauna and flora and included more than forty animal, vegetable or mineral substances that either originated or were brought through Egypt, this prevalence is not surprising.[263] Additionally, according to Elizabeth Reymond, the way in which Dioscorides describes herbals indicates that he was actually using an Egyptian source, perhaps the works of Cretenas, a famous herbalist based in Alexandria during the first century BC.[264] The questions and answers included in this catechism are also very similar to some found in the writings of Oribasius.[265]

In addition to possible teaching aids such as lists and catechisms, other literary medical papyri consist of entire sections of medical treatises written by influential medical writers. Of the relatively small number of medical treatises that include the names of their putative authors, Hippocrates and Galen are particularly well-represented. One treatise dating to around AD 150 was actually written by a medical practitioner about Hippocrates, quoting from lost works and incorporating a doctrine on the theory of disease, in addition to interjections from the writer giving his opinion of the doctrine.[266]

A consideration of the medical conditions written about in literary papyri could be quite informative regarding the concerns of medical practitioners in Egypt during the Roman period. Nineteen ophthalmological papyri survive, in addition to twenty four papyri containing recipes for collyrium. Twelve dermatological papyri survive, dealing with skin conditions such as alopecia, baldness, carbuncles, herpes, psoriasis and ulcers. In addition to these, pharmacology seems to have been a particularly popular subject and the texts include elaborate illustrated herbals as well as unillustrated extracts from pharmacological treatises such as Dioscorides' *On Medical Materials*.[267] Almost as numerous are lists of products known to have pharmacological properties, and the high numbers found are not surprising when it is considered that although urban centres contained apothecaries from whom medicinal ingredients and medicine could be acquired, these were not always entirely trustworthy.[268]

Regarding the sub-literary papyri, those consisting of medical recipes written in unskilled hands on single

papyrus sheets, often being reused to do so, are very likely to have been employed by professional medical practitioners. Their quality, or rather lack of quality, indicates that these would likely have been for personal use rather than general circulation. According to Andorlini, 'from texts like these, one can argue that the therapies accepted and recommended by practitioners in Egypt were often deeply affected by the accessibility of specific ailments in a rural setting'.[269] These texts indicate that the natural environment of Egypt played a significant role in medical practice, perhaps going so far as to influence the composition of a professional medical practitioner's training and certainly influencing their practices.

3. Medical Practitioners in Temple Complexes

Religious Medical Practitioners
The ancient Egyptian medical tradition dated back thousands of years prior to the arrival in Egypt of either the Greeks or the Romans. The first authenticated doctor in the world, Hesy-ra, was practising medicine as *wer ibeh swnw*, 'chief of dentists and doctors', under the Pharaoh Netjerkhet (King Djoser) in the Third Dynasty of the Old Kingdom, *c.* 2650 BC.[270] The earliest Egyptian medical papyrus, the Kahun gynaecological papyrus, can be dated from a note written on the verso to the twenty ninth year of the reign of the Pharaoh Amenemhat II, *c.* 1825 BC.[271]

According to Rosalie David, 'magic and religion, which were virtually indistinguishable concepts in ancient Egypt, played a significant role in medical practice'. Consequently, during the Pharaonic period, medical practitioners could be classed as being either *swnw*, physicians who practised what modern scholars tend to describe as 'rational' medicine, or *wa'abu*, priests who practised said 'rational' medicine in addition to what modern scholars tend to describe as 'irrational' medicine, which involved invoking the temple gods and practising magic; two significant types of *wa'abu* were the priests of Sekhmet and the priests of Serket.[272]

I discussed above the tendency for scholars to view Egypt as a conservative culture, particularly in respect of medical practice. One reason for this is that given by Diodorus Siculus, writing in the *Historical Library* in the early first century BC, who recorded how physicians were subject to punitive measures if they attempted to be innovative:

> The physicians draw their support from public funds and administer their treatments in accordance with a written law which was composed in ancient times by many famous physicians. If they follow the rules of this law as they

[262] Dioscorides, *De Materia Medica* 1.30; Gal. *San. Tu.* 3.6.
[263] *P. Aberd.* 8; *P. Mich.* Inv. 3; *PSI* Inv. 3011.
[264] Reymond (1976) 60.
[265] Oribasius, *Collectiones* 6.12, 15; 7.1, 2, 5-12, 23, 24; 8.1, 4, 6, 34, 38.
[266] *P. Lond. Lit.* 165.
[267] Hanson (2001); Leith (2006).
[268] Nutton (1985).

[269] Andorlini (2007) 26.
[270] Nunn (1996) 124.
[271] Nunn (1996) 34.
[272] David (2004) 133-5. For priests of Sekhmet, see Nunn (1996) 134-5; for priests of Serket, see Nunn (1996) 135.

read them in the sacred book and are yet unable to save their patient, they are absolved and go unpunished; but if they go contrary to the law's prescriptions in any respect, they must submit to a trial with death as the penalty.[273]

This description of the role of the physician towards the end of the Ptolemaic period is in accordance with the definition of the *Oxford English Dictionary* definition of the adjective 'professional' as someone 'engaged in an activity as a paid occupation rather than as an amateur', as well as with that of the noun 'professional', as 'a person having impressive competence in a particular activity'.

However, there is something of a hiatus in the scholarship of both Roman Egypt and ancient medicine regarding evidence for the *swnw* and the *wa'abu* in Egypt during the Roman period; scholars have preferred to focus on evidence for the Greek *iatros* or Roman *medicus* instead, despite the similarity between the Egyptian word *swnw* and the Coptic word for physician, *saein*. Despite devoting an entire chapter to healers in ancient Egypt, Nunn's *Ancient Egyptian Medicine* only utilises references to Pharaonic *swnw* and *wa'abu* in the Egyptian medical papyri and archaeological evidence such as grave stele and consequently is concerned primarily with medicine during the Pharaonic period.[274] However, the fact that a significant amount of medical literature written in both Demotic and Hieratic in addition to Greek has been recovered from the vicinity of the temple of Soknebtunis in Tebtunis, as well as from other villages in the Fayum, suggests that *swnw* and more significantly *wa'abu* were actively involved in practising medicine in the Roman period, although they may not have been referred to as such. In addition to this, it appears that they were incorporating Greek and Roman medical practices into their treatment of the sick in conjunction with their native Egyptian methods. A fragment of papyrus dating to the late first century BC contains a receipt stating 'you have paid as tax for the drugs of the Serapeum forty silver *drachmae'*.[275] One papyrus known as the *Crocodilopolis Medical Book*, written in Demotic, recovered from Dime and dating from the second century AD, preserves up to six different and independent medical works.[276] These were copied from older medical texts and evidently intended for use by individuals who were both well-educated and had a high level of technical competence in various aspects of medical practice.[277] However, although the diseases and ailments that the medical books are concerned with healing are familiar from the Pharaonic medical papyri, particularly Papyrus Ebers, the methods recommended to treat them are innovative in comparison with those older texts.[278] Instructions are given regarding which medicaments to prescribe and how these should be prepared, and these medicaments contain a variety of new pharmacological ingredients including herbs, minerals and metals that are not present in the Pharaonic papyri.[279]

Temple priests were themselves prohibited from learning a trade or having a profession. However, the temple *pastophori*, whose main duty was to carry the shrine of the deity in ritual processions, were not subject to the same sort of strictures. They were allowed to engage in trade and, like the priests, had living quarters within the temple compound which were known as *pastophoria*.[280] According to Clement of Alexandria, writing in the late second century AD, when the Egyptian priests processed, each carrying the symbols and books that were associated with his position in the temple hierarchy, it was the *pastophori* who carried the six sacred medical books:

> There are then forty-two books of Hermes that are indispensable and necessary; of these, the thirty-six containing the whole philosophy of the Egyptians are learned by the aforementioned personages; and the other six, which are medical, by the *pastophoroi*, treating of the structure of the body, and of diseases, and instruments, and medicines, and about the eyes, and the last about women. Such are the customs of the Egyptians, to speak briefly.[281]

David Frankfurter interprets Clement's assignment of different books to different ranks and tasks as emblematic, 'first of the way priestly roles were believed to be based in sacred writings, and second of the varieties of knowledge contained in the temples' scriptoria and the varieties of priestly expertise: not only sacred liturgy but astrology, geography, genealogy, anatomy, and healing'.[282] However, the location of medical practitioners in temples, whether they were priests or *pastophori* or held another position entirely, indicates the importance of religion and the role of the gods, whether Egyptian, Greek or Roman, in medicine and healing in Roman Egypt. This aspect of healing practice is not necessarily apparent from the documentary papyri that provide evidence for the existence of lay professional medical practitioners in the cities, towns and villages of Roman Egypt, although it is important to remember that even the smallest village had some sort of religious institution, whether this was an entire temple complex or just a shrine.[283] One specific example of this

[273] Diod. Sic. 1.82; Nunn (1996) 121 considers this unlikely as such a high level of control over standards of medical practice would have been difficult to enforce and maintain.

[274] Nunn (1996) 6.

[275] *P. Ryl.* 4.574 (late first century AD, unprovenanced): διαγεγράφατε τὸν φόρον του φαρμάκου τοῦ Σαραπείου [ἀρ]γυρίον δραχμ[ὰς] τεσ[σα]ρά κοντ[α].

[276] *P. Vindob.* D. 6257; I have not included a detailed discussion of the individual prescriptions contained in this papyrus because the translation and interpretation has been widely derided by scholars.

[277] Reymond (1976) 39, 61.

[278] Reymond (1976) 40; Ritner (2004).

[279] Reymond (1976) 59.

[280] Whitehorne (1980) 222.

[281] Clem. Al. *Strom.* 6.4

[282] Frankfurter (1998) 240-1.

[283] *P. Mert.* 2.63 (AD 58, Arsinoite nome), a private letter between a woman and her father, makes it clear that on occasion, even individuals

pervasiveness is Bes, a dwarf god originating in the Pharaonic period, who remained popular through the Late, Ptolemaic and Roman periods because of his protective and apotropaic function that specifically concentrated upon fertility, gynaecology and obstetrics.[284] During the Pharaonic and Ptolemaic periods, ritual specialists were associated with Bes through their capacities as healers; a house excavated at Kahun in the Fayum and dated to the Twelfth Dynasty was found to contain a large Bes mask painted on canvas and a pair of ivory clappers, and it has been suggested that the resident, presumably their owner, was a midwife or obstetrical healer associated with a local temple.[285] However, examination of documentary papyri associated with religious contexts and archaeological excavation of temple complexes dating to the Roman period has revealed a certain amount of continuity in these practices. An inventory from a temple at Soknopaiou Nesos, dating to AD 177-80, includes a bronze and silver statue of Bes, while the Heidelberg Festival Papyrus indicates that an annual festival celebrating Bes was held at Denderah.[286]

Since by definition a professional is an individual who engages in a specified occupation or activity for money or as a means of earning a living, it is evident that religious medical practitioners, that is individuals practising medicine within temple complexes, whether priests or temple staff, can be classified as such. Consequently, I will now proceed to examine the evidence for professional medical practitioners and medical practice within temples in Roman Egypt.

Case Study: The Temples of Sarapis and Isis at Canopus

According to Frankfurter, 'the Roman period [saw] several incubation cults grow to regional prominence while maintaining roots in traditional sacred space and cultic practice through association with temples, local deities, and their rites and priesthoods'.[287] Among these were the temples of Sarapis and Isis at Canopus. The town's close proximity to Alexandria combined with its geographical location on the Mediterranean coast ensured that it saw a succession of prominent Romans visit it for reasons pertaining to both health and recreation.[288] Strabo described both the positive and negative aspects of visiting Canopus during the early Principate.[289] However, nearly four centuries later, Ammianus Marcellinus was more positive as he enthused that 'the place is most delightful because of its beautiful pleasure-resorts, its soft air and healthful climate, so that anyone staying in that

region believes he is living outside of the world, as oftentimes he hears the winds that murmur a welcome with sunny breath'.[290] Unfortunately, Canopus' coastal location ensured that, like the Brucheion district of Alexandria, the town subsided into the sea centuries ago and is only now being excavated by maritime archaeologists from the University of Oxford. The results of these excavations have yet to be published in their entirety.[291] However, some previously recovered archaeological evidence for the town and its healing cults has been published such as votive statues and inscriptions set up there in gratitude after healing.[292]

Strabo specifically mentioned the Temple of Sarapis in his description of Canopus, but the Temple of Isis was also significant. Diodorus Siculus discussed how Isis was also venerated for her ability to heal the sick through incubation:

> For standing above the sick in their sleep she gives them aid for their diseases and works remarkable cures upon such as submit themselves to her; and many who have been despaired of by their physicians because of the difficult nature of their malady are restored to health by her, while numbers who have altogether lost the use of their eyes or some other part of their body, whenever they turn for help to this goddess, are restored to their previous condition.[293]

Frankfurter has suggested that Diodorus is specifically referring to the Temple of Isis at Canopus in this passage, stating that Isis' powers of healing through incubation are not known to have been recognised anywhere else during the Ptolemaic period.[294] The Temple of Isis at Canopus was particularly associated with women's fertility and conception until AD 391, when both it and the Temple of Sarapis at Alexandria were destroyed by a Christian mob.[295]

This particular association of Canopus with health and healing is evident from elsewhere in the Roman Empire. According to Pausanias, there were two temples dedicated to Sarapis in Corinth: one of these was the standard deity that was worshipped through the empire while the second was specifically called Sarapis 'in Canopus' (ἐν Κανώβῳ).[296] This particular aspect of Sarapis is also known from Delos, Athens, Epirus, Rome, Beneventum and Carthage. While the worship of Sarapis of Canopus had appeared in Delos as early as the second century BC, all the other instances seem to have

---

living outside the immediate vicinity of a temple were expected to contribute towards its upkeep: 'They are asking from everywhere for pious offerings for the sanctuary of Souchos from everyone, Romans and Alexandrians and settlers in the Arsinoite nome...I haven't paid, as I was today expecting you to come. Either give the request your attention and act on it or otherwise we shall pay it'.

[284] For detailed discussion of Bes, see Frankfurter (1998) 124-31.

[285] Frankfurter (1998) 126.

[286] *BGU* 2.387 (AD 177-80, Soknopaiou Nesos); *P. Heid.* Inv. 1818.8.

[287] Frankfurter (1998) 162.

[288] According to Dio 78.15.5-7, one of these eminent Romans was the emperor Caracalla.

[289] Strabo, *Geographica* 17.17.

[290] Amm. Marc. 22.16.14; see also Epiphanius, *Panarion* 12.1-4 and Rufinus of Aquileia, *Historia Eremitica* 26-7 for the persistence of religious activity at Canopus during the fourth century AD.

[291] See Goddio (2007) for preliminary excavation reports.

[292] Abdalla (1991) 192.

[293] Diod. Sic. 1.25.3.

[294] Frankfurter (1998) 162-3.

[295] Zachariah of Mytilene, *Historia Ecclesiastica* 5.

[296] Paus. 2.4.6.

originated during the Roman period, perhaps indicating the increased popularity of Canopus during the Roman period.

In addition to the religious evidence for health and healing at Canopus, there also appears to have been a thriving industry for the production of medicine and aromatics, which is not surprising considering the fact that Strabo described Canopus as a place of both healing and revelry at public festivals and thus would have utilised large quantities of both. Celsus describes a medicament known as the 'salve of Canopus'.[297] The fact that it contained cinnamon and frankincense indicates that it was a luxury product and was perhaps specifically produced for the wealthy tourists and pilgrims who visited Canopus.[298]

So who was practising medicine at Canopus? Since the temples that seem to have been favoured by those seeking healing were incubation temples, it is questionable as to whether the temple priests were actually providing medical treatment. In Egypt, priesthoods were frequently passed down through families, from father to son and mother to daughter.[299] However, the consistency with which the appointments remained hereditary and the apparent importance of this factor has led to debate over the abilities of the individuals who inherited these positions, if their abilities were even relevant at all.[300] It was common practice for those working in a variety of professions to take their children or other family members as their apprentices in the ancient world, so it is feasible that part of an individual's preparation for a hereditary priesthood could involve basic medical training if medical knowledge and expertise was necessary for that particular priesthood.[301]

The fact that medicine was being produced at Canopus and presumably utilised there, as well as exported to elsewhere in the Roman Empire, suggests the presence of medical experts and by implication medical practitioners. G. A. Moss has suggested that the Therapeutae, a Jewish sect related to the Essenes, were resident at Canopus and attached to the Serapeum where they undertook medical practices, citing a series of similarities between the cult of Sarapis and the Therapeutae.[302] This is a somewhat broad interpretation of Philo's description of the Therapeutae in *On the Contemplative Life*, the result of translating θεραπεύω as 'to heal' rather than 'to serve', 'to wait on' or even 'to tend the sick'.[303] On the contrary, Joan Taylor and Philip Davies argue that rather than being related to the Essenes, the Therapeutae were actually simply

devotees of gods.[304] However, it is notable that the votive offerings that they cite as proof are all dedicated to gods and goddesses associated with healing. Additionally, when Philo describes their community, like Strabo and Ammianus Marcellinus he emphasises the healthy climate of the area.[305] He also makes it clear that the community, consisting of both men and women, was a reasonably affluent and educated one so it is feasible that at least some of it members possessed a certain amount of medical knowledge and the ability to put it into practice.[306]

During the Pharaonic and Late periods, members of the Egyptian priesthood seem to have practised medicine. Herodotus describes the priesthood as the first of seven major occupations which made up the population of Egypt, which also consisted of soldiers, cow and swineherds, merchants, interpreters and pilots.[307] This list is notable for the absence of physicians. However, if temple priests were filling the role that would otherwise have been filled by professional medical practitioners, there would presumably have been no need for the latter.

Things seem to have changed radically over the course the Ptolemaic and Roman periods, with professional medical practitioners becoming ubiquitous in the region. However, as the Egyptian temples were gradually impoverished during the Roman period, it is clear from locations throughout Egypt that many priests had to utilise their skills as ritual specialists in order to earn money, skills which included the practice of medicine and healing.[308]

Case Study: The Temple of Soknebtunis at Tebtunis
Frankfurter has observed that 'the religion of the Fayum is distinctive in Roman Egypt for its population's special veneration of such a uniquely Egyptian god as Sobek in a religion deeply affected by Hellenism and in a period of active religious synthesis'.[309] While the temples of Sarapis and Isis at Canopus seem to have relied upon the patronage of those residing in or visiting Alexandria and consequently catered to more cosmopolitan religious preferences, the Temple of Soknebtunis at Tebtunis catered for the inhabitants of the Fayum. Despite the fact that large numbers of Macedonian and Greek veterans settled there during the Ptolemaic period, these settlers appear to have been more amenable to the local cults and religious practices and consequently, an examination of it offers a unique opportunity to gauge the extent to which native Egyptian, Greek and Roman medicine and medical practices interacted during the Roman occupation of Egypt.[310]

---

[297] Celsus, *Med.* 6.6.25 B.
[298] See for example Lucian, *Navigium*; Lucian records a conversation between Lycinus and one of his colleagues in which Lycinus asks him to bring back 'those delicate pickled Nile fish and perfumes from Canopus'.
[299] Thompson (1990) 98; see for example the position of High Priest of Memphis during the Ptolemaic and early Roman periods.
[300] Thompson (1990) 101.
[301] Merkelback (1994) 85.
[302] Moss (2002) 264.
[303] Philo, *De Vita Contemplativa* 2.

[304] Taylor and Davies (1998) 6.
[305] Philo, *De Vita Contemplativa* 22-3.
[306] Philo, *De Vita Contemplativa* 13; Taylor and Davies (1998) 16-17.
[307] Hdt. 2.164.
[308] Frankfurter (1998) 213.
[309] Frankfurter (1998) 99.
[310] For Macedonian, Greek and Roman immigrants to Egypt practising traditional Egyptian religion, see Smelik and Hemelrijk (1984) 1885-91.

Medical Literature from Tebtunis

According to Peter van Minnen, during the Ptolemaic and Roman periods Fayum temples retained their traditional role with priests and scribes being trained in ancient Egyptian lore. However, these priests and scribes also seem to have been familiar with Greek literature.[311] Modern scholars have been unable to reach a consensus as to who provided this literature. Van Minnen argues that the priests at Tebtunis copied and collected Greek literature, in addition to reusing official Greek and Latin documents to copy Demotic and Hieratic literature, and surmised that 'the Greek culture provided a stimulus to the Egyptian priests and that it made them rethink and reformulate their own traditions, perhaps even to approach these traditions with the help of Greek ways of thinking'.[312] However, Ann Ellis Hanson proffered an alternative explanation. She suggested that it was in fact members of the local Greek elite living in the vicinity of Tebtunis who were responsible for providing the temple priests with Greek medical literature, as a means of ensuring the type and quality of healthcare that they were used to receiving in urban centres.[313]

It is clear that the temple priests were producing literature of some sort; a receipt recovered from a house at Tebtunis and dating to 9th November AD 174 details that 'Petesouchos son of Petesouchos, priest of Tebtunis, has paid to Ammonios and Theon, lessees of marshes and desert shore in the division of Ptolemon, the price of 20,000 papyrus stalks at Ibion Argaiou, which he has transported to Tebtunis by Herakleides, the brother of Ammonios'.[314] Other papyri, taken from the archive of Kronion, the *nomographos* of the Grapheion of Tebtunis, also record purchases of rolls of blank papyri and even black ink.[315] In addition to the Grapheion's accounts, these papyri also contain a record of all the documents prepared at the Grapheion after 23rd August AD 46, including the fee for each piece of work produced. This record includes an entry which states 'gratis, for Heron the physician'.[316] It is tempting to speculate why exactly something copied out for a physician might be free of charge; perhaps this item was a medical treatise, recognised as being particularly useful to the temple and its priests.

There is a great deal of variety in the range of medical papyri recovered from Tebtunis, written in both Greek and Demotic. The earliest Greek medical treatise is a collection of ophthalmologic prescriptions and collyria recipes, dating to the late first century BC and written on the verso of a Demotic astronomical text.[317] There is a commentary on an extract from Nicander's *Theriac*, dating to the first century AD and written by a professional scribe.[318] The inclusion of this text in the temple's library is particularly interesting considering the number of wild animals that posed a danger to the inhabitants of Egypt during the Roman period. There are fragments of recipes dating to the first and second centuries AD, poorly written so unlikely to have been the work of a professional scribe and perhaps, consequently, written by a medical practitioner.[319] There is an extract from Herodotus Medicus' *Remedies*, dating to the late second century AD and written on the verso of accounts, which corresponds to information contained within a section of Oribasius' *Medical Collections*.[320] There is an illustrated herbal, dating to the second century AD, as well as an extract from a separate herbal, also dating to the second century AD.[321] There is a treatise describing the symptoms of various ailments, dating to the second century AD.[322] There is a therapeutic manual dealing with pulmonary diseases and the appropriate application of medicine and pharmacology, written by a professional scribe and dating from the second century AD.[323] This treatise has been tentatively associated with the medical writer Apollonius Mys on the basis of similarities between it and fragments of his work preserved by Galen, although this identification has been disputed.[324] There is an anonymous treatise on astrological medicine with references to gynaecology, dating from the second century AD.[325] There is an extensive collection of recipes aimed at medicating a variety of different diseases, dating from the second century AD.[326] There is also an extensive collection of recipes aimed at medicating eye diseases, written on the back of a tax report and dating to between the late second and early third centuries AD.[327]

So far, only three Demotic medical papyri have been published. The first is a herbal without illustrations, dating to the second half of the second century AD.[328] The second is a collection of medical recipes written on poor quality papyrus and dating to between the second and third centuries AD.[329] The third is a treatise combining magic and medicine, dating to the early third century AD, also written on poor quality papyrus.[330]

The Greek and Demotic medical papyri were all found within the temple precinct, in conjunction with numerous small wooden containers that appear to have been used

---

[311] van Minnen (1998) 101.
[312] van Minnen (1998) 169.
[313] Hanson (2006) 401.
[314] *P. Tebt.* 308 (AD 174, Tebtunis).
[315] *P. Mich.* 123 (AD 46, Tebtunis); this particular column gives an account of expenditures after 20th December AD 46.
[316] *P. Mich.* 123.
[317] *PSI Congr.* 21.3 (first century BC, Tebtunis).

[318] *P. Mil. Vogl.* 2.45 and 6.262 (first century AD, Tebtunis).
[319] *P. Tebt. Tait.* 43 Recto and *P. Tebt. Tait.* 44 Recto (first and second century AD, Tebtunis).
[320] *P. Tebt.* 272 Verso (late second century AD, Tebtunis).
[321] *P. Tebt.* 679 and *P. Tebt. Tait.* 39-41 Recto; *P. Tebt. Tait.* 42; for translation and discussion, see Hanson (2001) 585-604.
[322] *P. Tebt.* 678 (second century AD, Tebtunis).
[323] *P. Lund.* 6, *P. Mil. Vogl.* 16, *P. Tebt.* 677 and *PSI* Inv. 3054 (second century AD, Tebtunis).
[324] Hanson (2006) 392n.
[325] *P. Tebt.* 676 (second century AD, Tebtunis).
[326] *PSI* 1180 (second century AD, Tebtunis); see Marganne (1994) 174.
[327] *P. Tebt.* 273 (late second-early third century AD, Tebtunis); see Marganne (1994) 174.
[328] *P. Carlsb.* Inv. 230; *P. Carlsb. Dem.* 1; *P. Tebt. Tait* 20 (late second century AD, Tebtunis).
[329] *P. Tebt. Tait* 18 (second-third century AD, Tebtunis).
[330] *P. Tebt. Tait.* 19 (early third century AD, Tebtunis).

for storing unguents and powders.[331] At least one of these wooden pots still contained seeds.[332] There is a variety of evidence that attests to the use of different types of containers to optimise the conservation of unguents and other substances that could have been utilised as medical remedies. According to Pliny's *Natural History*:

> Unguents keep best in boxes of alabaster, and perfumes when mixed with oil, which conduces all the more to their durability the thicker it is, such as the oil of almonds, for instance. Unguents, too, improve with age; but the sun is apt to spoil them, for which reason they are usually stowed away in a shady place in vessels of lead.[333]

In addition to the numerous documentary papyri that mention such objects, there is archaeological evidence for the widespread use of containers such as those described by Pliny in Egypt during the Graeco-Roman period. Three examples of this practice: the first an alabastron currently exhibited in the British Museum that would have been used to store expensive unguents and oils (see Figure 4), and the second a mummy portrait currently exhibited in the British Museum that depicts its well-dressed and bejewelled female subject holding a glass unguentarium filled with a dark-coloured unguent or oil (see Figure 5).[334] The third is a mummy with an extensive assemblage of grave goods currently on display at the National Museum of Scotland. The assemblage not only included a painted plaque depicting a woman in labour on one side and a man that has been identified as an obstetrician on the other, but also a wooden box with a sliding lid, an ivory box without a lid, and six glass jars of different sizes, shapes and types of decoration.[335]

In his *On Medical Materials*, Dioscorides also wrote about the most suitable containers for different types of medicinal remedies. He included this information in the Preface, perhaps to aid the *rhizotomoi* in his or her initial preparations, as an ability to store both ingredients once they had been collected and remedies once they had been mixed was a fundamental part of ancient pharmacological practice due to the lack of effective methods of preservation:

> Flowers and such parts that have a sweet-smelling fragrance should be laid down in small dry boxes of lime wood, but occasionally they can be serviceably wrapped in papyrus or leaves to preserve their seeds. As for moist drugs, any container made from silver, glass or horn will be suitable. An earthenware vessel is well adapted provided it is not too thin, and, among

wooden containers, those of boxwood. Copper vessels will be suitable for most eye-drugs and for drugs prepared with vinegar, raw pitch or juniper-oil. But stow animal fats and marrows in tin containers.[336]

In her translation and discussion of the illustrated herbal from Tebtunis, Hanson explicitly linked this herbal with the work of Dioscorides, specifically a version of it encompassed in a parchment codex dating to AD 512, stating that there were significant similarities between the two at the textual level, and that 'the first editor [of the papyrus] left the matter open as to whether [the author] preceded Dioskourides and perhaps served as one of the latter's sources, or, in turn, was subsequent and drew on Dioskourides' *Materia medica*'.[337]

The fact that the priests at the Temple of Soknebtunis were in possession of a copy of a herbal containing very similar information to Dioscorides' *On Medical Materials*, along with the type of medical equipment recommended within the text is interesting for what it implies about medical practice in Egyptian temples. Yet, as is the case at the Canopus temples, it is unclear who exactly was providing this medical practice and whether they were priests, temple workers or professional medical practitioners attached to the temple complex.

Although it is unclear whether or not priests were practising medicine at temple complexes in Roman Egypt, the combination of votive offerings, medical literature and medical equipment recovered from these sites indicates that there were medical practitioners present at these complexes in order to provide medical care to those who needed it.

---

[331] Hanson (2006) 394.
[332] Rondot (2004) 58.
[333] Plin. *HN* 13.3.
[334] For the scientific analysis of organic residues left in ancient containers, see Colombin *et al.* (2005) and Ribechini *et al.* (2008).
[335] For discussion of the mummy and the grave goods, see Walker and Bierbrier (1997) 82-4.

[336] Dioscorides, *De Materia Medica* praefat. 9.
[337] Hanson (2001) 587.

Figure 4: Alabastron, Graeco-Roman period, Naukratis
(British Museum Inv. 1888,0601.16, image courtesy of the British Museum)

Figure 5: Mummy portrait in tempera on stuccoed linen, AD 100-20, Rubaiyat
(British Museum Inv. 1931, 0711.2, image courtesy of the British Museum)

Conclusion

It is clear that medical practitioners were present throughout Egypt during the Roman period. There is evidence for the existence of individuals who not only called themselves *iatros* or *medicus* but also practised medicine in Alexandria, the urban centres and the smaller rural settlements. Some of these individuals appear to have operated as part of the provincial hierarchy, others independently.

However, the fact that someone referred to himself or was referred to by others as an *iatros* or a *medicus* was no guarantee of professional competence. Even an 'official' position or role such as *archiatros* or *demosios iatros* seems to have been more concerned with the legal and administrative considerations of maintaining law and order in the province than actual medical treatment. Likewise, membership of the Museion and Library in Alexandria was frequently bestowed as a sign of imperial favouritism and patronage, rather than an indication of academic learning and professional expertise. What provides a clearer picture of the place of these individuals within the medical profession is the papyrological and archaeological evidence for how they acquired their learning and expertise and how they operated within the province.

Documentary papyri and archaeological excavations have revealed that the *iatros* sometimes practised medicine from a specific location, usually either his home or a

surgery attached to his home. He was often in possession of medical treatises, both works of literature by authors such as Herodotus Medicus, Galen and Oribasius, and collections of recipes for medicaments that were copied out by hand, probably by the *iatros* or *medicus* himself, on the back of whatever papyrus could be spared. He was also in possession of medical equipment such as surgical instruments and other apparatus. However, these items were not necessarily specially produced, or their usage restricted to medical practitioners: it is clear that a number of basic medical instruments such as knives, needles, shears, hooks and probes could be utilised in a variety of different ways. In all likelihood, this is precisely how they were used, since only large cities such as Alexandria could support medical specialists and a large number of general medical practitioners, particularly in rural areas, do not appear to have been wealthy enough to possess a substantial array of specialist equipment comparable to that owned by Eutyches of Rimini.

It is clear that during the Roman period, the role of the medical practitioner was very different to how it had been during the Pharaonic, Late and even the Ptolemaic periods. In earlier times, as attested not only by Herodotus but also archaeological evidence recovered from Egyptian temples and tombs, it was the temple priests who fulfilled the role of medical practitioner for both the urban and rural communities, often bearing medical titles in addition to their religious ones. While this practice seems to have continued during the Roman period, it was evidently on a much smaller scale than in previous generations. The foundation of the Museion and Library at Alexandria in addition to the influx of Greek and Roman immigrants, particularly to the urban centres, seems to have resulted in medicine and medical practice becoming professionalised and secularised. Despite this, it is also clear that native Egyptian medical practices did not just cease to exist but were instead incorporated into Greek and Roman ones, just as Egyptian ingredients were incorporated into the Greek and Roman pharmacopeia.

However, although there were undoubtedly medical practitioners operating in Egypt during the Roman period and providing medical treatment for the members of the population who sought them out, it is equally clear that not everyone experiencing ill health would automatically do so. Just as there is papyrological and archaeological evidence for members of the population of Roman Egypt patronising medical practitioners, there is also papyrological and archaeological evidence for members of the population preferring to treat themselves. The existence and significance of these amateur or domestic medical practitioners within the medical environment of Roman Egypt will be examined in the next chapter.

CHAPTER TWO

IDENTIFYING ALTERNATIVE HEALING STRATEGIES IN ROMAN EGYPT

1. Introduction

The assumption that modern scholars tend to make regarding the inhabitants of the Roman world is that, when suffering from an illness or an injury, they would automatically seek treatment from a so-called 'professional' medical practitioner such as an *iatros* or a *medicus*.[338] Chapter One has demonstrated that such individuals were available in certain parts of Egypt. However, the documentary papyri recovered from Egypt and dating from throughout the Roman period provide detailed evidence for certain aspects of the daily lives of a cross-section of the inhabitants of the province, one of which is the diverse range of healing strategies that was utilised for self-treatment. This evidence indicates that the default position for the inhabitants of Roman Egypt when healing was needed was that they tended to help themselves, their family members and even their friends as a matter of course.

A letter written to Apollonios, the *strategos* of the district of the Apollonopolites Heptakomia, by his wife Aline during the Jewish Revolt of AD 115-17 informs him that she was so worried about him that she had fallen into a deep depression and suffered a kind of nervous collapse: 'I take no pleasure in food or drink, but stay awake continually night and day with one worry, your safety. Only my father's care revives me and, as I hope to see you safe, I would have lain without food on New Year's Day, had my father not come and forced me to eat'.[339] A petition written to the prefect Aurelius Ammonius in AD 295 by a woman named Aurelia Techosis stated that she had nursed and tended her mother because such a thing was 'what is owed from children to parents'.[340] This sentiment was echoed in the verse epitaph of Lysandre, set up by her parents Philonike and Eudemon, which lamented her death in part because 'the breasts of my mother nourished me with their milk to no purpose at all, and to those breasts I cannot repay the favour of nourishment for their old age'.[341] A certain amount of

reciprocity was clearly expected; a letter written by Dionysius to his friend Nicanor in the second century AD states 'I request you, brother, to assist my brother Demetrius until he has measured out the corn, since I am still dangerously ill. You know that you do not give your help to an ungrateful person...For I in my turn, when I was with you, was attentive to your wishes'.[342]

It is evident that such help was given even if it was inconvenient for all involved. In the third century AD, Titianos wrote to his sister (or perhaps his wife) to explain his long absence: 'My father, on whose account I have stayed on till now in spite of illness, is also ill; and it is for his sake that I am still here'.[343] He goes on to say that everyone in the household was ill, and they all had to take care of each other. In the fourth century AD, Judas wrote from Babylon to his brother Joseph and sister Maria back home in Oxyrhynchus: 'Make every effort, my lady sister, send me your brother, since I have fallen into sickness as a result of a riding accident. For when I want to turn on to my other side, I cannot do it by myself, unless two other persons turn me over...Please come yourself as well and help me, since I am truly in a strange place and sick'.[344] However, it is clear that those who nursed their sick family members and even friends back to health took care of more than just their physical needs. The healing strategies utilised could extend far beyond this, to the actual preparation and provision of medicinal or magical remedies. The term used most frequently in modern scholarship to classify and describe this approach to healing is 'folk medicine', the definition of which is 'medicine originating from the beliefs, cultures and customs of ordinary people'.

During the twentieth century, folk medicine received little objective scholarly attention; according to Richard Gordon, 'the inexplicit character of Graeco-Roman folk-medicine, together with the distorted and haphazard nature of our evidence, has led to denigration of its aims

---

[338] See for example Pleket (1995) 28: 'City-based physicians apparently were not in the habit of regularly travelling around in the villages near towns...The villagers had to rely on wandering, passing doctors, not always of impeccable reputation or, in case they lived not too far away, on circuit doctors going around from their base in a market town'.

[339] *P. Giss.* 19 (AD 115, Hermoupolis): οὔτε πο[...ο]ὔτε [σε]ιτίοις ἡδέως προσέρχομαι, [ἀλλὰ συν]εχῶς ἀγρυπνοῦσα νυκτὸς ἡ[μέρας μ]ίαν μέριμναν ἔχω τὴν περὶ [τῆς σωτηρίας] σου. μόνη δὲ ἡ τοῦ πατρός [μου πολ]υωρία [ε] ἀνεγείρει με καὶ τῆι α [ἡμέρα] τοῦ νέου ἔτους, νὴ τὴν σὴν [σωτη]ρίαν, ἄ[γ]ευστος ἐκοιμώμην, [εἰ μὴ ὁ π]ατήρ μου εἰσελθὼν ἐβιάσατό [με].

[340] *P. Oxy.* 1121 (AD 295, Oxyrhynchus): ἡ προκειμένη μου μήτηρ Τεχῶσις νόσῳ κατα[β]λ[η]θεῖσα κατὰ τὴν ἐμαυτῆς μετριότητα ταύτην ἐνοσοκόμησα καὶ ὑπηρέτησα καὶ οὐκ ἐπαυσάμην τὰ πρέποντα γείνεσθαι ὑπὸ τέκνων γονεῦσι ἀναπληροῦσα.

[341] *I. Métr.* 83 (Roman period, Karanis): μαστοὶ μητρὸς ἐμῆς κενεὸν γάλα τοί με ἐκόμησαν, οἷς χάριν οὐ δυνάμην γηροτρόφον τελέσαι.

[342] *P. Oxy. Hels.* 47a (second century AD, Oxyrhynchus): παρακαλῶ σε, ἀδελφέ, τῷ ἀδελφῷ μου Δημητρίῳ συνλαβέσθαι, ἄχρι ἂν τὰ σῖ τάρια μετρήσῃ. ἐγὼ γὰρ ἔτι καὶ νῦν ἐπικινδύνως ἔχω. οἶδας δὲ ὅτι οὐκ ἀχαρίστῳ παρέχεις. τὸ δὲ σπουδαῖόν σου ἐπίσταμαι ... κα[ὶ] γὰρ ἐγὼ παρὼν πάλιν σοι προσεῖχον.

[343] *PSI* 299 (third century AD, Oxyrhynchus): ὁ δὲ πατήρ μου [μέχρι] [τ[ο]ύτου], δι' ὃν καὶ νοσῶν παρ[έ]μεινα [μέχρι ... τού[τ]ου], νοσεῖ· καὶ δι' αὐτὸν ἔτι ἐνταῦθά εἰμι.

[344] *P. Oxy.* 3314 (fourth century AD, Oxyrhynchus): πᾶν οὖν ποίησον, κυρία μου ἀδελφή, πέμψον μοι τὸν ἀδελφόν σου, ἐπειδὴ εἰς νόσον περιέπεσα ἀπὸ πτώματος ἵππου. μέλλοντός μου γὰρ στραφῆναι εἰς ἄλλο μέρος, οὐ δύναμαι ἀφ' ἐμαυτοῦ, εἰ μὴ ἄλλοι δύο ἄνθρωποι ἀντιστρέψωσίν με καὶ μέχρις ποτηρίου ὕδατ[ο]ς οὐκ ἔχω τὸν ἐπιδίδοντά μοι. Βοήθησον οὖν, κυρία μου ἀδελφή. σπουδαῖόν σοι γενέσθω ὅπως τὸ τάχος πέμψῃς μοι, ὡς προεῖπον, τὸν ἀδελφόν σου. εἰς τὰς τοιαύτας γὰρ ἀνάγκας εὑρίσκονται οἱ ἴδιοι τοῦ ἀνθρώπου. ἵνα οὖν καὶ σὺ παραβοηθήσῃς μοι τῷ ὄντι ἐπὶ ξένης καὶ ἐν νόσῳ ὄντι.

and methods'.[345] This denigration is particularly apparent in early twentieth century scholarship; one particular example defines folk medicine as 'the mass of superstitions [and] empirical beliefs held among the ignorant concerning materials useful as medicine' and claims that 'the more ignorant classes and peoples fall short according to the degree of their ignorance'.[346] A subsequent article, dating to the middle of the twentieth century, stated that 'the most enlightened ages display superstition, magic and revolting remedies that are comparable to those of less cultured periods', concluding that 'despite our approval or disapproval, the fact remains that otherwise intelligent people of ancient civilisations have put their trust in such remedies'.[347]

The primary objection raised by scholars with regards to folk medicine is the issue of efficacy or rather, lack of it; that is, the question of why individuals would rely on folk remedies that did not and could not possibly work when they had access to physicians who could provide them with medicinal remedies that did.[348] The validity of this objection has been questioned by John Riddle: 'What is it about modern medicine...that has its practitioners believing that they now have more information about the proper workings of the body, of biochemistry, and of myriad sciences and that no one without the knowledge and technology of today could possibly have done anything positive in the past?'.[349] Recent studies have shown that certain folk remedies are typically efficacious: for example, Dioscorides claimed that garlic 'cleans the arteries' and modern pharmacological investigation has shown that garlic does indeed help with hypercholesterolemia and its relation to atherosclerosis.[350] Likewise honey, beeswax and bee-glue have also been found to have antimicrobial, antibacterial and antifungal properties that can be harnessed in order to treat medical conditions ranging from simple skin wounds to more complicated and even chronic infections.[351] Both garlic and honey were cultivated extensively in Egypt during the Roman period.[352] Additionally, Renate Germer has observed that the herbs and spices cultivated in gardens in Egypt such as cumin, black cumin, coriander, dill and garden cress all share a common characteristic; they each possess a high essential oil content in either their seeds or leaves, and in turn these essential oils possess pharmaceutical properties.[353]

I intend to discuss both why and how folk medicine was practised in Egypt during the Roman period, first through an examination of the reasons why the inhabitants of the province might have preferred folk medicine to the services a physician could provide. Then I will use a combination of papyrological, palaeopathological and archaeological evidence from a range of sites and contexts (the village of Kellis in the Dakhleh Oasis of the Western Desert; the city of Oxyrhynchus in the Nile Valley, the quarry settlement of Mons Claudianus in the Eastern Desert; and the port of Berenike on the Red Sea coast) to examine the evidence for the actual practice of folk medicine in Roman Egypt. The common assumption with regard to folk medicine in the ancient world is that because the vast majority of it was not written down in the form of scientific treatises, it has been lost to us.[354] However, Roman Egypt demonstrates that this is not necessarily the case. I have selected the four communities of Kellis, Oxyrhynchus, Mons Claudianus and Berenike because, with the exception of Oxyrhynchus, all of them are not only attested by documentary papyri and ostraca, but have also been archaeologically excavated to varying degrees, with the result that human, animal and botanical remains as well as archaeological artefacts can also be considered here - features which open up the possibility of insight into the practice of folk medicine. In the case of Kellis, its strength is the palaeopathological findings that can be gleaned from the mummified and skeletal human remains recovered from the site's cemeteries, while Berenike is distinguished by the archaeobotanical evidence recovered from the site. For Mons Claudianus and Oxyrhynchus, the volume of papyri and ostraca recovered from these sites ensures a much more detailed reconstruction of these communities from papyri and ostraca than any other sites in Egypt.

With regard to the practice of ancient folk medicine, an understanding of the geographical and environmental contexts in which it was being practised is crucial; as the Hippocratic treatise *A Regimen for Health* stated: 'Diets...must be conditioned by age, the time of year, habit, country and constitution. They should be opposite in character to the prevailing climate, whether winter or summer. Such is the best road to health'.[355] Thus I have deliberately chosen to examine four very different communities: one in an oasis in the Western Desert; one located in proximity to the Nile in the Nile Valley; one amongst the marble quarries of the Eastern Desert; and one on the coast whose purpose was to trade with southern Africa, India and the Far East. I will assess what medicinal or magical ingredients these communities had access to and how the availability or lack of availability

---

[345] Gordon (1995) 363.

[346] True (1901) 105.

[347] MacKinney (1946) 150.

[348] True (1901) 107.

[349] Riddle (1996) 7.

[350] Dioscorides, *De Materia Medica* 2.152: *lamprunei arterias*. Riddle (1996) 7-8. Rahman and Lowe (2006). Galen also recognised the medicinal benefits that garlic could bring to a patient., *Alim. Fac.* 2: 'Garlic is eaten not just as an accompaniment to bread, but also as a medicine for health, because it contains aperient and discutient powers'.

[351] Greenwood (1993) 90-1; Postmes *et al.* (1993) 756-7; Visavadia *et al.* (2008) 55-6.

[352] On garlic cultivation in Egypt, see Crawford (1973). On apiculture in Egypt, see Sullivan (1973). For an interim summary of the findings of University of Manchester's *Pharmacy in Ancient Egypt* project, see David (2008), and also Cockitt and David (2010).

[353] Germer (1993) 71. In addition, each of these is highly aromatic and in antiquity strong scents were believed to possess a reviving and

---

regenerative effect, so aromatic substances were frequently incorporated into medicaments, Germer (1993) 76. This is particularly relevant to one element of Egyptian religious thought, as it was believed that one inhaled the breath of life through the nose.

[354] Nutton (2004) 1-2. He goes on to state 'they must be reconstructed imaginatively from case reports, educational treatises giving advice on what ought to happen, archaeological finds of instruments and drugs, and occasional artistic representations of an idealised moment'.

[355] Hippocrates, *Regimen* 2. See also Hippoc. *Aer.* for discussion of how the natural environment affects the health and constitution.

of these ingredients affected the practice of folk medicine. I will also consider how the social and cultural environment of these communities may have influenced the practice of folk medicine by examining factors such as the size of the community, the wealth and status of the individuals living there, and questions of religious affiliation and education. This will then lead into the second part of the study, which presents three case studies of, respectively, eye diseases, fevers and the injuries caused by wild animals. These were three categories of medical condition that despite being the subject of what modern scholars tend to refer to as 'high', 'professional' and 'rational' medical literature and treatment, also saw a sophisticated and widely practised set of 'low' and 'irrational' healing strategies develop around them, centred on domestic contexts and local communities.

2. Possible Reasons for Avoiding 'Professional' Medical Practitioners

In the previous chapter I discussed the wealth of evidence, both documentary and archaeological, for the activities of 'professional' medical practitioners in Egypt during the Roman period. However, there is also an abundance of evidence that suggests that such 'professionals', commonly designated as *iatroi* or *medici*, were not always consulted when an individual was experiencing health problems and was in need of medical treatment. Evidence from the ancient world suggests that there is a variety of reasons as to why this might have been the case: namely fear of incompetence, dishonesty or even outright malevolence on the part of the physician; a lack of availability, particularly in isolated and rural areas; and the often prohibitive cost of receiving medical treatment from a physician who might expect payment or at the very least, a 'gift' as evidence of the patient's appreciation for his or her intervention.

Fear

Even a cursory examination of the Latin and Greek literature dating from the Late Republic and early Roman Empire indicates that physicians were viewed in a decidedly negative light by Roman writers and, by implication, Roman readers.[356] This negativity pervades historical, scientific and even medical treatises if the subjects under discussion are other physicians with whose methods and practices the writer disagrees.[357] The very public and highly competitive nature of 'professional' medical practice undertaken by physicians such as Galen, through which they sought to undermine and lambaste their colleagues in order to promote their own expertise, may well have contributed to this.[358] With regard to Galen in particular, a significant proportion of his work was produced in an agonistic context, with the

specific purpose of refuting and (in extreme cases) humiliating his rival contemporaries or even his predecessors.[359] One particular example of this is recorded in Galen's *On Prognosis*, in which he records how he correctly diagnosed the philosopher Eudemos as suffering from a quartan fever, despite the fact that the man's other physicians (whom he takes great care to note are 'the best physicians of the city') insisted he was in good health.[360] Galen and the other physicians (Antigenes and Martianus, both very famous and influential) disagree four times; first over the initial diagnosis, then over whether or not Eudemos will suffer a relapse, then with regards to a remedy, and finally over whether Eudemos will die of his illness or not. As a result of this, Galen states that not only did he acquire 'no small reputation, not only for predictions but also for therapy', but Antigenes and Martianus were also 'very nearly leveled to the ground'.[361] This negativity about physicians is also present in poetry and prose literature. Consequently, whether an individual was reading for purposes of education or entertainment, they were absorbing variations on the same theme: physicians were not to be trusted.[362]

The most frequently cited reason to fear a physician is his or her incompetence, however good their intentions might initially have been. Martial wrote two epigrams about the undertaker Dialus, formerly a physician but evidently so bad at it that a career change was necessary, and this idea recurs in a subsequent epigram about a gladiator who was formerly an oculist: 'You used to do as a doctor what you now do as a gladiator'.[363] He also wrote about the physician Symmachus, who, as was not unusual amongst ancient physicians, brought his students with him on his house calls and encouraged them to manhandle the patient as a means of examining him, to the immediate detriment of his health.[364]

Incompetent (if well-meaning) physicians are also found in the novels *Apollonius, King of Tyre* and Achilles Tatius' *Leucippe and Clitophon*. In the first instance, the daughter of King Antiochus of Antioch supposedly dies in childbirth during a sea voyage. Her coffin is cast overboard and washes up on the beach at Ephesus where it is discovered by a physician and his students. The physician is unable to discern that the girl is actually alive although comatose and prepares to cremate her. It is one

---

[356] Amundsen (1974) 320.

[357] Historical treatises: Livy, *Ab Urbe Condita Libri* 40.56.11, 42.47.6; Tac. *Ann.* 12.67.2; Tac. *Agr.* 43.2; SHA *Gord. Tres.* 28.5. Scientific treatises: Plin. *HN* 29; Aul. Gell. *NA* 18.10. Medical treatises: Gal. *Praen.* 4.

[358] For instances where Galen discusses such public demonstrations and debates, see *Thras.* 2; *Nat. Fac.* 1.13; *De loc. aff.* 3.3; *Diff. Puls.* 2.3, 3.3; *MM* 2.5; *Libr. Propr.* 2.

[359] Mattern (2008) 15; see also *Diff. Puls.* 4.1; *Hipp. Epid.* 2.4.

[360] Gal. *Praen.* 2.4-5.

[361] Gal. *Praen.* 3.5; 3.6. For discussion of this episode and the importance of reputation - *fama* or δόξα - in the practice of ancient medicine, see Mattern (1999) 8-11.

[362] This did not prevent ancient writers such as Cicero or Pliny the Younger from having positive relationships with their physicians, but these were isolated cases originally written about in private correspondence rather than works of literature written specifically for public consumption. For a more positive view of ancient physicians, in which the gospel writers deliberately seek to present early Christian missionaries as physicians, see Bazzana (2009) 239-42. On the suggested readership of ancient novels, see Amundsen (1974) 321; Reardon (1989) 10-11; Stephens and Winkler (1995) 9-14.

[363] Mart. 1.30, 1.47, 8.74.

[364] Mart. 5.9.

of his students, 'of youthful appearance but mature judgment', who questions the cause of death and examines the girl, finding signs of life and succeeding in waking her up.[365] In the second case, the heroine Leucippe has some sort of fit, becomes violent and has to be forcibly restrained.[366] There is nothing technically wrong with the physician's treatment of her as he proceeds under the assumption that she is in fact insane and first dispenses medicine which is mixed with oil to rub on her head to induce sleep before administering a draught of medicine to purge her stomach. However, he fails to diagnose her condition correctly and simply states that 'Sleep is a remedy that suits every malady'.[367] In actual fact, an Egyptian soldier called Gorgias had spiked her drink with an aphrodisiac, but accidentally administered it undiluted and poisoned her instead.[368] At least in this case, the incorrect treatment was not harmful. Of course, these novels exploited stereotypes of unprofessional physicians, but it is entirely possible that certain physicians operating in Egypt during the Roman period were equally as incompetent. One papyrus dating from AD 142 records how a physician named Psasnis sought an audience with the prefect Valerius Eudaemon to complain about his fellow villagers compelling him to undertake civic duties from which, as a physician, he was supposedly exempt; Eudaemon responded by questioning his competence.[369]

In addition to the incompetence that might have arisen from issues such as a lack of training, misdiagnosis or even just bad luck, physicians were frequently considered to be casually dishonest and fraudulent. Martial depicts one physician, Herodes, as a thief who steals from his patients, while accusing others of committing adultery with a female patient in the name of medical treatment.[370] In Xenophon of Ephesus' *Ephesian Tale*, the heroine Anthia makes a physician named Eudoxas swear an oath to the goddess Artemis and promise to sell her poison so she can commit suicide in order to escape a forced marriage. However, instead of selling her poison, Eudoxas deliberately provides her with a soporific, not only cheating her but also violating his sacred oath to give her what she asked for. The result of this is that upon taking the drug and attempting suicide in good faith, she is presumed dead, entombed alive and only saved from death by suffocation or starvation by tomb robbers.[371] In Iamblichos' *Babyloniaka*, the heroine Sinonis attempts to commit suicide by stabbing herself in the chest. The hero

Rhodanes takes her to a nearby Temple of Aphrodite to be healed by a physician, and it is this physician who later informs on the couple to the mutilated eunuch Damas who is in pursuit of them, even joining in the pursuit of the couple himself until he drowns when crossing a river.[372]

There is also evidence that physicians were believed to be capable of outright malevolence and actively attempting to harm their patients. Pliny recounts the story of Archagathus, the first Greek physician to practise in Rome: 'On his arrival he was greatly welcomed at first, but that soon afterwards, from the cruelty displayed by him in cutting and searing his patients, he acquired the new name of 'Carnifex', and brought his art and physicians in general into considerable disrepute'.[373] He also records Cato the Elder's opinion of Greek medicine and medical practitioners: 'They have conspired among themselves to murder all barbarians with their medicine; a profession which they exercise for lucre, in order that they may win our confidence, and dispatch us all the more easily'.[374] Subsequently, in his own words Pliny states that 'a physician is the only person that can kill another with impunity'.[375] Martial warns a Rhaetian named Baccara against trusting a physician who is also a love rival.[376] Apuleius relates the story of a woman who wished to kill her husband, so went to a notoriously corrupt physician and paid him to administer poison disguised as intestinal medicine to him. However, the woman had simultaneously been planning to kill the physician too in order to remove all evidence of her crime, so she requested that the physician take some of the 'medicine' before he administered it to her husband, and then detained the physician so that he was unable to take the antidote. He did manage to get home in time to explain what had happened to his wife and to remind her to collect his fee, however.[377]

Whether ancient physicians were regarded with as much suspicion and hostility in life as they were in the works of literature that circulated among the Graeco-Roman elite is debatable. The negative portrayals such as those examined above could be dismissed as being extreme cases, or as stereotypes designed primarily for the purposes of entertainment.

Lack of Availability
Perhaps a more practical explanation as to why an individual might not consult a physician when suffering from an illness or injury would be some sort of logistical problem. According to Celsus, 'It is not possible for many patients to be cared for by one practitioner, and provided that he is skilled in the art, he is a suitable one

---

[365] *Historia Apollonii Regis Tyri* 27. This novel is known to have circulated in Egypt during the Roman period due to two fragments of papyrus originally from the same roll: *PSI* 151 and *P. Mil. Vogl.* 260 (late third or early fourth century AD, Oxyrhynchus).

[366] Achilles Tatius, *Leucippe et Clitophon* 4.9.1-2.

[367] Achilles Tatius, *Leucippe et Clitophon* 4.10.

[368] Achilles Tatius, *Leucippe et Clitophon* 4.15. This episode is discussed, and the doctor's actions are compared with recommendations in Celsus' *On Medicine*, in MacLeod (1969) 97-105.

[369] *P. Oxy.* 40 (AD 136, Oxyrhynchus): Εὐδαίμων εἶπεν· τάχα κακῶς αὐτοὺς ἐθεράπευσας.

[370] Mart. 9.96, 11.71.

[371] Xenophon, *Anthia et Habrocome Ephesiacorum* 3.4-5, 3.8. One papyrus fragment contains an episode possibly related to this novel: *PSI* 6.726 (late second century AD).

[372] Iamblichos, *Babylonaika* 75a30, 76a7.

[373] Plin. *HN* 29.6.

[374] Plin. *HN* 29.7.

[375] Plin. *HN* 29.8.

[376] Mart.11.74.

[377] Apul. *Met.* 10.23. This episode is discussed in Amundsen (1974), and his interpretation is that the physician's final words are a reference to the stereotype of the greedy and mercenary ancient physician.

who does not much absent himself from the patient'.[378] As an educated layman, Celsus' opinion of the capabilities of an individual medical practitioner did not necessarily accord with the reality of the medical profession, particularly since Galen portrays patients, admittedly ones who were members of the social elite, as being treated by multiple physicians at once. However, this does beg the question of how many patients each individual physician was responsible for, or alternatively how far one might have to travel in order to see a physician when the need arose.

It is difficult to reconstruct accurately the population of any settlement, no matter what the size, in Egypt during the Roman period. Diodorus Siculus states that during his lifetime, the population of Alexandria was over 300,000 ἐλεύθεροι.[379] When the number of women, children and slaves necessary to constitute an individual household are added to this, the total population has been thought by some to be over 1,000,000 people. This has been considered by Diana Delia to be far too large; when Alexandria is compared with Rome and other equivalent cities such as Seleucia, a range of between 500,000 and 600,000 people is preferred.[380] Roger Bagnall and Dominic Rathbone have lowered this even further to 500,000 at its peak.[381] In any case, there are no statistics for how many physicians lived and practised in Alexandria during the Roman period; it can only be inferred that there were significant numbers of physicians in the city, both teachers and their students, specialists and more general practitioners.

Likewise, estimates of the population of towns vary significantly. Consider the case of Oxyrhynchus: Richard Alston has tabulated figures of 11,901 in AD 199, 21,000 in AD 235, and 12,087 in the period AD 270-2 and surmised that while the figures for AD 199 and AD 270-2 are probably too conservative, those for AD 235 are probably much too high.[382] Peter van Minnen has suggested that in Late Antiquity the city had a population of 20,000, of which 10,000 were Greek.[383] The reports of the public physicians that survive from Oxyrhynchus all date from the fourth century AD, so roughly contemporaneous with van Minnen's suggested figures. Two public physicians are attested during the period AD 315-16; two more in AD 336; two in AD 338; three in AD 354; and two AD 376, so it would appear that at any one time there were only two public physicians tending to 20,000 people.[384] However, in addition to the public

physicians, there were probably numerous independent medical practitioners. With regard to the villages, Alston has estimated that the population of Karanis in AD 145-6 was around 3300 people, while in the period AD 171-4, it was between 1907 and 2135 people.[385] One ostraca from Mons Claudianus states that there were 920 people resident there on one day in the early second century AD, and there was at least one physician living there too.[386]

Although it is difficult (if not impossible) to assess the ratio of physicians to patients in Egypt during the Roman period, such figures are provisionally available from Egypt during the Ptolemaic period. According to Willy Clarysse and Dorothy Thompson, their analysis of a third century BC tax register from Themistos indicates that the ratio of physicians to patients was one physician to every 989 adult civilians.[387] However, if members of the army and children are added, the patient load increases to around 1640. It is possible that the physician to patient ratio was even smaller; if the privileged Greek members of society were treated separately from the Egyptians, there would have been one physician to every 493 Greek patients.[388]

Cost

As discussed in the previous chapter, 'professional' medical practitioners received payment for their services, whether in the form of a straight exchange of medical practice for money, or in the form of gifts received later.[389] During the second century AD, an average civilian worker located in the Nile Valley earned around twenty-five *drachmae* a month, with the maximum amount attested around forty *drachmae* a month.[390] There is a variety of papyrological evidence that testifies to the expense of medical practice and on occasion gives the specific amount owed, and so it is possible to assess the impact that the cost of consulting a physician might have on an individual's cash flow. In a papyrus thought to date to the third century AD, the writer specifies the amount owed for medical treatment; the woman writes to her brother to ask him to come to her as she and her children are ill and she owes the physician at least twenty

[378] Celsus, *Med.* 3.4.9.

[379] Diod. Sic. 17.52.6.

[380] Delia (1988) 284. According to Strabo, *Geographica* 16.2.5, Seleucia on the Tigris and Alexandria were comparable in manpower and physical size, while Pliny the Elder stated that in his lifetime, Seleucia had a population of approximately 600,000: Plin. *HN* 6.30.122.

[381] Bagnall and Rathbone (2004) 51.

[382] Alston (2001) 163 using figures tabulated from *P. Oxy.* 908 (AD 199, Oxyrhynchus); *P. Oslo* 3.111 (AD 235, Oxyrhynchus); and *P. Oxy.* 2892-5 (AD 270-2, Oxyrhynchus).

[383] van Minnen (2007)160.

[384] *P. Oxy.* 4441 (AD 315-6, Oxyrhynchus): Sarapias and Dioscorus; *P. Oxy.* 4366 (AD 336, Oxyrhynchus): Theoninus, Heron, Silvanus and Didymus; *P. Oxy.* 4528 (AD 338, Oxyrhynchus): Heron and Didymus;

[385] Alston (1995) 121. The figures for AD 171-4 were calculated from tax rolls *P. Mich* 4; the figures for AD 145-6 were calculated from poll tax receipts *P. Ryl.* 4.594 (AD 168-9, Arsinoite nome).

[386] Population: *O. Claud.* Inv. 1538 + 2921. Physicians: *O. Claud.* Inv. 2055; 3260; 2795; 3739; 1538; 2921. The latter two mention ἱππιατροί, horse doctors or veterinarians, who might also have treated humans.

[387] See *P. Sorb.* Inv. 211 + 212 Recto + *P. LilleDem.* 111.99 (June-July 229 BC, Arsinoite nome): *Count P.* 2. 485-7.

[388] Clarysse and Thompson (2006) 163. According to research undertaken by GMAP Consulting in 2005, the GP to patient ratio in the United Kingdom varied from 1:3428 in Greater Derby, to 1: 680 in the Western Isles, see http://www.medwire-news.md/news/article.aspx?k=51&id=32260, accessed 1st January 2012.

[389] For the question of a physician's income, see Kudlien (1976) 448-9.

[390] Cuvigny (1996) 141.

P. Oxy. 4370 (AD 354, Oxyrhynchus): Eulogius, Anubion, Didymus and Herodotus; *P. Oxy.* 4529 (AD 376, Oxyrhynchus): Dionysius and Eudaemon.

drachmae.[391] An account of expenditures lists the cost of two circumcisions; thirty-four and twenty *drachmae* respectively.[392] Having to pay out amounts such as these would put an individual earning only around twenty-five *drachmae* a month in severe financial difficulty, at least in the short term. In a papyrus dating to the second century AD, Aphrodite writes to her sister Taonnophris that while she was on the way to Alexandria, her foot was trodden on by a horse: 'I have been healed at great expense and until today I have been out of action'.[393] In a papyrus dating to the fourth century AD, Apollon requests that Herminos sends money at once: 'We are ruined by hunger; I have spent my portion on the doctor'.[394] However, there is evidence to suggest that even very wealthy individuals preferred to take care of their family members in times of serious illness themselves, so the prohibitive cost of medical treatment was not necessarily a definitive motivation for utilising alternative healing strategies. The will of Lucius Ignatius Rufinus, dating to 3rd June AD 211, includes a specific bequest to his wife: 'I give and delegate to Lucretia Octavia, my wife, who has laboured much during the course of my illness, five and a half *iugera* of land in wheat in the place of Potamon, adjacent to the property of Serenus, and half of my house...And if I have any possession in my house, I want this to be my wife's'.[395]

In addition to the cost of the physician, there was also the cost of the treatment that might be prescribed.[396] According to Pliny the Elder, nard, an oil derived from the *Nardostachys jatamansi*, a herb that grew in remote mountainous regions of India and was imported to the Roman Empire through the Red Sea port of Berenike, cost between forty and seventy five *denarii* per pound for the leaves and one hundred for the roots during the late first century AD.[397] Consequently, it was one of the most expensive imported plant products; in a list of medical prescriptions recovered from Oxyrhynchus and dating to the early first century AD, the amount of nard used in each is miniscule, while all the other ingredients are modest substances.[398] Likewise myrrh, the product of the *Commiphorua myrrha* tree that grew in Somalia and South Arabia, used in both mummification and medicine, particularly in the treatment of wounds and remedies for eye diseases, cost between eleven and sixteen and a half

denarii per pound, over twice the price of frankincense and four times the price of bdellium.[399] It was, however, much cheaper than nard or the other aromatics imported from India such as cinnamon and malabathron.[400] As is the case with nard, in a recipe for a plaster myrrh is used in conjunction with lower priced and more easily obtainable ingredients such as eggs, wax, oil and pig fat.[401]

One papyrus, a private letter sent to a man named Neicetes from his father and dating from the mid third century AD, contains a cryptic reference to a physician's account. The father makes several requests of his son: 'Write to me about my Leonidas. Not only have I shown you in my first letter how large the amount of [small change] is but you took 240 *drachmae* for the physician's account. If you have need of other supplies write to me and they will be brought to you at once'.[402] There are several possible readings of this. Depending upon how the term 'physician's account' is interpreted (as either an account that Neicetes has with a physician or that a physician has with him) it is possible that Neicetes (or perhaps Leonidas) has been ill to the point of requiring extensive medical treatment, but 240 *drachmae* seems an extremely large amount of money, even considering the prices quoted for ingredients with medicinal properties above. Conversely, it is also possible that Neicetes, along with his father and brother Dionysius who are also mentioned in the letter, serves as some sort of financier or money-lender and it is the physician who has the account with them, perhaps in order to borrow the money that enables him to purchase upfront such expensive ingredients so that he can then sell them on to his patients.

3. Domestic / Folk Medicine in Roman Egypt

Enumerating fear, lack of availability and cost as the principal reasons why an individual might choose to avoid a 'professional' medical practitioner might give the impression that alternative healing strategies were undertaken passively rather than actively, that individuals were taking care of themselves, their family members and friends as a last resort rather than a first one. This was not always the case. Although this tradition *seems* to appear infrequently in the surviving works of ancient literature that are commonly classified as medical treatises (those produced by writers such as Galen, Soranus, Rufus and Oribasius, practising physicians), folk medicine and self-help appear more frequently in pharmacological treatises such as Dioscorides' *On Medical Materials*, Scribonius Largus' *Compositions* and Gargilius Martialis' *Medicine from Oils and Fruits* as well as in agricultural treatises

---

[391] *P. Stras.* 1.73 (third century, unprovenanced): ἀλλὰ ἐχόμενα Ἐμοιτου ἰατροῦ συνλε ἐκπλέξας πρὸς αὐτὸν ἐπὶ δραχμὰς διὸ παρακαλῶ, ἄδελφε.

[392] *P. Thmouis* 1.123.1 and 128.4 (AD 170-1).

[393] *BGU* 13.2350 (second century AD, unprovenanced): ἐπατήθην ὑπὸ ἵππου εἰς τ[ὸν] πόδα καὶ ἐκινδύνευσα, ὥστε με καθαρισθῆναι καὶ πολλὰ ἀναλῶσαι, καὶ ἕως σήμερον ἀνέξοδος εἰμί.

[394] *P. Lond.* 3.982 (late fourth century, Lycopolite nome): τό γὰρ [μέρος] μου ἀνήλωσα εἰς τὸν ἰατρόν, ἕως ἄν [θεραπ]εύση με ἐν τῇ νόσω.

[395] *Diogenes P.* 10 (AD 211, Ptolemais Euergetis).

[396] See Nutton (1985) for discussion of the drug trade in antiquity, particularly 142-4 for the dangers of dishonest or unreliable traders.

[397] Casson (1989) 193; Miller (1969) 88-92. Nard is also known as spikenard and valerian.

[398] *P. Oxy.* 1088 (early first century AD, Oxyrhynchus).

[399] Plin. *HN* 12.70. See also Miller (1969) 104-5.

[400] Casson (1989) 118-20. For an account that contains both myrrh and malabathron, see *NNC: Col.* Inv. 137e (1) (second-third century AD, unprovenanced).

[401] *P. Mich.* 17.758 (fourth century AD, unprovenanced).

[402] *P. Wash. Univ.* 1.30 (mid third century AD, unprovenanced): Λεωνίδου μου καὶ διὰ τῆς πρώτης ἐπιστολῆς δεδήλωκά σοι [ὅτι] πόσον ἐστὶ ἡ ποσότης τοῦ κέρματος καὶ ἐξεκομίσω εἰς λόγ(ον) τοῦ ἰατροῦ (δραχμὰς) σμ εἰ δὲ χρείαν ἔχεις ἄλλων ἐ[π]ιμηνιδίων γράψον μοι κα[ὶ] εὐθέως σοι ὁμισθήσεται.

such as Cato's *On Agriculture*, Varro's *On Agriculture* and Columella's *On Country Matters*, commonly involving ingredients harvested from the household and/or the estate or the natural environment immediately surrounding it. In actual fact, there even appears to have been a thriving literary tradition associated with lay medicine in the ancient world (see for example Celsus' *On Medicine*), as exemplified not only by brief notations in those works which survive, but also by those which do not. For example, both Dioscorides and Galen produced pharmacological and medical treatises entitled *Family Medicines* (εὐπόριστικα), specifically designed for laymen, which are now unfortunately lost.[403]

One aspect of 'folk' medicine particularly well-attested in Egypt during the Roman period is belief in the 'evil eye' as being responsible for health problems.[404] The 'evil eye' represented the belief that envy, whether experienced by a fellow human or a deity, was able to harm or kill by supernatural means, and the concept is discussed in Plutarch's *Convivial Complaints* and Heliodorus' *Aethiopica*, the latter author specifically describing the 'evil eye' as infectious.[405] However, as well as evidence for the causes of health problems, there is also a particularly useful source of information for how they were treated: the extent to which individuals engaged in folk medicine and self-help is demonstrated through the contents of private letters sent by the inhabitants of the province to members of their family and friends. Consequently, it is not surprising that a number of letters survive in which the writer either asks the recipient to send them something that would be beneficial to their health, or thanks them for having already done so, or tells the recipient that they are in fact sending them something in conjunction with the letter, as a means of somehow circumventing such apparently pervasive malign influences. In some of these letters, the connection between the object sent or received and its use in the context of health or medicine is unambiguous, as this is expressly stated by the writer. During the first century AD, Heraclides wrote to Anchorimphis regarding the trees in his orchard: 'When these must be cut in order that the vines may not be shaded too much, send me a sweet palm crown since I am rather sickly'.[406] In the second century AD, Irene wrote to her friends Taonnophris and Philo informing them that she was sending them a case of dates from Ombos and pomegranates, and made a request of them in return:

'Please send me back in [the same container] two *drachmae* weight of purgative, in which I am in urgent need'.[407] Also in the second century AD, Serapias wrote to Ammonios and requested that he 'send me the scalpel - don't forget'.[408] Sometime during the second or third century AD, Thaisarion wrote to her siblings asking that they replace the two jars of radish oil they had borrowed from her 'for I have need of them when I give birth'.[409]

In other letters, the association is merely implied, as the object is something that could be utilised in a medical context. One example of this is a letter sent during the third century AD in which the unnamed writer wrote: 'I have ... sent you three letters. Be so kind as to send me a pair of bandages'.[410] Another is a contemporary letter sent from Sarapammon to his brother Andronicus in which he says that he has received his letter and 'the basket containing five salt fish and four fine loaves and a small quantity of unguent and two pieces of papyrus'.[411] The word that he uses for unguent, μύρον, indicates that this unguent was sweet oil such as balsam, which had numerous medical applications but was extremely expensive, hence the small amount stated here.[412] A third example is a letter sent during the third or fourth century from Tauris to his father Apitheon. He requests that his father sends 'two weaver's combs and two ounces of storax and also two large hair combs. Just as you said to me, "I shall send things like that to the farm for you", send them'.[413] Storax was a fragrant gum with medicinal properties, evidently frequently recommended by Galen if the remedies attributed to him by his successors are to be trusted, and the fact that it was being sent to Tauris' home indicates that it was for his personal use.[414] A fourth example is a letter sent during the fourth or fifth century AD, from Pares to his brother Papios. He requests that Papios acquire a range of medicinal spices and herbs for him: 'In the usual way, please buy me four pounds of kassamon and five pounds of pure Carian mastic and five pounds of common mastic and three ounces of saffron and five pounds of Cretan...and...pounds of cassia wood and...pounds of konaron and...pounds of costus root'.[415]

---

[403] Beagon (1992) 233-7.

[404] See for example *P. Oxy.* 292 (AD 25, Oxyrhynchus) and *P. Oxy. Hels.* 50 (third century AD, Oxyrhynchus. This belief in the power of the 'evil eye' to cause illness also extended to animals; two ostraca from a fort in Upper Egypt express concern for the horses of cavalrymen. See *O. Florida* 15 (mid to late second century AD, Apollonopolis Magna) and *O. Florida* 18 (mid to late second century AD, Apollonopolis Magna).

[405] Heliodorus, *Aethiopica* 3.7: 'The air by which we are surrounded and which reaches our inward parts through eyes, nostrils, breath, and other passages, brings with it qualities that it has received outside and implants in the person receiving it whatever affections it has required'.

[406] *P. Corn.* 50 (first century AD, Fayum): πότε δεῖ αὐτὰ κοπῆναι ἵνα αἱ ἄμπελοι μὴ σκιάζωνται, πέμψον μοι ἐνκεφάλιον γλυκὺ ἐπεὶ ἀσθενέστερός εἰμι.

[407] *P. Oxy.* 116 (second century AD, Oxyrhynchus): καλῶς ποιήσαντες πέμψατέ μοι ἐν αὐτῆι καθάρια διδράχμου, ἐπεὶ ἀναγκαίως χρεία ἐστί μοι αὐτῶν.

[408] *O. Max.* Inv. 279 + 467 (second century AD, Maximianon).

[409] *P. Mich.* 8.508 (second-third century AD, Karanis): καὶ γὰρ ἐγὼ χρείαν ἔχω [α]ὐτῶν ὅταν τίκτω.

[410] *P. Warr.* 18 (third century AD, unprovenanced): καὶ ἐγὼ ὑμῖν διεπεμψάμην τρεῖς ἐπιστολάς. καλῶς δὲ ποιήσεις πέμψας μοι τὸ ζεῦγος τῶν φασκιδίων.

[411] *P. Oxy.* 2596 (third century AD, Oxyrhynchus): ἐκομισάμην δὲ παρὰ τοῦ αὐτοῦ Ψαεις τὸ σφυρίδιον ἔχων ταρίχους ε καὶ καθαροὺς δ καὶ μυράφιον [καὶ] χαρτάρια β.

[412] For the medicinal properties of various different types of μύρον, see Dioscorides, *De Materia Medica* 1.42; Ath. 15.688 E.

[413] *P. Oxy.* 2599 (third-fourth century AD, Oxyrhynchus): πέμψον ἡμῖν δύο κτενία γερδιακὰ καὶ δύο ὀγκίας στυρακίου ἀλλὰ καὶ δύο κτενία μεγάλα τῆς κεφαλῆς. καθὼς εἴρηκάς μοι εἰς τὸ χωρίον πέμπω σοι τὰ τοιαῦτα, πέμψον.

[414] See for example Andromachus Junior 13.29.13, 30.1, 63.10 and 64.1.

[415] *P. Haun.* 20 (fourth / fifth century AD, unprovenanced): ὡ[ς] ἔθος ἔχεις ποιεῖν καλῶ[ς] ἵνά μοι ἀγοράσῃς κασσάμου λί(τρας) δ

The quantities mentioned are rather large, perhaps too large for personal use, so it is possible that Pares was an apothecary.

More intriguing is the lengthy shopping list given to a man called Achillas, who was evidently going to market, by a group of his friends and neighbours:

> Buy half a *cotyle* of sediment of good dry perfume at sixteen *drachmae*, some trodden grapes at eight *drachmae*, aromatic gum to the weight of four *drachmae*, onycha to the weight of four *denarii*, incense to the weight of one *denarius*, some large pine cones at one *denarius*, desiccated powder at twelve *drachmae*, thread at twenty *drachmae*, two hair combs at one *denarius*, sauce at one *denarius*. Horion the baker says, buy me four *obols* of marjoram. Diogenes says, buy a sheet of papyrus. Buy us a bedstead; buy us…some pomegranate wine.[416]

This shopping list contains a range of items that could be used either for medicinal purposes or even in the production of medicine such as aromatic gum, onycha, pine cones and marjoram; even pomegranate wine could be taken medicinally. Equally, the inclusion of ξηρομύρον, what seem to be either cakes or bars of dried perfume, in conjunction with aromatic substances like gum and onycha could imply that these ingredients are required for the production of aromatics, although ξήριον, desiccated powder, does seem to have been used specifically to treat wounds in antiquity.[417] The inclusion of household items such as thread, hair combs and a bedstead implies that the subjects of these requests were intended primarily for use in domestic contexts.

Finally, in a letter dating to the second century AD, Horion wrote to his father and brother-in-law Sarapion, requesting their help in obtaining materials to be used for the mummification of a friend of theirs. He states that the reason he is doing this is that the deceased's mother and sister, also acquainted with his father and brother-in-law, were too distraught to organise anything themselves and goes on to list the items he needs: 'I rolled up in this letter samples of herbs for a mummy. In addition, buy carpenter's glue, two pounds […] and half a pound of safflower seeds for dying the linen'.[418] Although the herbs were intended for use in mummification in this case, they would also have had medicinal properties and could equally have been utilised for medicinal purposes, as indicated by the use of the word φάρμακον, a drug that could be used as a dangerous poison or a healing remedy depending on the context. Likewise, although safflower and its seeds, κνῆκος, were used as cheaper substitutes for saffron to dye textiles, they were also used to make oil which could be used to flavour food or taken medicinally as a laxative.[419] Thus, when Horion purchased such items for use in mummification, he (or anyone else who wanted to) could just as easily purchase them for use in the preparation of medicaments.[420] Thus, it is possible that in some cases, the capabilities of those practising 'folk' medicine and undertaking domestic medical practice extended to the production of quite sophisticated medicinal remedies incorporating a range of expensive ingredients such as myrrh or even natron.

The Natural Environment of Roman Egypt

Dioscorides was well aware of the fact that the medicinal properties of plants varied in accordance with the nature of the environment in which they grew: the type of soil, the nutrients available, the associated flora, the climate and the level of cultivation all affected the strength of the medicine that could be made from a plant.[421] Despite its hot, dry climate, low levels of rainfall and extensive desert terrain, Egypt was a particularly fertile province and provided up to one third of Rome's total grain consumption each year; an estimated 135,000 tonnes.[422] This massive agricultural output was the result of the annual inundation of the Nile.[423] Agricultural land was at a premium and a wide variety of plants, herbs, fruit and vegetables were cultivated. The province was also home to numerous species of exotic animals. So, in addition to purchasing medicine from medical practitioners, the inhabitants of Egypt had the option of gathering wild flora, cultivating their own gardens and harvesting ingredients for medicinal and magical remedies from wild fauna.

That the diverse qualities of animal products, fruit, vegetables, herbs, spices, pulses and nuts were well known in the ancient world is indicated by the writings of

---

καὶ μαστίχης ἁπλῆς Καρίας λί(τρας) ε καὶ χυδαίας [μ]αστίχης λί(τρας) ε καὶ κρόκου οὐγ(κίας) γ καὶ κρητικῆς λί(τρας) ε καὶ … ειχειο λί(τραν) α καὶ ξυλοκασσί[ας] λί(τρας) κόνναρά λί(τρας) … καὶ κοσταρί[ού] λι(τρας).

[416] *P. Oxy.* 1142 (late third century, Oxyrhynchus): ὑποστάθμιον ἀγόρασον ἡμικοτύλην ξυρομύρου καλὸν (δ) ις, πατήματος (δ) η, βρέλλιον ὁλκῆς δ, ὄνυχος τέσσερα δηνάρια ὁλκῆς, στυράκιν ὁλκῆς δηναρίου, στοβ[ί]λια δηναρίου μεγάλα, ξήριον δ ιβ, στήμιον δ κ, κτένια πρὸς κεφαλὴν δύο δηναρίου α, αρτυματος δηναριου α. λέγει Ωρίων ὁ κλιβανεὺς ὅτι αγόραρόν μοι … τετρώβολα ὀριγάνου. Διογέ[ν]ης … ς ὅτ[ι] αγόραρόν χάρτον α. [ἀγόραρόν] ἡμεῖν χελάδριον … [ἀγόρα]ρόν ἡμεῖν ἐλέου ξέσ[τ]ις α, ἀγόρασον ἡμεῖν [γλ]ύκιον ῥουτικόν.

[417] Aët. 6.65; Alexander of Tralles, *Alexandri Yatros Practica* 1.15.

[418] *P. Haun.* 2.17 (second century AD, Arsinoite nome): σὺ οὖν ἐπίστασαι τὰ μέτρα αὐτῆς. καὶ ὁμοίως συνείλιξά τῆδε τῇ ἐπιστολῇ δείγματα φαρμάκων ὡς εἰς σορόν. ἀγόρασον δὲ καὶ τεκτονικὴν κόλλαν, μνᾶς δύο … καὶ ἡμιμνοῦν σπερμάτ(ων) κνήκου εἰς βάψαι λίνα.

[419] See for example *SB* 16.12564 (either AD 145 or AD 168, Arsinoite nome), in which the supervisor of an oil-press acknowledges receipt of safflower seeds to be converted into oil. For the medicinal properties of safflower seeds and oil, see Dioscorides, *De Materia Medica* 4.188; Plin. *HN* 21.90.

[420] See for example the list of spices found in *P. Harr.* 98 (fourth century AD, unprovenanced): 'Castor, pepper, spurge, costus, laurel berries, marjoram, vegetable salt, feverfew, frankincense, balsam juice, nard'.

[421] Dioscorides, *De Materia Medica* Praef. 6; Riddle (1985) 71.

[422] Jackson (2002) 273.

[423] Plin. *HN* 5.10,

Hippocrates, Pliny the Elder, Dioscorides, Galen and many others that circulated in the provinces of the Roman Empire.[424] Hippocrates stated simply that 'food is medicine', Cato observed that 'while a garden feeds people, it also heals them', and centuries later Galen echoed these statements: 'Everyone knows, even if they only have a little intelligence, that experience serves as a teacher, just as of many things, so too of which foods are easy or difficult to digest, which are helpful or harmful to the stomach, and which are purgative, laxative or costive of the bowels'.[425] It seems likely that the practitioners of medical self-help and folk medicine were experienced not only with regards to the nutritional properties of the foodstuffs available to them through agricultural cultivation of the land, foraging and gathering, and trade, but also the medicinal ones. Rather than asking why the inhabitants of Egypt during the Roman period would practice medical self-help and folk medicine when they had the option of engaging the services of a 'professional' medical practitioner such as a physician, we should consider asking why the inhabitants should have patronised a 'professional' medical practitioner when there was no guarantee that his or her treatment would work, and when they themselves could produce a remedy that was tried and tested.

Aspects of the Natural Environment: The Nile
According to Danielle Bonneau, seventy different ancient authors discuss the Nile flood, both questioning and then debating what caused it.[426] In turn, according to Robert Wild, fifty-six ancient authors discuss the properties and benefactions of Nile water.[427] During the fifth century BC, Aeschylus wrote that it was 'untouched by disease' and this idea seems to have persisted; during the second century AD Aelius Aristides stated that 'we benefit from the healing remedies of the saviour gods, of whom one is synonymous with the Nile'.[428] He also claimed that '[Nile water] does not spoil, when kept in Egypt or exported beyond the frontiers. The Egyptians are the only people we know who fill jars with water as others do with wine, keep it three, four or more years, and draw pride from its age as with wine'.[429] According to Theophrastus' *On Waters*, 'Nile water is very fecundating and very sweet, and that for this reason it relaxes the stomach of those who drink it with the natron mixed in it', and Oribasius also recommended Nile water as an aid to digestion and intestinal function, as well as menstruation and childbirth.[430] One fable in which Nile water was

expressly used medicinally was repeated in the works of a variety of ancient writers; it related how the klyster, or enema, was supposedly discovered when an ibis was seen performing one on itself with Nile water.[431]

The agricultural fertility that resulted from the inundation was attributed specifically to the Nile water, rather than the silt that it brought with it, and was thought to affect not only crops, but also animals, men and women.[432] However, it was not just water from the Nile that was coveted for its supposed healing properties. According to Galen, Egyptian soil processed into clay was also sought after for medicinal uses:

> Many people both in Alexandria and Egypt use it. Many do so by their own free choice, but many others are inspired by dreams to do so. At Alexandria I saw some people suffering from dropsy and spleen disorders who used the clay of Egyptian soil. And many clearly benefited from rubbing the clay of this soil onto their lower legs, thighs, forearms, upper arms, backs, sides and breasts.[433]

It is clear that, while the soil may have been mixed with Nile water in order to turn it into clay, it is the clay and thus the soil itself that is considered to be medicinal in this particular instance. Egyptian soil is also included as an ingredient in medical recipes incorporated into the corpora of magical papyri.[434]

In addition to water and clay, both the Nile and Egypt's lakes provided the Egyptians with large quantities and wide varieties of fish; as a case in point, during the second century AD a fisherman from Oxyrhynchus leased the right to fish in private waters in return for thirty jars of fish sauce, two jars of shad, two jars of Spanish mackerel, one jar of mullet and one jar of catfish.[435] These fish were eaten both fresh and salted, with salt taken from lakes, pans and deposits, and from the mines located between Egypt and Mount Sinai.[436] However, according to medical writers such as Dioscorides and Galen, salted fish and other fish products such as garum were also used as *materia medica*.[437] Garum was even recommended for the treatment of animal bites, particularly those inflicted by crocodiles.[438]

---

[424] For work currently being undertaken at the Smithsonian Conservation Biology Institute, involving DNA analysis of medicines found in an ancient shipwreck off the coast of Tuscany that has revealed the use of ingredients of vegetables including onions, carrots and cabbage and plants including parsley, alfalfa, hawthorn, hibiscus and chestnut, see Callaway (2010).
[425] Hippocrates, *De alimento* 19; Cato, *Agr.* 8.2; Gal. *Alim. Fac.* proem.
[426] Bonneau (1964) 213.
[427] Wild (1981) 86.
[428] Aesch. *Supp.* 560; Aristid. *Or.* 36.124; Wild (1981) 99-100 is of the opinion that this is not enough evidence to support the theory that Nile water was believed to actually give or restore health, believing instead that the water was venerated for its agricultural fertility.
[429] Aristid. *Or.* 2.573, 612.
[430] For Theophrastus, see Ath. 2.15.41 E-F. For Oribasius, see Oribasius, *Collectiones* 1.5, 3, 15.

[431] See Cic. *Nat. D.* 2.126; Plin. *HN* 8.97; Plut. *Mor.* 381C and 974C; Ael. *NA* 2.35; Gal. *Cur. Rat. Ven. Sect.* 6. This fable is not included in Wild's discussion of the properties and benefactions of Nile water.
[432] Wild (1981) 100. Accordingly, twins and multiple births were believed to occur very frequently in Egypt, see Strabo, *Geographica* 15.1.22; Plin. *HN* 7.3; Aul. Gell.10.2.
[433] Gal. *SMT* 9.1.2.
[434] See *PGM* 12.414 for soil included on a coded list made by temple scribes of ingredients, dating to the fourth century AD.
[435] *P. Lond.* Inv. 2143 (second century AD, Oxyrhynchus): excluding the Spanish mackerel, which is native to the Mediterranean, all of these fish are found in the Nile; see also Diod. Sic. 1.36.1; Xenocrates cited at Oribasius, *Collectiones* 2.58.148-50; Ael. *NA* 10.43.
[436] Vitr. *De arch.* 8.3.7.
[437] Gal. *Alim. Fac.* 3.40.1-6; for discussion of the medicinal uses of salted fish and garum see Curtis (1984) and (1991) 27-34.
[438] Plin. *HN* 31.97.

There is certainly evidence for the consumption of garum in Roman Egypt, particularly in the wealthier households such as those of the prefects of Egypt and even in that of the emperor Caracalla during his visit to the province in AD 216.[439] However, there is also evidence of the use of garum as *materia medica*. In a letter dating to the second century AD, a man wrote to his brother repeatedly asking him for updates regarding the state of his presumably poor health, and also enquiring as to whether he had received a care package containing lettuces, beets, bulbs, greens and three semi-salted fish (μαιώτας καλοὺς τρεῖς ἡμινήρους).[440] In a letter dating to the period from the late third to the early fourth century AD, Cornelius wrote to his mother first about his illness, then about the fact that he had received a quantity of garum (σπάθιν γάρους) from the wife of an acquaintance.[441]

The Built and Cultivated Environment of Roman Egypt

The natural environment of Roman Egypt had a profound effect on the living arrangements of the inhabitants of the province in a variety of ways. The scarcity of trees and the labour and logistics required to quarry stone and transport it to the Nile Valley meant that timber and stone were extremely expensive, so most houses were constructed out of mud-brick. Consequently, the style of the architecture was very different to that of the other provinces of the Roman Empire.[442] Houses in villages tended to be narrow and consist of multiple stories, while houses in cities and towns more commonly had one, these different uses of the space available reflecting the demands of the economic environment in which the houses were located.[443] Houses in urban environments were frequently constructed around an *aithrion*, a central integral courtyard. In addition to the courtyard, these houses seem to have had wells and space for animals and animal fodder. It is likely that the space in these courtyards, accompanied by a water source in the form of the wells, provided the inhabitants with the opportunity and location for the cultivation of kitchen gardens, although out of necessity these would have been extremely compact, perhaps simply consisting of several potted plants.[444]

However, there is much more papyrological and archaeological evidence for the cultivation of plots of 'garden land' surrounding villages and towns, land which was used to grow fruit, vegetables and herbs with medicinal properties. This garden land was subject to a garden tax and numerous receipts for payment of this particular tax survive on papyri and ostraca.[445] The fact that there was a separate tax on vineyards indicates that vines and grapes were not usually grown on these plots of garden land. The papyrological evidence indicates that these plots of garden land tended to be used to cultivate one crop at a time, with olive trees, palm trees and melon trees being particularly popular.[446] However, there is some evidence for the cultivation of multiple crops at the same location. A lease dating from AD 141 states that in return for the land and irrigation equipment that he was leasing, Primion would grow grapes, dates, pumpkins, melons, pomegranates, peaches, olives and figs in addition to whatever vegetables were in season and dried sebesten.[447] A fragmentary petition dating to the period during the late second and early third century AD states that the owner of an olive garden caught one of his neighbours stealing dates from palm trees that were also planted there.[448] There are also some references to vegetable gardens, although the vegetables grown are not generally specified.[449] One exception to this is the quarry settlement at Mons Claudianus in the Eastern Desert. Archaeologists recovered botanical remains of thirteen vegetables and herbs including onions, garlic, artichokes, cucumbers and cabbage, while the cultivation and consumption of additional vegetables and herbs are attested by the correspondence of Dioscorus, who had the enviable job of tending a garden and growing fresh vegetables while his contemporaries quarried marble for public monuments.[450]

In addition to the crops grown in these gardens specifically for commercial reasons, it seems likely that some plants, fruits and vegetables were also deliberately cultivated for personal use; remains of weeds retrieved from archaeological sediments dating to the Roman period from locations throughout Egypt have revealed thirty four species of flora, of which a significant proportion have medicinal properties including *Cyperus articulatus*, which can be used as a sedative.[451] In letters, mention is often made of roots that have either been given or received, and these needed to have been freshly gathered and prepared in order to be effective. In a letter dating to the second century AD and recovered from House T632 at Tebtunis, Thenpetsokis writes to her sister: 'Had it not been for the fact that I was ill, I should have sent them to you long ago; but if my health is good I will send a kotyle of orris-root for your daughter'.[452] The

[439] *P. Lond.* 1159 (AD 144-7, Hermopolis Magna). *P. Ryl.* 627-39 (AD 317-23, Hermopolis Magna). *P. Got.* 3 (AD 215-16, Panopolis). For discussion of the expense of garum, see Curtis (1983) 234-7, with particular reference to Egypt at 234 and 237.

[440] *P. Mich.* 8.496 (second century AD, Karanis).

[441] *P. Oslo* 3.161 (late third-early fourth century, unprovenanced); Curtis (1991) 137 n128 cites this papyrus as evidence for receipt of a salted fish product, but does not discuss the illness of the writer.

[442] Bagnall (1993) 49.

[443] Alston and Alston (1997) 209.

[444] Cappers (1998) 83; van der Veen (1998b) 229; see also Jashemski (1995) for courtyard gardens in Tunisia containing olive, fig and possibly apricot trees in addition to laurel, myrtle, rosemary, laurustinus, oleander, acanthus, ivy and box plants.

[445] See for example *P. Stras.* 9.846 and *P. Col.* 5.1, a list of taxes paid by the inhabitants of Theadelphia in AD 160, thought to have been compiled by tax collectors.

[446] See Strabo, *Geographica* 17.1.35 for discussion of the Arsinoite nome and the olive trees planted and cultivated there; and 17.1.51 for discussion of Alexandria, the Nile Delta and the Thebaid nome and the palm trees planted and cultivated in those areas.

[447] *P. Ross. Georg.* 2.19 (AD 141, Oxyrhynchus).

[448] *SB* 12.11113 (AD 180-210, Karanis).

[449] *SB* 14.12203 (AD 250-350, unprovenanced); *SB* 6.9242 A (AD 160-1 or AD 183-4, Ptolemais Nea).

[450] See *O. Claud.* 224-242 (mid second century AD, Mons Claudianus).

[451] Fahmy (1997) 241.

[452] *P. Oxy.* 46 (second century AD, Tebtunis): ἔπεμψά σοι διὰ Πρωτᾶτος ἰσχάδες ν, εἰ μὴ ὅτι ἠσθένηκα πάλαι πεπόνφην σοι,

letter implies that Thenpetsokis intended to cut and prepare the root herself; why else would she need to be in good health in order to acquire it? Orris root was another name for the dried root of the *Iris germanica* and was highly sought-after for its medicinal properties and fragrant scent during the Roman period. Not only it is a powerful diuretic that can be used to alleviate excess water retention problems such as dropsy and edema, but it is also a purgative, expectorant and emetic. Strabo stated that it was used to make ointment, while Celsus recommended it pounded up, mixed with vinegar and applied topically in order to treat a headache.[453] One medical recipe recovered from Oxyrhynchus and dating to the first century AD includes it in a recipe for treating nasal polyps.[454] In a contemporary letter, Dorion wrote to his son Serenus to inform him that he was sending him a basket of parsley root, just as his son had requested.[455] Parsley root's medicinal properties are particularly effective in the treatment of digestive disorders, kidney and liver problems, menstrual irregularities, and cleansing the blood and body of toxins; Pliny recommended it for the treatment of headaches.[456] The fact that Thenpetsokis and Dorion were sending the roots in their raw forms also implies that the recipients would have known exactly what to do with them.

The utilisation of these gardens for the growing of crops that are intended for personal use in addition to those being grown specifically for sale is evident in one condition that is commonly included in leases of agricultural land; that part of the rent will be paid in the form of fruit or vegetables presumably grown there. A lease dating from AD 87-8 states 'the lessee shall pay to Hierakiaina the rent...at the threshing floor at Nesla in fresh, clean, unadulterated, sifted radish seed', while a lease dating from the third century AD states 'I will deliver as payment, on a daily basis, from the day of the beginning of the harvesting, ten cucumbers, four melons [and] four gourds'.[457]

While none of this is direct, irrefutable evidence for alternative healing strategies, it is clear that the raw materials for a wide range of medicaments were both present and easily obtainable in Egypt during the Roman period.

4. Domestic Medicine and Self Help in Roman Egypt
The so-called 'professional' medical practitioner was not always the first person from whom an individual sought to obtain medicine, ingredients for medicine or other medicinal apparatus, let alone medical treatment. On the contrary, the supply and demand for such items are frequently mentioned in documentary papyri and ostraca exchanged by family members, that have been recovered

from sites all over the province. However, it is important to remember that these amateur medical practitioners and the knowledge that they espoused were extremely diverse. Their methods derived from personal experimentation, undertaken either by themselves or their ancestors and subsequently transmitted, and utilised primarily the products of their own individual natural environments; what was available to amateur medical practitioners in the Nile Delta was not necessarily available to those in Upper Egypt, or the Eastern and Western Deserts. Consequently, this section will first examine how medical self-help and domestic medical practice was undertaken during pregnancy and childbirth (conditions experienced throughout Egypt) before turning to examine medical self-help and domestic medical practice in four specific (and very different) geographical locations, in an attempt to establish why such healing strategies were preferred.

Pregnancy and Childbirth
High mortality placed a heavy burden on the women of Egypt during the Roman period, as the population's survival depended on sustaining a high level of overall fertility.[458] Consequently women married during their late teenage years and usually remained married until either their own deaths or those of their husbands. Motherhood is attested in women as young as nine and as old as fifty one.[459] The peak period of fertility seems to have been between the ages of seventeen and thirty, and families with as many as eight children are attested.[460]

Soranus' *Gynaecology* recommended the use of midwives to facilitate childbirth. Soranus himself not only studied in Alexandria and used Egyptian examples in his work, but his treatise is also known to have circulated in Egypt.[461] Three papyri contain definitive mentions of midwives. The first mention is found in a letter dating to the second century AD and it uses the term ἰατρίνη: 'The midwife greets you warmly'.[462] A different term for a midwife, μαῖα, is used in two other papyri. The first is from the Arsinoite nome, dating to during August and September AD 147, when one was called to examine a pregnant woman whose husband had died.[463] Her purpose on such occasions was not only to

ἀλλὰ ἐὰν κομψῶς σχῶ πέμψω [τ]ῆ θυγατρί [σ]ου κοτύλην ἴριδος.
[453] Strabo, *Geographica* 12.7; Celsus, *Med.* 3.10.
[454] *P. Oxy.* 1088 (first century AD, Oxyrhynchus).
[455] *P. Mich.* 212 (second-early third century AD, unprovenanced).
[456] Plin. *HN.* 25.90.
[457] *P. Princ.* 147 (AD 87-8, Oxyrhynchus); *P. Princ.* 39 (third century AD, unprovenanced).

[458] Bagnall and Frier (1994) 135.
[459] See *P. Lond.* 2.324 and *BGU* 1.115.i respectively. However, these could also be mistakes resulting from the difficulty of accurately assessing an individual's age in the ancient world or deliberately false declarations. For discussion of age awareness in the Roman world, see Duncan-Jones (2002) 79-92.
[460] Bagnall and Frier (1994) 136. Eight children: *BGU* 1.115.i.
[461] Sor. *Gyn.* 2.6: 'The midwife herself is to receive the infant, covering her hands first with pieces of cloth, or, as those in Egypt do, with thin scraps of papyrus, so that the baby won't slip off'; the presence of the *Gynaecology* in Egypt is known from *PSI* 2.117, a fragment of Book 3, and possibly Pack³ 2347, a fragment containing five columns from a treatise of 'Soranian' gynaecological writing.
[462] *P. Oxy.* 1586 (second century AD, Oxyrhynchus): ἡ ἰατρίνη σε ἀσπάζεται. The publication of this papyrus translates ἡ ἰατρίνη as 'midwife', although the term could also be translated as 'female physician', which would make it the only reference I have found to one in Egypt during the Roman period.
[463] *P. Gen.* 103 (AD 147, Arsinoite nome): διεπέμψατό σοι καταμεμακηχέναι με σὺν μαίαί καὶ ἐγνωκέναι κατὰ γαστρὸς

protect the interests of a legitimate child born posthumously, but also those of a deceased father's family, seemingly similar to the *demosioi iatroi* called to examine victims of assault of illness for legal purposes.[464] A corroborative example of a midwife serving such a purpose is found in the third papyrus, from Oxyrhynchus and dating to 2nd February AD 326, when she was dispatched to examine a pregnant woman who had been the victim of an assault in order to contribute to a medical report to accompany a petition:

> I make submission of this petition requesting that…midwife should be officially instructed by you to come and take note of her condition and report in writing [and that] when the report has been made and the outrage investigated, they should provide guarantees so that if anything should befall my wife, the appropriate action for retribution may take place.[465]

There is a fourth papyrus, a private letter dating to the second century AD and recovered from Oxyrhynchus, that could be interpreted as containing a reference to a midwife being used in conjunction with a physician, but the papyrus itself is particularly fragmented at the relevant point in the letter: 'Look to my mother and the house and the physician and the [midwife?]'.[466] The fact that only four papyri refer to the use of a midwife (and that two of these references are rather questionable) could be an indication that trained midwives were rare in Egypt during the Roman period, and so not generally available to guide women through pregnancy and childbirth.

It is clear that the prevalence of medical self-help in Roman Egypt was not restricted to incidents of illness and injury; it is also evident with regard to pregnancy and childbirth in the province (this in itself could be an explanation for the lack of references to midwives: they were considered entirely unnecessary). It seems that in Roman Egypt, pregnancy and childbirth were family affairs that involved not only the female members of the family, but the male ones as well. In the late second or early third century AD, Thaisarion wrote to her sister and brothers, requesting two jars of radish oil which she specifically stated she needed for when she gave birth, as well as a jar of salve.[467] In the mid to late second century AD, Maximus wrote to his sister (and possibly his wife) Tinarsieges, with a detailed list of instructions for her regarding her labour:

> If you are coming to your days of giving birth, write to me so that I may come and perform your delivery, since I do not know your month. I wrote to you in advance for this reason, so that you might also act in advance and write to me so that I would come in the provisions-boat, so that I might also remain with you and perform your delivery. For I advise you that I will wait with you for the birth. If you do not send [word] to me you do me no favour. For I was going to send you jars for your delivery; for this reason I did not send them, that I might bring them when I come and two matia of lupines.[468]

Presumably the jars mentioned would be filled with oil or unguents, as was the case with Thaisarion's labour, but the provision of lupines is interesting considering that, although lupine seeds were primarily used as a foodstuff in Roman Egypt, Dioscorides and Pliny the Elder recommend them as a means of preventing birthmarks and other skin conditions, as well as preventing wounds from becoming infected.[469] In the early third century AD, Serapias wrote to her son-in-law Herminos, requesting that he bring her daughter to her so that she could assist with the birth of her grandchild.[470] In the late third - early fourth century AD, an unnamed son wrote to his parents, requesting that they take care of his wife Theonilla (who was also his sister, and thus their daughter) during the late stages of her pregnancy and labour: 'I repeatedly pleaded

---

ἔχουσαν, μὴ δύνασθαι δὲ παρ' αὐτῇ ἀπο [κυ]ῆσαί με, ὑπεσχῆσθαι δὲ αὐτὴν ἐποπτεῦσαί μέ εἰ συνέχω ἕως ἅπαντα τὰ κατ' ἐμὲ πεπλη[ρ]ῶσθαι, καὶ μηδὲν παρ' ἐμὴναἰτίαν γεγονέναί, ἵν' ᾧ εὐεργετημένη.

[464] Rowlandson (1998) 290.

[465] *P. Oxy.* 3620 (AD 326, Oxyrhynchus): τὴν βιβλιδίων ἐπίδοσιν ποιοῦμαι ἀξι[ῶν]…μαῖαν ἐπισταλεῖσαν ὑφ' ὑμῶν ἀπαντῆσαι καὶ σημειώσασθαι τὴν διάθεσιν αὐτῆς καὶ ἐνγράφως προσφωνῆσαι [τὴν] <καὶ> τῆς προσφωνήσεως γεγενημένης καὶ γνωσθέντος τοῦ ἀτοπήματος ἐγ'γύας αὐτὰς παρασχέσθαι ἵν' εἰ συμβαίη τι τῇ συμβίῳ μου ἡ δέουσά ἐκδικία γένηται.

[466] *P. Oxy.* 3642 (second century AD, Oxyrhynchus): ἐπισκέψαι τὴν μητέρά μ[ου] καὶ τὴν οἰκίαν καὶ τ[ὸν] ἰατρὸν καὶ λοχίαδα[...]. The term used here that could be translated as 'midwife' is λοχίαδα, which could have originated from λοχεύτρια, meaning 'midwife' or even λοχείαδα, 'woman in childbed'.

[467] *P. Mich.* 8.508 (late second-early third century AD, Alexandria): πέμψα[τέ μ]οι ῥαφαν[ελαίο]υ κεράμια δύο ὡς τῆς τιμῆς οὐ δε δαπάνηκα. καὶ γὰρ ἐγὼ χρείανξ ἔχω [α]ὐτῶν ὅταν τίκτω. καὶ ὑμῶν γὰρ ἀδ[ε]λφός ἐστιν… καὶ κάδιόν μοι πέμψατε κολλουρίου.

[468] *O. Florida* 14 (mid-late second century AD, Apollonius Magna or Thebes): ἐὰν ἔλθῃς εἰς τὰς ἡμέρας σου τοῦ τεκεῖν, γράψον μοι ἵνά εἰσέλθω καὶ τὴν λοχίαν σου ποιήσω, ἐπεὶ οὐκ οἶδά σου τὸν μῆνα. χάριν τούτου προέγραψά σοι, ἵνά καὶ σὺ προλάβῃς καὶ γράψῃς μοι ἵνά εἰσέλθω ἐν τῷ πλοίῳ τῶν κιβαρίων ἵνά καὶ ἐγὼ μείνώ ἐχόνομά σου καὶ τὴν λοχίαν σού ποιήσω. σοὶ γὰρ προσέχω ὅτι ἐχόνομά σου μενῶ τεκεῖν. ἐὰν μὴ πέμψῃς ἐπ' ἐμὲ οὐ χάριτάν μοι ποιεῖς. ἔμελλόν σοι πέμψαι ἀγγεῖά εἰς τὴν λοχίαν σου· χάριν τούτου οὐκ ἀπέστειλά ἵνά εἰσερχόμενος ἐνέγκω καὶ δύο μάτια θερμίων. There is some dispute over whether Maximus was a man or a woman; the name Maximus is a male name and the Florida Ostraca come from a military encampment, but some of the pronouns used in the letter are female. However, this does not fundamentally affect the content of the letter; either way, Maximus is coming to help Tinarsieges give birth and bringing her supplies specifically for that purpose.

[469] Dioscorides, *De Materia Medica* 2.109. Plin. *HN.* 22.74.

[470] *P. Oxf.* 19 (early third century AD, unprovenanced): ἐρωτηθεὶς ποίησον τὴν χάριτα, ἵνα ἐνέγκῃς τὴν ὑγατέρ<α> μου ὥστεκη, ἵνα εὐχαριστήσω σοι, ὡς Μεσωρὴ α. μὴ σύλα μου περὶ τοῦ ναύλου τοῦ ὄνου, ἵνα φιλιάζω σου.

with them by letters to furnish the same concern for her and to make all the customary preparations for her delivery. For god knows that I wanted to send unguents and all the other things to be used for the delivery'.[471] His use of the word 'customary' here implies an awareness of and concern for tradition and continuity.

During the Roman period women appear to have laboured either sitting or squatting on a birthing stool, as demonstrated by numerous terracotta figurines (see Figures 6 and 7).[472] These two figurines, the first 14.2 cm in height and the second 14.3 cm in height, would have been moulded out of Nile mud, fired and brightly painted - although only traces of white paint are still present on the first figurine, the second retains pink flesh tones, black for the hair, green for the clothing and red to highlight the vulva, placing particular emphasis upon this part of the body to indicate what these figurines were intended to portray. It is possible that figurines such as these were simply decorative, but it is also possible that they served a religious or ritualistic purpose - utilised as amulets or even kept in household shrines during pregnancy and labour, family heirlooms that were used by successive generations of women.

The dangers of childbirth for both the mother and the child are readily attested not only by the epitaphs of women who died in childbirth, but also by human remains recovered from Egypt and dated to the Roman period. Of a collection of such epitaphs from Leontopolis, Arsinoe's, dating to 5 BC, poetically states 'Fate led me to the end of life in the labour-pain of my first-born child', while Dosarion's, dating to 25 BC, states that she was aged twenty five when she died.[473] The epitaph of Kleopas, dating to 7 BC, does not state her age, but it does name her husband Petos, while another woman who died during the first century BC or AD is only referred to as 'the daughter of Sabbataios'.[474] So in just a matter of years four young women are all recorded as having died in childbirth. Since this small corpus of inscriptions is part of a larger corpus of Jewish inscriptions from Roman Egypt, the fact that all four date from the same period and originate from the same town indicates that the loss of these four young women of childbearing age would likely have been a significant loss for their religious, social and cultural community.

Due to the climate of the Dakhleh Oasis and the burial practices of its inhabitants, a large number of foetal skeletons have been recovered from Kellis 2; out of 450 skeletons, 149 (34%) were aged under one year old and over half of those were foetuses or aged under one month old.[475] When eighty-two foetal and perinatal skeletons

dating to between the third and fourth centuries AD, were examined, it was concluded that the majority of them had been born prematurely and consequently would have either been stillborn or died soon after birth. There is evidence for at least one woman having died during or shortly after childbirth; one foetus was buried alongside the left leg of an adult female, a joint inhumation.[476]

While the inhabitants of Egypt were fully cognisant of the dangers of pregnancy and childbirth, they did not automatically refer pre- and post-natal care to a 'professional' medical practitioner such as a physician or midwife, unless there was a legal dimension to the proceedings. Rather, family members and friends (both male and female) assisted each other with both the preparations for labour (providing the necessary oils and unguents and perhaps even apparatus such as a birthing stool) and with the actual physical process.

---

[471] *PSI* 895 (third-fourth century AD, Oxyrhynchus); see also *P. Oxy.* 3642 (second century AD, Oxyrhynchus).
[472] Vassilika (1994) 181. See Sor. *Gyn.* 2.2-3 for Soranus' recommendation of the use of a birthing stool during labour.
[473] Arsinoe: *CIJ* II: 1510. Dosarion: *CIJ* II: 1515.
[474] Kleopas: *CIJ* II: 1530B. The daughter of Sabbataios: *CIJ* II: 1481.
[475] Tocheri *et al.* (2005) 334; documentary papyri record the dangers of childbirth to both the mother and the baby, for example see *P. Mich.* 5.228, a petition dating from 23rd November AD 47: 'He also

mercilessly inflicted on my wife Tanouris many blows on whatever parts of her body he could, although she was pregnant, with the result that she gave birth to a dead child and she herself is confined to bed and is in danger of her life'; *SB* 16.12606, a letter dating from AD 290: 'My sister Techosous is fearfully ill, and I expect that she will give birth today to a seven months' baby. If then she comes through it successfully, I will let you know what happened'.
[476] Tocheri *et al.* (2005) 337. The foetal and infant skeletons were not found in separate areas of the cemetery; infants, children and adults were buried side by side.

Figure 6: Terracotta figurine, first century BC, Alexandria
(British Museum Inv. 1992, 0811.1, image courtesy of the British Museum)

Figure 7: Terracotta figurine, first-second century AD, Fayum
(British Museum Inv. 1982, 0406.11, image courtesy of the British Museum)

Case Study: Kellis, Dakhleh Oasis, Western Desert
The ancient village of Kellis (modern Ismant el-Kharab) is located in the central part of the Dakhleh Oasis in the Western Desert of Egypt. The entire oasis is approximately seventy-five kilometres from east to west and fifteen kilometres north to south, covering an area approximately 2000-3000 km² and within this Kellis covers an area of approximately 1050 m north-east to south-west and 650 m north-west to south-east.[477]

The climate of the Dakhleh Oasis is hyperarid with an annual rainfall of 0.7 mm and water is only available from underground artesian springs and bores; there is papyrological and archaeological evidence of an irrigation system.[478] There are no mineral resources to be exploited in the Western Desert as there are in the Eastern Desert and consequently attempts to sustain any kind of economic activity have been concentrated on agricultural land. Although there is evidence that the oasis had been continuously occupied for thousands of years prior to the Roman conquest of Egypt, the Roman period saw a major influx of people into the area and so far around 250 sites have been discovered, ranging from single farmsteads to large villages.[479] Roger Bagnall has suggested that the primary crop cultivated by the settlers of the Dakhleh Oasis during this period was the olive, for the production of olives and olive oil for the Nile Valley and beyond.[480] There are certainly numerous papyrological references to

the cultivation of olives and olive oil at Kellis in particular.[481]

The most comprehensive evidence for agricultural and economic activity at Kellis comes from the *Kellis Agricultural Account Book* (hereafter *KAB*), a codex recovered from a house in the residential area of the village and dating to the middle of the fourth century AD.[482] Before I discuss the evidence for alternative healing strategies that can be gleaned from the contents of the *KAB*, I will briefly discuss the implications of the contents of the house in which it was found. House 2 is located in Area A of Kellis, a residential area comprising primarily of mud-brick houses of varying sizes, roofed with mud-coated palm ribs supported on beams of date palm and arranged around a central courtyard.[483] The house is believed to have been occupied by carpenters and weavers, based on the tools and materials that were recovered from one of the rooms; it is thought that the carpenter was responsible for producing codices such as the *KAB*. I discussed the possibility that craft tools and domestic utensils could have been employed in household medical practice in the previous chapter, and in addition to these a kohl stick was recovered. In ancient Egypt, from the Pharaonic period through to the Roman period, two types of kohl were applied to the eyes to reflect the glare of the sun, ward off insects and prevent eye infections and blindness; malachite was green and galena was black, and the two minerals were ground up

[477] Hope (1997) 5.
[478] Climate and rainfall: Mills (1997) 1; Fairgrieve and Molto (2000) 320. Irrigation system: *P. Kellis* 1.3 (mid fourth century AD, Kellis).
[479] Mills (1997) 1-2.
[480] Bagnall (1997) 80. See also Mattingly (1996) 213-53 for discussion of olive cultivation in the Roman world.
[481] *P. Kellis* 1G. 45, 49, 52, 61, 65, 74, 80, 90, 5C. 44.8-9, 11, 14, 19-20, 31-2. *O. Kellis* Inv. A/6/64, D/1/141, D/1/144, D/6/6, D/6/10, D/6/53, D/6/85, D/6/86.
[482] *P. Kellis* 4. Gr. 96.
[483] For detailed discussion and digital reconstruction of House 2, see Bowen *et al.* (2005) 54-5, 59-61.

on palettes, mixed with fat and then applied using a small stick or other type of applicator.[484] The fact that the carpenter was also in possession of a sizeable quantity of acacia and date palm wood implies access to acacia and date palm trees; acacia gum, dates and date palm crowns were frequently used as ingredients in medicinal remedies and consumed by individuals in poor health.[485]

The *KAB* contains the accounts of an agricultural estate owned by a man called Faustianus. Both the estate's income in the form of its tenants' rent and its expenditure on other necessary items are recorded, and these are generally in the form of commodities rather than money. Numerous items which could have been utilised specifically for their medicinal properties in addition to their use as foodstuffs are included amongst the commodities that the tenants provided to pay their rent, in addition to the olives, ἐλαία, and olive oil, ἔλαιον, thought to have been produced by the estate. One individual mentioned is Myron the honey-seller, Μύρων μελιτοπώλ[ης], and honey, μέλι, appears elsewhere in the accounts as the rent paid by an individual called Louia.[486] Honey was used to wean infants on the recommendation of medical writers such as Soranus and Galen and was not only included as an ingredient in medicinal remedies, but also in magical ones.[487] In addition to this, wine, οἶνος, and must wine, γλεῦκος, were also included and these items were utilised as ingredients in a wide range of medicinal and magical remedies for conditions as diverse as ulcers, gout, ear infection and erectile dysfunction.[488]

Although the agricultural potential of the oasis was readily exploited by the inhabitants in order to produce a range of crops for consumption as well as export to the Nile Valley, the communities were not entirely self-sufficient and supplies were also brought in. It was particularly important that the military garrison at Kysis be provisioned.[489] Roads certainly connected the Dakhleh Oasis with the Kharga Oasis, further east and thus nearer and more conveniently located to the settlements of the

Nile Valley; one papyrus records that a journey was made between the two and covered the 200 km between them in four days.[490] Despite the fact that the inhabitants of the Western Desert considered the Nile Valley to be 'Egypt' and themselves separate from it, the Small Oasis was under the administrative control of Oxyrhynchus and part of the Oxyrhynchite nome, while the Great Oasis was linked to the Heptanomia.[491]

Since the Dakhleh Oasis was located at a distance of around 300 km from the Nile, supplies transported overland, probably by camel or donkey, would have taken around a week to arrive.[492] It is likely that the sheer distance as well as the conditions of the journey would have affected the type of products that could have been transported in this manner. Perhaps this is why, despite the evident wealth of Faustianus, items such as saffron, pepper and myrrh are absent from the *KAB*; they were not necessarily accessible to those residents of Kellis who were his tenants. However, there is some evidence that the inhabitants of Kellis had access to exotic oils and unguents; seven glass vessels dating to the fourth century AD were recovered, three of which still contained residues.[493] Unfortunately, only one of the residues could be identified, and was revealed to be of pine, cedar or fir resin.[494]

That the foodstuffs recorded in the *Kellis Agricultural Account Book* were genuinely consumed by the inhabitants of Kellis has been confirmed by analysis of forty-nine mummies excavated from the Kellis 1 burial site, used in the period from the end of the second century BC to the end of the third century AD.[495] Analysis of the mummies has revealed that the inhabitants of Kellis lived on a diet that consisted primarily of plants, primarily wheat, barley and fruits. This was supplemented by the meat from birds and animals which themselves lived solely on plants.[496] There was also evidence of the consumption of Nile fish and oyster shells from the Nile Valley, as well as marine snails indicating some trade with the Mediterranean.[497] More specifically, analysis of coprolite material recovered from six of the mummies identified numerous different types of seeds, most notably grape seeds.[498] The beneficial effects of this healthy diet were augmented by seasonal consumption of

---

[484] Allen (2005) 19-20.

[485] A recipe for an eye salve containing acacia gum: *SB* 14.12046 (second-third century AD, unprovenanced); a magical spell to cure a stiff foot containing acacia fruit: *PDM* 14.1024-5 (third century AD, unprovenanced); a request for a date palm crown to treat sickness: *P. Corn. 50* (first century AD, Fayum); a recipe for a date palm plaster to treat ulcers and promote cicatrisation: *P. Mich* 17.758 (fourth century AD, unprovenanced).

[486] Myron: *KAB* 686; Louia: *KAB* 1669-70.

[487] Weaning: Dupras *et al.* (2001), Tocheri *et al.* (2005); remedy for an infection of the windpipe: *P. Oxy.* 3724 (first century AD, Oxyrhynchus); magical spell to cause 'evil sleep': *PDM* 14.716-24 (third century AD, unprovenanced); three magical spells 'to stop liquid in a woman': *PDM* 14.970-7, 978-80, 81-4 (third century AD, unprovenanced). For discussion of the detrimental effect being weaned with honey could have on the health of infants, see Dupras *et al.* (2001).

[488] Poultice for ulcers: *P. Mich.* 17.758 (fourth century AD, unprovenanced); magical spell to cure poison or a hangover: *PDM* 14.563-74 (third century AD, unprovenanced); magical spell to cure 'watery ear': *PDM* 14. 935-9 (third century AD, unprovenanced); magical spell to cure gout: *PDM* 14. 985-92 (third century AD, unprovenanced); magical spell to cure erectile disfunction: *PDM* 61.58-62 (third century AD, unprovenanced).

[489] Adams (2007) 30.

[490] Adams (2007) 45; *Chrest.Mitt.* 78 (AD 376-378, Mothis).

[491] Adams (2007) 237; papyrus in which the Nile Valley is referred to as Αἴγυπτος, 'Egypt': *P. Kellis* I. G. 23.20 (AD 353, Kellis).

[492] Bagnall (1997) 57; for evidence of a camel-driver living in Kellis, see *P. Kellis* 1.38a (AD 331, Kellis).

[493] Kaper *et al.* (2006) 32-4.

[494] 31420 - D6 -1/D/7/0/3; *Treasures of the Dakhleh Oasis* 7.1. See Dioscorides, *De Materia Medica* 1.77 for medicinal uses of cedar resin.

[495] Aufderheide *et al.* (2003) 1-8; see also Aufderheide *et al.* (2004) 63-86 for discussion of the unusual mummification techniques practised at Kellis.

[496] Aufderheide *et al.* (2003) 3; see also Kaper *et al.* (2006) 12 for discussion of a farmstead with a pigeon loft on the second storey, the consumption of pigeon and the use of pigeon dung as fertiliser in Roman Egypt.

[497] Aufderheide *et al.* (2003) 4.

[498] Aufderheide *et al.* (2003) 5.

grain contaminated with the antibiotic tetracycline, which helped prevent infections.[499]

Case Study: Oxyrhynchus, Nile Valley

Oxyrhynchus was one of over thirty nome capitals in Egypt during the Roman period. Despite the fact that virtually nothing remains of the ancient city, attempts have been made to reconstruct it according to the information gleaned from the documentary papyri.[500] It was a significant enough settlement that the designation λαμπρὰ καὶ λαμπροτάτη, 'illustrious and most illustrious', was added to its official title in AD 272.[501] Unlike Mons Claudianus, a small quarry settlement located out in the middle of the Eastern Desert, Oxyrhynchus was a city built up on the Bahr Yūsuf canal adjacent to the Nile and thus connected to the rest of Egypt; the inhabitants were easily able to sail down the Nile to Alexandria, a journey that would take around a week.

The presence of 'professional' medical practitioners in Oxyrhynchus was discussed in the previous chapter. However, despite their presence in the city, it is clear that a number of the inhabitants did not necessarily engage their services. In addition to professional medical practitioners, apothecaries and druggists operated in Oxyrhynchus, and they did not restrict their wares to physicians.[502] On 18th May, AD 257 Aurelius Neoptolemus, a φαρμᾱκοπώλος or druggist, wrote to the Aurelii Arruntius Heraclianus, Hierax and Theon, lessees of the monopoly of the alum industry, to register his stock which included alum, split alum, melanteria, miltos, misy, ochre and salt.[503] In AD 300, Aurelius Macrobius, a subsequent lessee of the alum monopoly, sent 'one Italian pound of alum and two ounces, eight carats of nasturtium powder' to one of his agents.[504] A fragmentary receipt for the purchase of drugs either made out by or to Dioskoros the φαρμάκος or druggist survives from the second and third centuries AD.[505]

Like the evidence for 'professional' medical practitioners, a significant proportion of the evidence for alternative healing strategies in Oxyrhynchus has been presented in this chapter already: the efforts that Aurelia Techosis, Titianos, and Joseph and Maria made on behalf of their sickly parents and siblings, as well as the arrangements made by Irene, Sarapammon, Tauris, Achillas and Theonilla's husband to obtain items with medicinal properties and uses have already been discussed.[506]

However, there are a number of other examples of alternative healing strategies being utilised in Oxyrhynchus. One papyrus letter, recovered from Oxyrhynchus and dating to the fourth century AD, provides an interesting counterpoint to the recipes for oxen medicine found in Cato's *On Agriculture*, despite its having been written around five centuries later. Isidorus wrote to his son Demetrius and made a request: 'Give your brother Ammonianus the colt to be brought to me and the salt of ammonia, both the pounded and un-pounded, and the basil-seed, in order that I may doctor him away here'.[507] This letter provides clear evidence of the head of the household exercising his authority by instructing his sons and acting as family healer and veterinarian, but in addition to this, it also provides explicit proof of the transmission of knowledge about domestic medicine and the utilisation of the natural environment for medicinal remedies.

The reference in the letter to salt of ammonia is also interesting. Salt of ammonia, τὸ ἅλας τὸ ἀμμωνιακὸν or hammoniacum, is included in Pliny's *Natural History*, in his discussion of the different types of salt. Both salt and salt of ammonia seem to have been particularly associated with Egypt.[508] Basil, *Ocimum basilicum*, is known to have been cultivated at various locations in Roman Egypt. In addition to being an edible condiment, it also has a range of medicinal uses and can be utilised as a diuretic or a stimulant, as well as for treating skin and stomach complaints and diarrhoea.[509] Although the leaf of the herb is the edible part, the excavations at Mons Claudianus recovered basil seeds, indicating that the herb was grown there in pots.[510] The excavations at Kom el-Nana, possibly the site of the Late Antique Roman town of Pejla, also recovered basil.[511]

According to James Adams, in antiquity the *ars ueterinarii* was considered sordid, with specialist *ueterinarii* being despised by their peers.[512] Vegetius observed in his *Equine Medicine* that veterinary medicine lacked *dignitas* and was traditionally practised by men lacking in distinction.[513] He also stated that veterinary medicine was not particularly lucrative: 'because of the vice of greed and the slimness of the rewards, no-one devotes the requisite study to the learning of the

[499] Cook *et al.* (2005) 137-43.
[500] See Turner (1952); Alston (2002).
[501] See Turner (1952) 78 for the possibility that the title was awarded in preparation for the *IsoCapitolia* being held at the city the following year.
[502] See *P. Oxy.* 3065 (third century AD, Oxyrhynchus) for reference to a myrrh seller.
[503] *P. Oxy.* 2567 (AD 257, Oxyrhynchus).
[504] *P. Oxy.* 1429 (AD 300, Oxyrhynchus).
[505] *P. Oxy.* 1727(second-third centuries AD, Oxyrhynchus).
[506] See *P. Oxy.* 1121 (AD 295, Oxyrhynchus); *PSI* 299 (third century AD, Oxyrhynchus); *P. Oxy.* 3314 (fourth century AD, Oxyrhynchus); *P. Oxy.* 116 (second century AD, Oxyrhynchus); *P. Oxy.* 2596 (third century AD, Oxyrhynchus); *P. Oxy.* 2599 (third-fourth century AD,

Oxyrhynchus); and *P. Oxy.* 1142 (late third century, Oxyrhynchus); *PSI* 895 (third-fourth century AD, Oxyrhynchus).
[507] *P. Oxy.* 1222 (fourth century AD, Oxyrhynchus): δὸς τῷ Ἀμ<μ>ωνιανῷ τὸν πῶλον ἵνα ἐνεχθῇ μοι καὶ τὸ ἅλας τὸ ἀμ<μ>ωνιακὸν τὸ τετριμ<μ>ένον καὶ τὸ ἄτριπτον καὶ τὸ σπέρμα τοῦ ὠκίμου ἵνα θεραπεύσω αὐτὸν ὧδε ἔξω. This papyrus is overlooked by Adams (1995) in his monograph on Roman veterinary medicine. A similar, roughly contemporary example has been recovered from Antinoopolis; see *P. Harr.* 109 (late third / early fourth century AD, Antinoopolis): 'Take care of my donkey, and if his condition improves and he can be disposed of, then sell him'.
[508] Plin. *HN* 31.39.
[509] Smith (2003) 80.
[510] van der Veen (1998a) 107.
[511] Smith (2003) 52-3.
[512] Adams (1995) 66.
[513] Vegetius, *Digesta Artis Mulomedicinae* 2.

discipline'.[514] The difficulty in finding a suitably competent specialist practitioner of veterinary medicine could explain why Isidorus was treating his horse himself. However, the cost of employing someone else to do something that you could feasibly do yourself may also have been a consideration; although Vegetius thought that veterinary medicine as a profession was not sufficiently well-paid, he also commented on the exorbitant cost of drugs: 'Because of a desire for profit certain potions have been put together in such a way that they entail an enormous price, and the cost of treatment seems to almost equal the value of the animal, so that generally the mean or at any rate the cautious abandon their animals to disasters or neglect a financially damaging treatment'.[515] Several of the documentary papyri discussed above contain complaints about the cost of medical treatment the writer had cause to undertake.[516] However, while someone might be willing to pay for expensive medical treatment for themselves, he or she may not have been willing to do the same for their livestock, thus resorting to amateur medical practice as a means of saving money; Pliny records that camels were smeared with cheap and easily obtainable fish oil to ward off insects such as gadflies, to which they were particularly susceptible because of their thin coats.[517] Even if they were willing to pay, the lack of a local specialist practitioner of veterinary medicine may well have likewise resulted in them undertaking amateur medical practice.[518] It is clear that Isidorus knew what he was doing in this instance and in addition to this, was using easily obtainable natural ingredients to treat his horse's ailment. This begs the question, if the inhabitants of Roman Egypt were in the habit of undertaking amateur medical practice and domestic medicine as far as their livestock was concerned, what was to stop them from applying the same knowledge to themselves, particularly if they had passed the knowledge necessary to do so down through the generations, from father to son (as in the case of Isidorus), or mother to daughter?

A household account dating from the late second century AD records expenditures over a period of nine days.[519] In addition to supplies necessary for visiting the bath-house, it lists a variety of different foodstuffs that were also utilised in medicinal or magical remedies. These include lupines, vetch, asparagus, beets, radishes, lemons, eggs, oil, pomegranate wine, pickled fish, coriander and wine. While these may well have been intended for meals rather than medicine or magic, the fact remains that the members of this household were well-equipped to utilise these ingredients for medicinal or magical purposes if the need arose, just as Isidorus did with regard to his horse.

Case Study: Mons Claudianus, Eastern Desert
Mons Claudianus was a settlement based around a series of granodiorite quarries in the Eastern Desert; quarrying activity was at its most intense during the late first and early second centuries AD.[520] It has been suggested that the quarries were not used constantly; rather they were opened and exploited only when stone was needed for building projects.[521] However, when the quarries were in operation, the population of the settlement consisted of the soldiers from the Roman army and government officials who administered the site; the skilled and unskilled quarry workers; and a number of women and children, presumably the families of the workers. An ostracon dating from the early second century AD concerned with the distribution of water records that 920 people were present on the site on that particular day.[522]

The common assumption made regarding desert communities is that their inhabitants exist at subsistence level, not only suffering physical hardship due to the climate but also social isolation due to the difficulty in travelling to and from the settlements.[523] However, the documentary, archaeological and palaeopathological evidence recovered from Mons Claudianus indicates that this was simply not the case here. Although both male and female skeletons exhibited Schmorl's nodes and osteophytosis, evidence of heavy lifting and hard physical exercise, they did not exhibit any evidence of dietary deficiency or malnutrition. On the contrary the presence of caries (particularly in females) indicates a diet with a significant component of sugar (found in honey, or sweet fruits such as dates and figs).[524] The inhabitants of the site not only had access to a variety of both basic and luxurious foodstuffs, but they were in frequent touch with members of their families and friends living in the Nile Valley.[525] The recovery of thousands of ostraca from Mons Claudianus make it clear that the residents wrote letters to members of their families and friends living elsewhere in the hope of obtaining a range of items from them that were not easily available to them at the settlement. Although these letters were primarily concerned with obtaining items such as foodstuffs, often requests were made for medicine, ingredients for medicine or other medicinal apparatus, despite the fact that there was at least one physician in residence.[526] These requests indicate that there were amateur medical practitioners among the inhabitants of Mons Claudianus; individuals who preferred to treat themselves rather than resort to or rely upon a professional medical practitioner. Archaeological excavation has revealed that the main fort was surrounded on three sides by ditches and rubbish dumps containing organic and human waste, which would have constituted a major health hazard for the

---

[514] Vegetius, *Digesta Artis Mulomedicinae* prol. 1.
[515] Vegetius, *Digesta Artis Mulomedicinae* prol. 5.
[516] See for example *BGU* 13.2350 (second century AD, Alexandria).
[517] Plin. *HN* 32.4.
[518] Veterinarians are attested at Mons Claudianus and Apollonius Magna, but these were places with a military presence. For Mons Claudianus, see *O. Claud.* Inv. 1538 and 2921. For Apollonius Magna, in Upper Egypt, see *O. Florida* 15 (mid to late second century AD, Apollonius Magna): 'I sent you via Quintus the veterinarian the andromax and the boiled wood-bird, since there is no meat for sale'.
[519] *P. Mich.* 11.619 (late second century AD, Oxyrhynchus).

[520] Mons Porphyrites, Mons Claudianus' sister site, was reportedly discovered by Gaius Cominius Leugas on 23rd July AD 18, according to an inscription recovered from the site.
[521] Peacock and Maxfield (1997) 115.
[522] *O. Claud.* Inv. 1538 and 2921.
[523] van der Veen (1996) 137.
[524] Maxfield and Peacock (2001) 33-5.
[525] van der Veen (1998a) 101; van der Veen (1998b) 221.
[526] *O. Claud.* 220 (AD 137-45, Mons Claudianus).

occupants (however many there were at any one time) and a breeding ground for diseases such as plague, cholera, dysentery and typhoid.[527] If the occupants of the fort and the quarry settlement did contract such diseases, this would certainly have rendered some level of medical care necessary.

During the early second century AD, Isidorus wrote to his sons Isidorus and Paniscus, requesting two sticks of salve and a cushion to rest his sore arm on.[528] The elder Isidorus seems to have been living out in the desert, probably at one of the smaller quarries, while his sons were living at the main settlement where they presumably had easier access to medical supplies. The nature of collyrium sticks means that, provided they were kept in suitable conditions, there was no reason why they could not be acquired in advance and then kept until it was necessary for them to be used. If Isidorus meant collyrium in the sense of an eye salve, he might have been suffering from an eye infection at that point in time, or he might have been anticipating suffering from one in the near future. Alternatively, if the collyrium was intended to treat his sore arm, the same applies; the fact that he is asking for two indicates a certain amount of forethought on his part, and perhaps a desire to treat any health problems that arose as quickly and efficiently as possible. A second ostracon, dating to between AD 100 and 120, reveals that one Menelaus wrote to another Menelaus, requesting a second flask of rose oil because his own had been stolen.[529] Rose oil or *rhodinum* was frequently recommended by ancient writers as a cure for conditions such as reptile bites, headache and sunstroke.[530] Papyri recovered from Egypt include it in a number of different medical and magical recipes. One of these, attributed to Dionysius and taken from a fourth century AD medical codex, lists it as an ingredient in a plaster to treat spreading ulcers, wounds, abscesses and lichen-like skin eruptions.[531] In AD 145, Bekis wrote to his son Petearoeris, requesting that he send a bandage suitable for a head injury.[532] During the reign of Antoninus Pius, an unnamed individual wrote to his brother, claiming that his life was in danger and he needed a remedy for an inflammation of the tonsils.[533]

With regard to Isidorus and Menelaus, they themselves actually specified that the reason they were asking for these things was that they had not been able to obtain them where they were, and presumably the same rationale applied to Bekis and the unnamed individual; after all, why go to all the trouble of getting something sent out into the Eastern Desert, perhaps from as far away as the Nile Valley, if it was available right there at Mons Claudianus? However, it seems strange that a physician practising at a quarry settlement out in the desert would lack remedies such as eye salve for eye infections, rose oil for headaches and sunstroke, and something as basic as a bandage. The logical explanation for these requests is that these individuals were amateur medical practitioners, either out of choice or necessity.[534]

One of the reasons why an individual might self-medicate would be their inability to afford treatment by a professional medical practitioner, as discussed previously. However, it is clear that the inhabitants of Mons Claudianus were not poor by any means.[535] The skilled workers were craftsmen such as stone-masons, blacksmiths and quarry-men and their salary was forty seven *drachmae*, in addition to a monthly allocation of wheat, oil, lentils, onions and a ration of wine.[536] The unskilled workers were also paid a salary and received an allocation of wheat, lentils and oil each month. The soldiers earned more than the civilians; during the second century AD a legionary infantryman based in Egypt earned 100 *drachmae* per month.[537] If there were comparatively few professional medical practitioners based at Mons Claudianus, and those that were there lived and practiced at the fort, perhaps lack of availability was an issue; for those like Isidorus who were living and working at subsidiary quarries some distance away, it would have been far easier and more convenient for them to take care of themselves, and even stock up on remedies in advance if they suffered from periodic bouts of ill health caused by their occupation or environment.

Case Study: Berenike, Eastern Desert, Red Sea Coast

Berenike is the furthest south of all the Red Sea ports. Despite its remote location and the fact that the journey overland from there to the Nile Valley is much longer than from the other Red Sea ports such as Myos Hormos, Berenike was significant because the sea voyages from there to the East were much shorter.[538] Despite its strategic location and importance for trade, Berenike was not a large port; it measured approximately 700 m east-west and 300 m north-south and may only have

---

[527] Maxfield and Peacock (2001) 35.

[528] *O. Claud.* 174 (early second century AD, Mons Claudianus): πέμψατέ μοι τὸ ὑπανκόνιον τὸ μικρὸν ἐπεὶ πάσχο καθεύδον καὶ οὐκ ἐπέμψατε. πέμψατε οὖν αὐτὸ καὶ τὸ μελάνιον καὶ κολοιρίδια.

[529] *O. Claud.* 171 (early second century AD, Mons Claudianus): ἐρωτῶ σε, ἐπὶ διε[ρ]πάγη μοι ῥώδινον, καλος ποιήσις πέμψας μοι τὸ λοικύθιν, ἐπὶ οὐχ εὕρω ν ἐνθάδε ἀγοράσαι.

[530] Dioscorides, *De Materia Medica* 2.82.3; 2.234.1.

[531] *P. Mich.* 17.758 (fourth century AD, unprovenanced): 'The white plaster with rose oil: one *drachma* of fresh young pig fat, 1/4 ounce of litharge, 1/4 ounce of birthwort Longa, 1/4 ounce of wax, 1/4 *drachma* of myrrh, five ounces of oil, the whites of three cooked eggs. Prepare and use'.

[532] *O. Claud.* 221 (AD 145, Mons Claudianus): πέμψον μοι σπληνάριν [ις] τὴν κεφαλήν μου ἐπὶ.

[533] *O. Claud.* 222 (second century AD, Mons Claudianus): [ἐρωτηθε]ὶς βοήθησον [...]ορι ἡμῶν κὲ πέμψον αὐτῷ φ]άρμακον ἐπὶ κι[ν]δυ[νεύει διὰ] τῶν παρισθμίων.

---

[534] See also MacKinnon (2010) 302 for zooarchaeological evidence of a pet dog receiving special care from its owner at Mons Claudianus; the animal suffered numerous severe bone fractures, and survived for long enough for these to heal.

[535] Cuvigny (1996) 139-45.

[536] See *O. Claud.* Inv. 4751 for the example of Pachoumis, a member of the *pagani* class of workers at Mons Claudianus. There is documentary evidence that at least 106 workers were classed as such a Mons Claudianus.

[537] van der Veen (1998a) 109-10.

[538] Cappers (1999) 185; the journey overland from Berenike to the Nile Valley took around twelve days, see Wendrich *et al.* (2003) 51. See Strabo, *Geographica* 17.1.45 for description of the ancient harbour.

comprised an area of around 2 km² at its maximum extension.[539] A conservative estimate puts the population of the port at around 500 but presumably this refers to permanent residents and excludes the transient members of port society such as merchants and sailors.[540]

The climate of the Eastern Desert is hyperarid with temperatures ranging from 33 to 40°C. The mean annual rainfall in the region ranges from 22 mm in Suez to 4 mm in Hurghada to 3.4 mm in Quseir.[541] However, the proximity of Berenike to the Red Sea ensures significant amounts of water through condensation, sufficient for plants adapted to arid conditions.[542] Attempts were certainly made by the Roman imperial government to regulate the water supply of Berenike and the surrounding region.[543] One result of this regular water supply would have been sufficient water to actually cultivate plants for foodstuffs and medicinal purposes at Berenike, rather than relying solely upon them being transported from elsewhere.

The most comprehensive literary evidence for the trade in substances that could have been utilised as ingredients in medicinal and magical remedies at Berenike is the *Periplus of the Erythraeian Sea*, a work dating to AD 40-70 that offers guidelines for merchants sailing to India from Berenike and Myos Hormos. The *Periplus* is supplemented by the documentary papyri and ostraca excavated from rubbish dumps at Berenike. One account recovered from near the Temple of Sarapis and dating from the period AD 50-75 contains information for the period from the 22nd to the 27th of an unknown month, listing amounts received for a range of items with possible medicinal uses including cabbage, parsley and salt fish.[544] A contemporary account lists amounts received for figs, olive oil and wine.[545] In a letter written by Aphrodite to her husband Lucius, she mentions that she has provided utensils.[546] In a letter discussing matters of business, Herennius writes to his brother Satornilus, 'What do you think about the roses for 200 *drachmae* and 180 *drachmae*, inquiring also about the transport costs?'; roses had numerous medicinal uses, for example as discussed above, as a constituent of rose oil, used to treat sunstroke and thus particularly useful out in the desert.[547] A second letter between Herennius and Satornilus discusses the price of incense which Herennius has ordered from a slave called Stichus, indicating that the

brothers were certainly in the habit of purchasing aromatics, which could have been utilised for medicinal purposes.[548]

There is also a significant amount of archaeobotanical evidence for the cultivation of certain foodstuffs at Berenike, a number of which could have been utilised as ingredients in medicinal and magical remedies. According to René Cappers, remains of over sixty cultivated plant species have been recovered from the site, representing not only the foodstuffs available to the inhabitants of the port, but also the items traded between the Roman Empire and East.[549] These include fairly common items such as garlic, onion, fennel, dill and cucumber that are thought to have been cultivated in kitchen gardens, but more unusual items are also attested.

There are a number of foodstuffs that would have been regularly imported to Berenike from the Nile Valley and could have been utilised for their medicinal properties as much as their culinary ones. Carob seeds could have been used to treat eye diseases and coughs and white lupin seeds could have been taken orally to treat stomach disorders in children or ground up in a plaster to treat intestinal worms.[550] Pomegranate cultivation is well documented in the Nile Valley and the root and bark of the tree can be used to expel tapeworm, while the rind can be used as an astringent for the treatment of diarrhoea and bleeding.[551] The pomegranate is also frequently employed in recipes relating to fertility, pregnancy and abortion.[552] However, there is also evidence of goods that were either harder to acquire locally or were imported from farther away. The fruit and seeds of the balsam tree, which only grows in the Gebel Elba area of Egypt, have been recovered from Berenike; the bark produces the unguent balsam, used to make perfumes and ointments.[553] Large amounts of rice, probably imported to Berenike from the Near East, have also been found and this was used to treat stomach complaints.[554] It was also mixed with beans and used by women to preserve the smoothness of their skin.[555] However, perhaps the primary motivation for maintaining the trade route to India was pepper. Different varieties were available, both white and black (*Piper nigrum*) and long (*Piper longum*).[556] Huge quantities of black pepper have been found at Berenike, including an Indian dolium storage jar containing over 7.5 kg of pepper corns.[557] In addition to its culinary uses as a condiment and a spice, pepper was

---

[539] Cappers (1998) 75; Cappers (2006) 17.

[540] Cappers (2006) 17.

[541] Cappers (2006) 21.

[542] Cappers (1998) 77.

[543] See *O. Berenike* 2.120, a Latin inscription from Sikait, commemorating the dedication of a hydraeum by Iulius Ursus, the Prefect of Egypt, in AD 76-77.

[544] *O. Berenike* 2.210 (AD 50-75, Berenike). For a medical prescription containing juice extracted from the stalk of a cabbage, see *P. Yale* 2.133 (third century AD, unprovenanced): σκοτοῦσθαι κράμβης καυλία ι[γ] 'κ' λύσας ἐν θερμῷ προσλάμβ[ανε] διασησάμενος τὸν χύλον καὶ πίν[ε] ἀφ' ἑψέματος κυάθους γ οἴνου α[...] τρου α ἐλαίου τὸ ἀρκοῦν συν [...].

[545] *O. Berenike* 2.209 (AD 50-75, Berenike).

[546] *O. Berenike* 2.130 (AD 50-75, Berenike).

[547] *O. Berenike* 2.95 (AD 50-75, Berenike).

[548] Incense has not been found at Berenike, although there is indirect evidence for it in the remains of shrines, see Wendrich *et al.* (2003) 80.

[549] Cappers (1999) 185.

[550] White Lupin: Plin. *HN* 18.36.136.

[551] Cultivation: *P. Ross. Georg.* 2.19 (AD 143, Oxyrhynchus). Medicinal properties: Plin. *HN* 13.44. See also Cappers (2006) 123.

[552] Sor. *Gyn.* 1.62.

[553] Balsam: Plin. *HN* 12.54.

[554] Gal. *Alim. Fac.* 1. Plin. *HN* 18.20.93. See Strabo, *Geographica* 15.1.18 for rice growing in Bactria, Babylonia, Susis and lower Syria. See *Periplus Maris Erythraei* 37.12.13-5 for rice being exported from Parsidai and the Gulf of Terabdoi.

[555] Cappers (2006) 105.

[556] Milne (1969) 80-3.

[557] Wendrich *et al.* (2003) 69.

utilised in medicinal remedies for female complaints and quartan fever.[558]

The presence of gardens at Berenike indicates that, just as in the case of Isidorus at Oxyrhynchus, the inhabitants of the town were in possession of botanical knowledge and expertise, presumably passed down through the generations, which could well have included an understanding of the medicinal applications of the plants, fruit and vegetables that they grew. This also indicates planning and forethought, just as in the case of Isidorus at Mons Claudianus, and the ability to make preparations to treat episodes of ill health as quickly and conveniently as possible.

Conclusion

I began this chapter with a discussion of the reasons why an individual in need of medical treatment might not consult a professional medical practitioner and suggested three possible explanations: fear, lack of availability and cost. While there are numerous references in ancient literature to the stereotypical incompetence, dishonesty and malevolence of physicians, it is not clear how significant a factor this was in the day to day life of the inhabitants of Egypt during the Roman period. With regard to possibility that the lack of availability of a physician led to the inhabitants managing their own health and that of other family members, papyrological and epigraphic evidence from the province suggests that there were many individuals who claimed to be physicians, although this is obviously no indication of their level of competence. Public physicians are attested in Alexandria and Oxyrhynchus, army physicians are attested at Alexandria, Luxor and Mons Claudianus, and those who just referred to themselves as 'physicians' appear to have been everywhere. The Nile and a comprehensive network of roads and way-stations facilitated trade and travel, so while a professional medical practitioner might not have been immediately available in the need for the expertise was urgent, they could arrive within a matter of days. In any case, letters sent between family members and friends indicate a certain amount of forethought and planning was undertaken with regard to engaging a physician or obtaining medical supplies for future events such as the birth of a child, and the anticipated onset of recurring conditions such as eye infection or sunstroke.

If automatic consultation of a professional medical practitioner was considered the norm, the most reasonable explanation as to why an individual might sometimes prefer to self-medicate is the prohibitive cost of medical treatment and/or prescriptions. The letters examined frequently comment on the cost of hiring a physician, and it is notable that in each of them, such a course of action was undertaken when the health problem requiring treatment was an unanticipated one such as an accident or a sudden outbreak of illness afflicting an entire family, or alternatively an elective surgical procedure such as a circumcision. Professional medical

practitioners were also hired for medical conditions in which there was a legal interest, such as a midwife hired to oversee the birth of a posthumous child or a physician engaged to verify injuries suffered during an attack for which compensation was now being sought. If, however, an individual suffered from a chronic or recurring condition that was not necessarily life threatening, hiring a physician at the onset of each episode would probably be out of the question for all but the wealthiest individuals.

However, the continuing assumption that the inhabitants of the ancient world ordinarily consulted a professional medical practitioner when suffering from health problems and only self-medicated as a last resort is unnecessarily short-sighted and does not engage with the range of evidence that survives indicating that individuals not only provided each other with ready-made medicaments, the ingredients for medicaments and medicinal apparatus, but also physically nursed each other through sometimes lengthy periods of convalescence. The animal products, fruit, vegetables, herbs, spices, pulses and nuts available to the inhabitants of Egypt during the Roman period are readily attested by both papyrological and archaeological evidence from sites in the Western Desert, the Fayum, the Nile Valley and the Eastern Desert. Admittedly, it is difficult to determine the precise context in which an item with medicinal properties was being utilised in the majority of cases and, as detailed above, foodstuffs such as garlic, salted fish and olive oil could be consumed for their medicinal properties just as readily as for their culinary and nutritional ones. Likewise, aromatics such as myrrh could be used in incense, perfume and cosmetics as well as in medicinal remedies. The widespread availability of raw ingredients for medicaments and the widespread knowledge of alternative healing ensured that approaches to healing were integrated into the rhythms and patterns of daily life rather than compartmentalised as in the fashion of modern medical practice.

The combination of Egypt's natural agricultural fertility and its convenient position in the trade networks of the Roman Empire ensured that a wide variety of produce was available; items such as olive oil and wine were exported from the Great Oasis in the Western Desert and the ports and quarries of the Eastern Desert exported luxury goods such as aromatics, gems and marbles to the rest of the Roman Empire and received produce to sustain their communities in return. However, an individual's financial situation was relevant here as well; while expensive items such as nard, myrrh and saffron were on sale does not mean that individuals could afford to buy them in anything but the tiniest quantities. In a hot country with very little means of preserving organic substances and often hardly any storage space, such items would be utilised in a variety of different ways in order to maximise their potential for the duration of their shelf-life.

It is evident that future historians of medicine examining healing strategies in Roman Egypt (and other provinces) need to develop a more sophisticated understanding of

---

[558] Hippoc. *Mul.* 2.205, 395, 654.

the integration of 'professional' medical practice alongside domestic, localised healing traditions. Surviving evidence suggests that the inhabitants of Roman Egypt clearly not only utilised medicaments which they could have obtained from a physician, but also possessed the medical knowledge, contacts and supplies to create medicaments of their own, or utilise objects such as utensils or foodstuffs used on a daily basis in alternative ways as and when necessary. It also suggests that families (and even communities) ensured that their own particular healing traditions survived by passing them down through successive generations, ensuring continuity of knowledge. Rather than viewing medical self-help as a last resort only to be undertaken out of desperation, the inhabitants of Egypt were empowered not only to take care of themselves, but to organise areas of their lives and homes in such as way that they were able to do so as quickly, easily and conveniently as possible.

CASE STUDIES

The first part of this study surveyed the evidence for both 'rational' and 'irrational', 'religious' and 'secular', and 'natural' and 'supernatural' healing practices and strategies in Egypt during the Roman period, focusing on the institutions and the individual inhabitants of the province in turn. The second part will provide an opportunity to explore further the concepts examined there by using three very different types of health problem particularly prevalent in Egypt as case studies: eye complaints, fevers and the injuries inflicted by wild animals.

Whatever their origin (whether bacterial, viral, traumatic or degenerative) in antiquity eye complaints were extremely localised ailments that seemingly affected only one part of the body. This part (or parts, if both eyes were affected) was easily accessible not only to a 'professional' medical practitioner, whether a general practitioner or a more specialised one who dealt solely with conditions affecting the eyes, but also to a layperson who wished to self-medicate. In addition to this, while the cause of eye complaints remained a mystery, the nature and structure of the eye itself was reasonably well understood, particularly by those scholars and medical practitioners who had been fortunate enough to study at the Museion in Alexandria and other institutions, and certain healing strategies such as ophthalmic surgery or topically applied pharmacological remedies had been proven to be efficacious under certain circumstances. On the contrary, febrile conditions (again, whether bacterial, viral or traumatic in origin) were poorly understood in antiquity and seen as a disease in themselves rather than a symptom of an entirely separate condition. Unlike an eye complaint, a fever seemingly affected the whole of the body, often without an obvious cause, and treatments could often be more hazardous to the health of the sufferer than the original illness itself. Also unlike a number of different eye complaints, a fever could pass within a couple of days even without any medical intervention, leaving the individual seemingly cured and in perfect health.

The bites, stings and scratches inflicted by wild animals had a very obvious cause; it is significant that when an individual suffered injuries inflicted by another person or persons, or even a domestic or industrial animal owned by another, they could seek both legal redress and financial compensation from the relevant authorities, but if injuries or damage were inflicted by a wild creature, there was nothing to be done about it as the wild animal or animals in question were beyond the remit of the provincial or local administration.

This approach of examining particular conditions (all particularly prevalent in Egypt) will ensure a more detailed and nuanced study of the precise ways in which the natural environment of Egypt impacted upon certain aspects of health by contributing to eye problems and febrile conditions, and exposing the inhabitants of the region to injuries inflicted during attacks by wild animals, in addition to demonstrating the significance of peculiar historical, cultural and environmental factors in the development of healing strategies in a specific province. It will also enable an understanding of how closely healthcare was integrated into every aspect of life in Egypt during the Roman period. It is apparent that no single medical condition was dealt with in one specific way; rather there was a whole range of possible treatments, whatever the cause, and a great deal of individual autonomy. Eye complaints could have bacterial, viral, traumatic or even degenerative causes and equally could be treated with surgery, pharmacology, non-invasive treatment such as a simple dressing, a magical spell, a charm or amulet, an oracle, a prayer or a votive offering. Likewise fever could have a bacterial, viral or traumatic cause, last for any number of days and be a one-off or recur on a regular or semi-regular basis. Surgical, medical and pharmacological treatments could be attempted, magical spells, charms and amulets could be utilised as both preventative and curative measures and divine intervention could be sought from a deity specifically associated with the condition. Injuries inflicted by animals might be superficially simple to treat, but the possible ramifications of such an injury to an individual's physical and psychological welfare were more problematic.

CHAPTER THREE

EYE COMPLAINTS IN ROMAN EGYPT

1. Introduction

Eye problems seem to have been prevalent in Egypt during the Roman period.[559] These problems, often caused by the effects of the hot and dry climate with its resultant dust and sand, as well as insect fauna such as flies, were exacerbated by the crowded and unsanitary conditions in which many people lived - particularly in cities and towns but also in large villages.[560] All of these factors combined to ensure that eye disease was rife and in addition to infectious diseases, eye problems could also result from accidents and assaults, not to mention the natural aging process.[561]

As early as the fifth century BC, the Hippocratic writers were associating specific types of eye disease or ὀφθαλμια with the hotter regions of the known world.[562] According to the writer of *Airs, Waters, Places*, the inhabitants of cities exposed to hot winds tended to experience eye diseases that were 'of a humid character, but not of a serious nature, and of short duration, unless they attack epidemically from the change of the seasons'.[563] Such eye diseases were considered to be particularly common during the summer months.[564] The Hippocratic treatment of *ophthalmia* was later paraphrased by Celsus in *On Medicine*, indicating that it continued to be employed in the early first century AD.[565] This link between climate and eye disease (as well as a number of other conditions) was made explicit:

> Not only does the weather of the day but also of the preceding days matter. If a dry winter has been accompanied by north winds, or again a spring by south winds and rain, generally there ensue runnings from the eye, dysenteries, fevers, and most of all in more delicate bodies, hence especially in women. If on the other hand south winds and rain have prevailed during winter, and the spring is cold and dry...other people are attacked by dry *ophthalmia*, and if

elderly by choked nostrils and runnings from the nose...but if the autumn is dry owing to a north wind continuing to blow...the harder constitutions...may possibly be attacked by dry *ophthalmia*.[566]

In ancient ophthalmological and medical treatises, ὀφθαλμια is used specifically to signify an eye disease involving discharge from the eye or eyes - the Latin equivalent seems to have been *lippitudo*, indicating a more general inflammation of the eyes. Thus it is not surprising that these terms were also regularly used in documentary papyri from Roman Egypt to refer to eye infections in which the eyes were suppurating and inflamed, such as conjunctivitis or trachoma. One example of this is found in a letter dating to the late third century AD in which Titianos regaled his sister with descriptions of his symptoms: 'My eyes began to suppurate and I had granulations and suffered greatly'.[567]

Conditions such as *ophthalmia* would have been inconvenient but not necessarily debilitating unless they were chronic. For example, during the second century AD Flavius wrote to his brother Morus, 'After I arranged with my partner to come up for our business meeting, I went and got *ophthalmia*. That is why I didn't come up'.[568] Although Flavius evidently did not feel up to travelling for a business meeting with his partner, he was apparently well enough to either write or dictate a long letter to his brother, providing Morus with a comprehensive list of instructions to be followed in his absence.

The focus of this chapter will be upon the ways in which the inhabitants of Roman Egypt dealt with eye problems that were contracted, acquired or developed at various points during life. There is evidence to suggest that defective vision that arose from eye strain (perhaps caused by the demands of occupations that required long periods of close or finely detailed work) and/or the natural aging process, which would today be treated with glasses or contact lenses, was treated similarly in Egypt during the Roman period. A number of different types of glass lenses have been recovered by archaeologists excavating houses and workshops; two plano-convex glass lenses dating to AD 174 and recovered from Tanis (one of which is currently exhibited in the British Museum (see Figure 8)) have been shown to provide a 2.5 x rate of magnification, while two other lenses (one a white plano-convex lens and the other a yellow conical

---

[559] Boon (1983) 4. See also Al-Rifai (1988) and Tower (1963) for general surveys of the history of eye disease in Egypt.

[560] For the role of flies (particularly Diptera) in spreading eye diseases such as trachoma in ancient Egypt, see Panagiotakopulu (2004) 1675 and Panagiotakopulu and Buckland (2009) 349.

[561] See Strouhal and Jungwirth (1980) 62-4 for the high level of traumatic injuries to the frontal and parietal bones of the skull experienced by the inhabitants of four late Roman and early Byzantine cemeteries in Egyptian Nubia, seemingly caused by daggers and swords. See also Appenzeller *et al.* (2001) for suggestions regarding the extent to which it is possible to retrospectively diagnose congenital eye problems such as *tropia* and *corectopia* from mummy portraits.

[562] Hippoc. *Aer.* 10 and *Epid.* 1.5.

[563] Hippoc. *Aer.* 3; according to 4, inhabitants of cities exposed to cold winds, however, tended to experience eye diseases 'of a hard and violent nature, and soon ending in rupture of the eyes'.

[564] Hippoc. *Aer.* 10.

[565] For discussion of the extent to which Celsus plagiarised Hippocrates, see Pardon (2005).

[566] Celsus, *Med.* 2.1.13-16.

[567] *PSI* 299 (late third century AD, Oxyrhynchus): ἐπύθετό μοι ὁ ὀφθαλμὸς καὶ τραχώματα ἔσχον καὶ δεινὰ πέπονθα.

[568] *P. Oxy.* 3058 (second century AD, Oxyrhynchus): ἔτυχέν μοι ὀφθαλμιᾶσαι.

lens) dating to the second century AD were found at Hawara.[569] However, glass lenses were specially made and consequently extremely expensive and highly sought after, so this means of coping with failing eye sight was certainly not available to all.

It is worth remembering, however, that such conditions could also have been interpreted as the result of an eye disease and treated accordingly.[570] Thus those so afflicted sought to affect a cure and utilised a range of healing strategies that incorporated elements of medical, surgical, magical or religious healing. There is also evidence for the undertaking of a certain amount of preventative measures through the use of black and green kohl.[571] Although kohl was considered a cosmetic and worn primarily by women elsewhere in the Roman Empire, in Egypt it was utilised by men, women and children and this wide usage across both genders and all age groups implies that is was *not* worn simply for cosmetic purposes.[572] Certain types of kohl have been found not only to protect the lens of the eye from the glare and reflection of the sun, but also to have antibacterial properties. Ground into a paste, kohl was applied from a tube or a palette with a stick or a needle and numerous examples of these instruments survive in the archaeological record.[573]

Although most are without a definite provenance, archaeologists excavating at Kellis in the Dakhleh Oasis discovered one kohl stick in House 2, while archaeologists excavating at Karanis in the Fayum recovered thirty-two kohl sticks made from a range of materials including wood, glass, bone and stone from locations throughout the village.[574] Kohl tubes, pots and sticks not only come in a range of different materials, but also vary in their decoration from entirely plain to elaborately carved and decorated; despite being made from Nile silt, one such kohl pot (exhibited in the British Museum (see Figure 9)) is carved into the shape of an Atef crown while the wooden kohl stick exhibited with it (which did not necessarily originally belong with the pot) is surmounted by a finely whittled standing falcon. Thus it can be inferred that kohl was utilised on a regular basis by individuals at all levels of society; access to it was not restricted as it did not need to be prescribed by a physician or obtained from an apothecary.

In addition to the kohl sticks, tubes, pots and palettes that have been recovered from Egypt, mummy portraits and masks that portray the deceased (men, women and children) wearing kohl provide the opportunity to see precisely how it could be applied around the eyes. One mummy portrait (currently exhibited in the British Museum (see Figure 10)) depicts a woman wearing a garland of rosebuds and bejewelled collar with an extremely pale face (perhaps an attempt to indicate the use of a cosmetic such as white lead) and eyes that are ringed with kohl.

2. Life with an Eye Complaint in Roman Egypt

It is clear from a wide variety of documentary papyri that the inhabitants of Roman Egypt frequently experienced problems with their eyes and that such problems could have a significant impact upon their lives. The examination of two family archives from the Nile valley provides invaluable information as to how eye problems affected not only the two individuals who suffered from them, but also members of their families, their finances, business interests and status within the local community.

Figure 8: Glass lens, AD 174, Tanis (British Museum Inv. 1885, 0101.378, image courtesy of the British Museum)

---

[569] See Sines and Sakellarakis (1987) 193 and Plantzos (1997) 455 for discussion of these lenses. For the lenses from Tanis, see British Museum Inv. 1885.0101.255 and 1885.0101.378 (diameter 66 mm). For one of the lenses from Hawara, see University College London Inv. 16764 (diameter 53 mm).

[570] Boon (1983) 10; hence the many recipes and collyrium stamps which proclaim *collyria ad claritatem*, 'clear-sightedness'.

[571] See Trinquier (2002)104-6 for discussion of the use of green kohl / malachite.

[572] For the use of kohl in conjunction with an amulet and a religious ritual to ward off the 'evil eye' and ill health and protect a sickly child, see a mummy portrait of a young boy, dating from AD 150-200 (J. P. Getty 78.AP.262), discussed in Ikram (2003) 251.

[573] See Olson (2009) 298-9 for discussion of Roman eye makeup including kohl.

[574] Kohl sticks are easily identifiable due to their distinctive shape; they tend to have a triangular spatula at one end to aid with the application of the substance.

Figure 9: Terracotta kohl stick and pot, second century BC, Egypt
(British Museum Inv. 2612, image courtesy of the British Museum)

Figure 10: Painted plaster and cartonnage mummy mask, AD 100-20, Egypt
(British Museum Inv. 1897, 0511.192, image courtesy of the British Museum)

Tryphon from Oxyrhynchus (mid first century AD)
Tryphon, the son of Dionysius and Thamounis, was a member of a high status family of weavers, possibly descended from one of Alexander the Great's Macedonian soldiers, living in the Nile Valley at Oxyrhynchus during the first century AD.[575] In AD 52, he was released from military service specifically because of his eye problems: 'Release from service was granted by Gnaeus Vergilius Capito, praefect of Upper and Lower Egypt, to Tryphon, son of Dionysius, weaver, suffering from shortness of sight, of the metropolis of Oxyrhynchus. Examination was made in Alexandria'.[576] This papyrus states that Tryphon was given some kind of medical examination prior to being excused from military service. Ralph Jackson interprets this examination as having been an eye test that was part of a medical examination given to new recruits as standard procedure, although this interpretation of the papyrus is disputed.[577] If this interpretation is correct, it follows that Tryphon's affliction, 'shortness of sight' (ὀλίγον βλέπων), was discovered during the course of a standard medical examination and thus rendered him unfit for military service. However, it is also possible, if not probable, that the examination took place specifically to prove that Tryphon's vision was defective to enable either his exclusion from military service prior to beginning it, or his discharge from military service having already begun it. The fact that Tryphon would have been around forty-four years of age in AD 52 supports one of these

alternatives rather than Jackson's interpretation.[578] It is also worth noting that, despite Tryphon living with his family in Oxyrhynchus, the examination took place in Alexandria. However, whether this was done for legal, military or medical reasons is unknown.

Tryphon's being declared unfit for military service could have been either a cause for celebration or a great disappointment, depending upon whether or not he actually wished to remain in the army. The fact that his father Dionysius was a weaver, as were both his brother Onnophris and his son Thoönis, raises the question as to whether or not Tryphon was physically capable of weaving himself. Thoönis' apprenticeship contract, which dates to AD 66, when Tryphon would have been around fifty-eight years of age, makes it clear that at this point he was certainly a weaver by profession.[579] However, the fact that he apprenticed his son to a fellow weaver for the unusually short period of one year raises the possibility that, due to his affliction, he had started but was unable to complete his son's training himself.[580]

Gemellus Horion from Karanis (late second century AD)
Gemellus Horion, also known as Gaius Gemellus Horigenes, was the grandson of Gaius Julius Niger, an Antinoopolitan army veteran granted Roman citizenship, living in the Fayum at Karanis during the late second century AD. He was a member of the local social elite and, as the documents in his family's archive testifies, a

---

[575] Brewster (1927).

[576] *P. Oxy.* 39 (AD 52, Oxyrhynchus): ἀπελύθη [ὑ]πὸ Γναίου Οὐεργιλίου Καπίτων[ο]ς τοῦ ἡγεμόνος ἀμφοτέρων Τρύφων Διονυσίου γέρδιος, ὑπο<κε>χυμένος ὀλίγον βλέπων, τῶν ἀπ᾽ Ὀξυρύγχων τῆς μητροπόλ(εως). ἐπεκρίθη(ἡ ἐν Ἀλεξανδ(ρεία).

[577] Jackson (1996) 2229; for discussion of different interpretations of the papyrus see Baker (2004) 38 and Hirt Raj (2006) 145-7.

[578] *P. Oxy.* 288 (AD 22-5, Oxyrhynchus).

[579] *P. Oxy.* 267 (AD 37, Oxyrhynchus) and 275 (AD 66, Oxyrhynchus); discussed in Westermann (1914) 309.

[580] See, coincidentally, *P. Oslo* Inv. 127, a petition dating to the late first century AD: 'Since I am no longer able to practice as a weaver, due to failing eyesight and old age - I am about eighty years old - I ask to be exempt from the weavers' tax'.

substantial landowner. However, on a number of occasions he felt he was not accorded the respect due to his rank. His first petition was sent to Quintus Aemilius Saturninus, prefect of Egypt, in the spring of AD 197: 'Julius and Sotas, both sons of Eudas, wrongfully, with violence and arrogance, entered my fields after I had sown them and hindered me therein through the power which they exercise in the locality, contemptuous of me on account of my weak vision'.[581] The term he uses to refer to his condition on this occasion is τὴν ὄψιν μου ἀσθένειαν, although he does not explain how or more precisely why his vision was weak. However, it appears that, in his opinion, this infirmity was the reason that he was being mistreated.

A subsequent petition, dating to 22nd May AD 197 and sent to Hierax Nemesion, *strategos* of the division of Herakleides of the Arsinoite nome, reiterates the original offence of Julius and Sotas. However, it also details a subsequent offence committed by Julius alone, Sotas having died in the intervening time, when he took olive shoots and heath plants from Gemellus Horion's olive grove. Then Julius, his wife and another man called Zenas cast a spell upon Gemellus Horion to prevent either him or any of his companions from obstructing them, and stole yet more of Gemellus Horion's crops. On each of these occasions, Gemellus Horion attributes the behaviour of Julius, Sotas and their cronies to their contempt for his weak vision (τὴν ὄψιν μου ἀσθένειαν) and, presumably, their wish to take advantage of this: 'I appealed, my lord, by petition to the most illustrious prefect, Aemilius Saturninus, informing him of the attack made upon me by a certain Sotas, who held me in contempt because of my weak vision and wished himself to get possession of my property with violence and arrogance'.[582]

Another petition on a different matter was sent in the August of AD 198, not only to Calpurnius Concessus, *epistrategos*, but also Saturninus, prefect of Egypt. This petition details abuse that Gemellus Horion received from another individual, and once again the reason he gives for this treatment is his disability:

> I appeal, my lord, against Kastor, tax collector's assistant of the village of Karanis in the division of Herakleides of the Arsinoite nome. This person, who held me in contempt because of my infirmity - for I have only one eye and I do not see with it although it appears to have sight, so that I am utterly worthless in both - victimised me, having first publicly abused me and my mother, after maltreating her with numerous blows and demolishing all four doors of mine with an axe so that

our entire house is wide open and accessible to every malefactor.[583]

Whereas in his previous petitions Gemellus Horion merely described himself as having weak vision, in this one he gives a more detailed account of the nature of his infirmity. He states that he only has one eye, μονόφθαλμος, but unfortunately this eye is πονηρὸν, useless.

The final petition, on an entirely separate matter, dates from AD 199-200 and was sent to Arrius Victor, *epistrategos*, asking for exemption from liturgical service that Gemellus Horion had been signed up for without his knowledge or consent. The reason he gives for wishing to be exempt from the duties is, once again, his disability:

> The elders of the village of Karanis of the same division of Herakleides, men without the least scruple, with their habitual violence and arrogance [...] me whom they nominated as their colleague under the name 'Horus, son of Apolinarius', a fictitious name which I do not know. For this reason I do not know it, for neither did it set forth 'disabled' or 'infirm' or any other of my distinguishing marks...Since not only am I one-eyed, but I also do not see with the eye that supposedly remains, because a cataract has appeared in its pupil and my sight is impaired.[584]

This petition provides further details regarding the nature of Gemellus Horion's infirmity; he repeats that he only has one eye and that this eye is unfortunately blind, but he then goes on to attribute this blindness to a cataract (λευκώμᾶ τος ἐκ τῆς κόρη[ς]).

It is clear from the contents of these petitions that Gemellus Horion's visual impairments had serious negative consequences for both himself and his family; he was prevented from harvesting the crops grown in his fields, attempts were made to seize his property, magical spells were cast upon him and his house was vandalised.[585] He was illegally signed up for liturgical

---

[581] *P. Mich.* 422 (AD 197, Karanis).

[582] *P. Mich.* 423-424 (AD 197, Karanis).

[583] *P. Mich.* 425 (AD 198, Karanis).

[584] *P. Mich.* 426 (AD 199-200, Karanis); see also *P. Oxy.* 39 and *P. Fay.* 106, a petition from the Arsinoite nome, dating to AD 140, in which M. Valerius Gemellus asks the prefect G. Avidius Heliodorus to excuse him from liturgical service due to both ill health and the fact that he is a physician: 'Have pity on me and order me to be released from my task, in order that I may be able to recover from the effects of my labours, having at the same time appended precedents by which complete exemption is granted to those practising the art of medicine' (ὅθεν ἀξιῶ σέ τὸν σω[τῆρα] ἐλεῆσαί με καὶ κελεῦσαι ἤ[δη με] ἀπολυθῆναι τῆς χρείας ὅπ[ως δυ]νηθῶ ἐμαυτὸν ἀνακτήσα[σθαι ἀ]πὸ τῶν καμάτων οὐδὲν δ[ὲ δεῖ] τον καὶ ὁμοιώμ[ατα] ὑποτάξα[ι ὅτι] τέλεον ἀπολύονται τῶν [λειτουρ]γιῶν οἱ τὴν ἰ(ατρικὴν ἐπιστή[μην] μεταχειριζόμενοι μάλ[ι]στα [δὲ οἱ δε] δοκιμασμένοι ὥσπερ καὶ ἐγ[ώ]).

[585] Frankfurter (2006).

service, a drain on both his time and his finances.[586] In addition, both he and his mother were physically assaulted, with him being unable to protect either himself or her sufficiently because of his blindness. To add insult to injury, all of these events occurred while Gemellus Horion was in his early twenties; he was not an older man simply suffering from the aging process, but a young man who had been unlucky enough to lose one eye before developing problems with his sight in his remaining eye.[587]

Gemellus Horion's disability seems to have been his defining characteristic, both in the way he viewed himself and the way he was viewed by others. In the same way that in a number of legal contracts other people refer to scars they bear as their distinguishing marks, presumably to aid identification and prevent fraud, Gemellus Horion states that his distinguishing marks are πηρὸς ἢ ἐπισινὴς ἢ, 'either "blind" or "impaired"'. Whether he was born with only one eye or he lost it later in life is, of course, unknown. What is clear, however, is that this would have been a permanent physical impairment with absolutely no chance of a cure being forthcoming. However, he does state that the reason he has lost sight in his remaining eye was due to his having developed a cataract. This condition was well known in the ancient world and is frequently mentioned in the documentary papyri from Roman Egypt.[588] According to Celsus, treatment was possible under certain circumstances: Gemellus Horion could have been cured either by the use of an ointment or a fairly simple operation and was presumably wealthy enough to have been able to afford either.[589] In the event that Karanis or any of the other villages of the Fayum lacked a physician experienced in eye surgery, it would have been both possible and feasible for Gemellus Horion to travel to Alexandria in search of a specialist. Considering Gemellus Horion's reaction to the magical spells that Julius attempted to cast upon him in AD 197, it is entirely possible that he would not have been tempted to try magical spells as a means of curing his afflictions.[590]

Discussion

Both Tryphon and Gemellus Horion suffered from eye problems that affected not only themselves, but also their families, their finances, their business interests and their standing in the community. While Tryphon's weak vision appears to have started affecting him later in life, Gemellus Horion was still very young when he not only lost one eye but began going blind in the remaining one; it is impossible to tell how severely Tryphon was affected

by his weakening vision, but the fact that he was still working as a weaver fourteen years after being released from military service indicates that he was probably not as unfortunate as Gemellus Horion, who repeatedly states that he cannot see at all. Both of them used their visual impairments, presumably to their own advantage, as a way of avoiding certain possibly undesirable duties; in Tryphon's case military service and in Gemellus Horion's, a liturgy. However, their visual impairments also had significant negative impacts upon their lives; Tryphon sent his son elsewhere to train as a weaver and Gemellus Horion was systematically terrorised by his neighbours, probably because they saw him as an easy target. It is interesting that, relying solely upon what is stated in the documents of their family archives, neither of them seems to have undergone any treatment for their respective conditions. Considering the importance of sight for a full range of activities in ancient life, and considering the problems that impaired vision evidently caused, we can expect that Tryphon and Gemellus Horion attempted some kind of healing, but if so it appears to have been ineffective. For the remainder of this chapter, I will examine the different types of treatment that seem to have been available in Egypt during the Roman period for those suffering from these and other eye complaints.

3. Medical and Surgical Healing

According to Celsus, 'There is scarcely any one of the eye disorders…which it may not be possible to clear up by simple and readily procured remedies'.[591] The most frequently attested treatments for eye infections such as *ophthalmia* are medicinal remedies such as salves or *collyria*. These salves appear to have been fairly standardised, generally containing active and aromatic ingredients blended together with some sort of gum as an agglutinant.[592] The reason Celsus gives for this is 'gum, amongst other properties, has this particular advantage, that when salves made of it have become dry, they stick together and do not break up'.[593] This would have been particularly useful in a country with a hot, dry climate such as Egypt. The gum taken from the *Acacia nilotica* was particularly popular; Pliny stated 'it is universally agreed that the best gum is that produced from the Egyptian thorn'.[594] While this gum sold outside Egypt for three *denarii* per pound, the trees grew abundantly within in Egypt and acacia gum would have been easily accessible as well as being cheaper without the import costs that would have been added onto the price in cities outside the Nile Valley, such as Alexandria and Rome, thus a salve might have been considered a particularly accessible and reasonably priced means of treating eye conditions.[595]

There is evidence to suggest that some eye salves were either invented or used in Egypt, or at least contained ingredients that were associated with Egypt, whose

---

[586] Lewis (1982) 96; the earliest evidence for exemption from public services on the grounds of ill health or physical impairment is the edict of Vibius Maximus (AD 103-7).

[587] *P. Oxy.* 424 states Gemellus Horion's age as being 'about twenty-six'.

[588] See for example *P. Mich.* 5.321, a will from Tebtunis, dating to 2nd December AD 42: 'About sixty-five years old, with a prominent right eye and a cataract on the left eye'.

[589] Celsus, *Med* 6.6.35; 7.7.13 A.

[590] *P. Mich.* 423-424 (AD 197, Karanis). For discussion of the magical spells, see Frankfurter (2006).

[591] Celsus, *Med.* 6.6.39.

[592] Jackson (1996) 2239.

[593] Celsus, *Med.* 6.6.3.

[594] Plin. *HN* 13.20.

[595] Manniche (1989) 65-7. For acacia as a standard ingredient in ancient eye salves, see Youtie (1977) 39 and (1979) 150.

names alluded to their Egyptian origins and connections. One collyrium stamp recovered from Lugdunensis seems to have been used in the preparation of a salve entitled *aegyptiacum*, which contained balsam.[596] Another eye salve was evidently either invented or used at Canopus, and was well known enough for the recipe to have been given by Celsus: 'But thick scars are thinned...by the salve of Canopus which contains: cinnamon and acacia four grams each; washed oxide of zinc, saffron, myrrh, poppy-tears and gum eight grams each; white pepper and frankincense twelve grams each; roasted copper thirty-two grams'.[597]

A papyrus of unknown provenance but thought to date from during the second and third centuries AD contains recipes for eye salves on either side, both written by the same small, rapid cursive hand. The recto side of the papyrus contains a recipe, complete with instructions as to its preparation and intended recipients: 'For children; burnt copper, four *drachmae*; calamine, six or eight *drachmae*; opium, two or four *drachmae*; myrrh, 2.3 *drachmae*; erica, two *drachmae*; acacia, six *drachmae*; gum, six *drachmae*; use water until it becomes sufficiently glutinous in thickness'.[598] The ingredients used were all available in Egypt during the Roman period and this recipe corresponds closely with that of the famous salve of Theodotus, included in Celsus' *On Medicine*.[599] Apparently, this particular salve was known as the ἀχάριστον, 'ungrateful', because it relieved the condition so quickly that the patient felt no gratitude for the cure.[600] This rapid relief could be why the author of the papyrus specifically prescribed the eye salve for children.

It seems that eye salves such as the ἀχάριστον could be prescribed by and obtained from a physician, who either made them himself or acquired them in another way; a fragmentary letter from Mons Claudianus dating to AD 137-45 states 'Go to the physician's house...return the saffron...collyrium sticks of medicine'.[601] In a letter dating to the fourth century AD, Eudaimon, who seems to be a physician himself in addition to coming from a family of physicians, writes to his mother and grandmothers: '[My brother] furnished in place of the container of animal fat, a jar of salve ... [*In the left margin*] Also send three pounds of salve mixed from all...astringent substances'.[602] However, it is equally

clear that eye salves could be obtained with a view to use at some point in the future, as and when necessary. Another letter from Mons Claudianus, dating to the second century AD, was written from Isidorus to his two sons who seem to have been living at the main camp not too far away. He writes 'Send [the small elbow-rest] and the ink and two sticks of salve'.[603] There is plenty of evidence from Mons Claudianus to suggest that eye infections occurred frequently.[604] The reason for this was probably the combination of the hot, dry climate in the Eastern Desert, the dust and grit from the quarries and the close confines of the living quarters. With eye infections occurring so routinely, perhaps it was not practical or financially viable to see a physician every time, hence Isidorus asking his sons to provide him with sticks of salve so that he could self-medicate as the need arose. While sticks of salve would be usefully portable, salve was also available in larger jars. In a letter dating to during the second and third centuries AD, Thaisarion writes to her sister Serapous, asking for a jar of salve (καὶ κάδιόν μοι πέμψατε κολλουρίου).[605]

Although Celsus was of the opinion that the majority of eye infections could be cured by the application of salves, some cases required more extensive medical or even surgical intervention. In addition to ophthalmological prescriptions, a number of extracts from ophthalmological treatises have also been discovered in Egypt.[606] These include three general treatises, three questionnaires with questions on symptoms to facilitate diagnosis, a treatise on the aetiology of eye infections, and a treatise on ophthalmological surgery. The importance of a functioning sense of sight aside, the conditions that resulted in such cases might be extremely debilitating, not to mention painful, thus needing to be dealt with once and for all. As mentioned previously, Gemellus Horion lost the sight in his one remaining eye to a cataract and under certain circumstances surgery was a way of correcting this.

When listing the medical specialists that one might find in Alexandria (since like Rome the city was large enough to accommodate both general and specialist medical practitioners) Galen indicated that in addition to the ὀφθαλμικός ἰατρός, an eye doctor, there was also a specialist that dealt specifically with cataracts.[607] Celsus

---

[596] Boon (1983) 10.
[597] Celsus, *Med.* 6.6.25 B.
[598] *SB* 14.12086 / *P. Princ.* 3.155 (second-third century AD, unprovenanced); see Youtie (1976) for translation and discussion. See also Youtie (1977) and (1979) for other examples of *achariston* eye salves.
[599] Celsus, *Med.* 6.6.6.
[600] Gal. *Oss.* 3.
[601] *O. Claud.* 220 (AD 137-45, Mons Claudianus): ὕπαγε πρὸς τὸν ἰατρὸν ἵνα δώσι σοι τὴν κρόκον καὶ πέμψις μοι ἐπὶ ταῦτα ἃ ἔπεμψές μοι οὔπ ο ἔλαβα ... κολλύρια ἰατρικά.
[602] *P. Oxy.* 4001 (fourth century AD, Oxyrhynchus): ὅθεν σπουδασάτω ὁ ἀδελφὸς ἡμῶν Θεόδωρος ζητῆσαι ηπο...τον να... καὶ γνῶναι περ[ι] αὐτοῦ... ὑδρίαν, παρέσχεν ἀντὶ τοῦ

ὀξυγγίου κολλουρίων ὑδρίαν... τάδιον... ἀπόστειλον δὲ καὶ κολλουρίων λίτρας τρεῖς μεμιγμένων ἀπὸ πάντων.
[603] *O. Claud.* 174 (second century AD, Mons Claudianus): πέμψατε οὖν αὐτὸ καὶ τὸ μελάνιον καὶ κολλυρίδια.
[604] *O. Claud.* 212, 213 and 217 are all lists of sick and injured personnel that include people suffering from *ophthalmia*.
[605] *P. Mich.* 8.508 (second-third century, Alexandria).
[606] See Marganne (1994) for publication, translation and discussion of six such extracts: Pack³ 2343 (early third century AD, Hibeh); *P. Ashm. Libr.*s.n. (second century AD, Arsinoite nome); *P. Aberd.* 11 (second century AD, Fayum); *P. Ross. Georg.* 1.20 (second century AD, Dime); *P. Strasb.* Inv. gr. 90 + *P. Ryl.* 1.29a+b (second century AD, unprovenanced); and *P. Cair. Craw.* 1 (third century AD, Fayum). See also *P. Gen.* Inv. 486 (third century AD, unprovenanced), a fragment from an ophthalmological treatise; and *P. Strasb.* Inv. G 839 (fourth century AD, Fayum), an ophthalmological questionnaire.
[607] Gal. *Ars Med.* 2-3.

APPROACHES TO HEALING IN ROMAN EGYPT

provides a set of instructions as to how a physician should conduct the procedure.[608] It is evident that Gemellus Horion did not undergo this procedure. However, there is plenty of literary and archaeological evidence to suggest that others did both elsewhere in the Roman Empire, and in Roman Egypt.[609] The sender of a private letter dating to the early fourth century AD writes 'If it's possible let him come with your mother so that his cataract can be cured - I myself have seen others cured'.[610] The term used is λεύκωμα, the same used by Gemellus Horion to refer to his cataract.

There were also a number of other eye conditions that required surgical intervention to either cure them or at least alleviate the symptoms. The corpus of mummy portraits recovered from the Roman cemetery at Hawara in the Fayum, produced from the first to the third centuries AD, comprises primarily of encaustic or tempera portraits painted onto wooden panels that covered the head of a mummified individual and was then buried with him or her. The purpose of the portraits may have been to serve as a record of how the individual had appeared during life; the portraits are highly detailed, extremely varied and thus presumably realistic, to the point that it has been suggested that it might be possible to identify certain medical conditions from them.[611] Close examination of a mummy portrait currently exhibited in the Metropolitan Museum of Art has led to the suggestion that it is possible to diagnose *trachoma*, an eye infection that results from *Chlamydia trachomatis*, a sexually transmitted infection. *Trachoma* is caused by direct contact with bodily fluids or an object contaminated with them, and between five and twelve days after exposure the tissue lining the eyelids becomes inflamed. If left untreated, the infection can result in the eyelashes turning in and rubbing against the cornea, causing eye ulcers, scarring and deformity of the eyelids, and even blindness. *Trachoma* has been particularly common in Egypt throughout history, leading to it being described as 'Egyptian Ophthalmia' by Napoleon's army during the invasion of Egypt during the nineteenth century.[612] This diagnosis was possible because the artist responsible for painting the portrait included a healed surgical scar upon the skin around the subject's right eye. The nature of this scar resulted in the putative identification of an ancient blepharoplasty, the surgical technique that was the only effective remedy for the symptoms of the condition.[613]

Celsus describes the simple operation that would have been required to treat this condition in *On Medicine*:

> If eyelashes have grown where they ought not, a fine iron needle flattened like a spear point is put into the fire; then when the eyelid is turned up, so that the offending eyelashes can be seen by the operator, the red hot needle is passed along their roots, from the angle, for a third of the length of the eyelid, then for a second and for a third time, until the opposite angle is reached; this causes all the roots of the eyelashes so cauterised to die. A medicament is then applied to check inflammation, and when the crusts have become detached, cicatrisation is to be induced.[614]

It has been observed that the way in which the pupil of the right eye has been depicted in comparison to the left eye could be seen to indicate that, unfortunately for the young man, the blepharoplasty failed to save the sight in that eye.[615] However, the operation would certainly have alleviated the pain caused by the chronic infection of his eye and eyelid. The fact that the surgical scar was included in his portrait (if it is in fact a surgical scar) could indicate that he was not ashamed of his condition; perhaps its inclusion could be viewed as an indication that he was proud of the fact that he had been able to afford surgical treatment, or perhaps his ability to withstand the pain of an operation probably undertaken without any kind of anaesthetic. If cataracts were as common in Roman Egypt as the documentary literature seems to suggest, it is likely that others around him were suffering from similar conditions; perhaps they were unable to afford or even bear the treatment that he could? If this was the case, his scar could have set him apart from them, perhaps even distinguishing him in their eyes.

4. Magical Healing

In addition to the judicious application of kohl or eye salve, the inhabitants of Roman Egypt also employed magical spells and amulets both as a means of protecting their eyes from infection, and of curing an infection once contracted. A magical spell, dating from the third century AD and written in Demotic, is specifically aimed at male sufferers of *ophthalmia*:

> To heal *ophthalmia* in a man: "O Amoun, this lofty male, this male of Ethiopia, who came down from Meroe to Egypt and found my son Horus hurrying on his feet. He beat him on his head with three spells in the Ethiopian language. When he finds NN, whom NN bore, he will hurry on his feet, and he will beat him on his head with three spells in the Ethiopian language:

---

[608] Celsus, *Med* 7.7.14 B-F.

[609] For a set of medical instruments identified as being suitable for eye surgery recovered from a shipwreck and assumed to belong to a passenger rather than a ship's doctor see Gibbins (1988); for three cataract needles and other implements for eye surgery see Feugère *et al.* (1985).

[610] *P. Oxy.* 2601 (early fourth century AD - after AD 303, Oxyrhynchus): καὶ εἰ δυνατόν ἐστιν ἐρχέσθω μετὰ τῆς μητρός σου ἵνα θεραπευθῇ τὸ λευκωμάτιον· ἐγὼ γὰρ εἶδον ἄλλους θεραπευθέντας.

[611] Walker (2000) 23. On retrospective diagnosis, see Leven (2004).

[612] For discussion of the history of *Chlamydia trachomatis* in Egypt, see Tower (1963) and Al-Rifai (1988).

[613] Johnson (2005) 31; the mummy portrait in question has subsequently been re-titled 'Youth with a Surgical Cut in the Right Eye'.

[614] Celsus, *Med* 7.7.8 B.

[615] Johnson (2005) 31.

68

"GENTINI tentina qyqybi [ak] khe akha".[616]

The caster is instructed to say the spell over oil, before adding salt and nasturtium seed to it and then anointing the sufferer, although the instructions do not specify where the sufferer should be anointed; anointing the eyes would make sense considering that they were the parts affected, but it does not follow that this was done. Oil, salt and nasturtium seeds were all readily accessible; according to Pliny, nasturtium in particular was believed to sharpen the senses.[617] In addition to anointing the sufferer with oil, the caster is instructed to write the spell on papyrus and make it into a roll upon the sufferer's body, perhaps echoing the actions referred to in the verbal part of the spell itself. Papyrus is also employed in a magical spell dating from during the third and fourth centuries AD and written in Greek: 'For discharge of the eyes: Write [this] on a piece of papyrus and attach it as an amulet: "ROURARBISAROURBBARIASPHREN"'.[618]

The breast milk of a woman who had borne a son was a popular ingredient in both medical and magical remedies as well as protective spells; the substance was equated with the breast milk of maternal goddesses such as Isis or Hathor and thought to be imbued with overwhelmingly positive qualities such as vitality and strength.[619] Thus breast milk was used to treat a variety of complaints including eye infections; modern research has even found breast milk and colostrum to contain immunological and antimicrobial properties that would have been particularly effective against infections such as *Staphylococcus aureus* and *Chlamydia trachomatis*.[620] The incorporation of aspects of pharmacology and thus medicine into magical practices indicates the extent to which elements of medical, magical and religious healing were integrated into healing strategies and, in turn, the ways in which healing strategies were integrated into daily life, whether this integration involved the purposeful gathering of weeds or the cultivation or purchase of specific species of flora, or even the expression of extra breast milk after having nursed a baby.

5. Religious Healing
The god Asclepius was the most prominent healing deity in the Roman Empire. However, in Egypt the god Sarapis was preferred and was particularly popular in Alexandria, where there was an immense temple, the Serapeum,

dedicated to him.[621] Prayers for health, dedications and offerings to Sarapis on behalf of family and friends are a common feature of letters surviving amongst the documentary papyri that can be definitively identified as having been sent from Alexandria.[622] Demetrius of Phaleron, writing in the late fourth to the early third century BC, indicates that faith in Sarapis as a god of healing originated in the royal court during the reign of Ptolemy I.[623] There was another major centre of the cult of Sarapis further along the coast at Canopus where, according to Strabo, numerous 'reputable' people had undertaken incubation in an attempt to cure their illnesses or receive oracles from the god.[624]

Demetrius himself visited Egypt, staying for several years at the court of Ptolemy Soter. According to Diogenes Laertius, writing much later in the third century AD, 'He lost his eye-sight in Alexandria, and recovered it again by the favour of Serapis; on which account he composed the paeans which are sung and spoken of as his composition to this day'.[625] The possibility that in subsequent years the inhabitants of Roman Egypt came to consider Sarapis to be particularly capable of curing eye problems is supported by the famous Canopus eye salve discussed above, which could have been used at the Serapeum in Canopus, as well as an oracle question addressed to Zeus-Helios-Sarapis Nikephoros, recovered from Oxyrhynchus and dating from the second century AD, which questions the god regarding treatment for the worshipper's *ophthalmia*, wishing to know the best physician from whom to seek treatment (εἰ ἐπιτρέπεις μοι χρήσασθαι Ἑρμείνωι [Ἑ]ρμοπολίτηι ἰατρῶι πρὸς θεραπείαν τῶν ὀφθαλμῶν καὶ τοῦτό μοι συμφέρει, τοῦτό μοι δός).[626] This oracle question illustrates the intersection of medical and religious healing in Egypt during the Roman period, particularly with regard to eye complaints. Although the individual in question intended to seek medical treatment for their condition, he or she saw no reason not to involve a god as well, in the hope of maximising the chances of the treatment being successful and (perhaps) saving them both time and money.

Also writing in the second century, Tacitus and Suetonius mention an event that occurred while the emperor Vespasian was in Egypt in AD 69. Tacitus reports the story that while Vespasian was in Alexandria Sarapis showed great favour towards him by endowing him with the divine power to heal two men, one blind and one

---

[616] *PDM* 14.1097-1103.
[617] Plin. *HN* 19.44; 20.50; Pliny also states that Pythagoras believed that nasturtium was beneficial to sight at *HN* 20.51.
[618] *PGM* 7.197-198.
[619] See Bonfante (1997) 187-8 for the magical power of even the *image* of a nursing mother. The way in which the milk is poured into and then out of a jar decorated with the image of the goddess is very similar to the way in which water is poured into and then out of a basin attached to a Horus *cippus*. See also *P. Mich.* Inv. 593 (fifth century AD, unprovenanced) for a recipe containing, conversely, the milk of a woman who has suffered a miscarriage as a remedy against inflammation.
[620] Laskaris (2008) 460.

[621] For the archaeological evidence for the Serapeum in Alexandria, see McKenzie *et al.* (2004).
[622] See for example *P. Oxy.* 1070 (third century AD, Alexandria): 'The prayer which I previously made to all the gods for the preservation of yourself and our child and your brother and father and mother and all our friends now goes up to them with far greater force in the great Serapeum, and I beseech the great god Sarapis for your life and that of all our friends'.
[623] Diog. Laert. 5.78.
[624] Strabo, *Geographica* 17.1.17.
[625] Diog. Laert. 7.
[626] *P. Oxy.* 3078 (second century AD, Oxyrhynchus). The discovery of votive eyes made from gold and silver at the Serapeum on Delos indicates that healing eye problems was a particular speciality of the Delian Sarapis in any case.

lame.[627] About a decade later, this same episode was included by Suetonius in his biography of Vespasian.[628] Tacitus prefaces his account of the miracle by stating 'many marvels continued to mark the favour of heaven and a certain partiality of the gods toward him'.[629] Vespasian's purpose in disseminating the miracle was to confirm that he had been the right man to be emperor, chosen by the gods themselves, and presumably this was also Tacitus' purpose in repeating it. Suetonius presented his account slightly differently, choosing to emphasise first the fact that Vespasian was of relatively humble origins before relating his abbreviated version of the miracle, presumably with a view to making sure the tale had more of an impact on the reader. He stated that 'Vespasian as yet lacked prestige and a certain divinity, so to speak, since he was an unexpected and still new-made emperor; but these also were given him'.[630] Both Tacitus and Suetonius were both writing primarily with the Roman senatorial and equestrian elite in mind as their readers, and consequently Barbara Levick interprets these miracles as 'a metaphor of the new regime's healing powers, reluctant though the physician was'.[631] However, it is likely that the inhabitants of Alexandria and Egypt viewed this story in a very different light.[632]

Tacitus' account includes the information that the blind man was 'well known for his loss of sight' (*quidam oculorum tabe notus*) presumably as a way of authenticating the miracle; since the man was known to be blind, Vespasian could not be accused of orchestrating a stunt, pretending to restore sight to someone who was in turn pretending to be blind. Indeed, Tacitus then recounts that Vespasian's first thought was to consult a physician regarding the severity of the man's condition, indicating his own belief in the power of medicine over religious faith. However, the blind man told Vespasian that he had been advised by Sarapis (*monitu Serapidis dei*) to ask the emperor to 'moisten his cheeks and eyes with his spittle' (*ut genas et oculorum orbis dignaretur respergere oris excremento*). Suetonius' account differs here slightly, stating that the man was visited by Sarapis in a dream (*opem valitudini demonstratam a Serapide per quietem*) and that he requested that Vespasian spit in his eyes (*restituturum oculos, si inspuisset*). However, in both accounts, once Vespasian obliged, the blind man could see again (*ac caeco reluxit dies*). If, as Tacitus records, the man was truly blind and had been for some time, presumably he had exhausted all other options such as medical treatment or magical spells before turning to Sarapis. If, as Suetonius says, the man was visited by Sarapis in a dream, it is possible that he had even undergone an incubation ritual within the Serapeum in his desire to be cured.

For the inhabitants of Alexandria and Egypt, in all probability the most important detail included in Tacitus and Suetonius' accounts of the miracle would have been the fact that it was Sarapis who was responsible for it, validating belief in Sarapis as a healer and as a healer of eye problems in particular. Indeed, Tacitus even comments on Sarapis being the god 'whom this most superstitious of nations worships before all others' and that, if Vespasian had been unsuccessful, 'ridicule would fall only on the poor suppliants'. In antiquity, saliva was believed to be a cure for a number of different medical conditions, whether it came from someone of importance or not. For while Tacitus and Suetonius give examples of healing occurring from the saliva of an emperor, the New Testament incorporates the superstition into miracles performed by Jesus, and Pliny includes a whole section on saliva in the twenty-eight book of his *Natural History*, which details remedies derived from living creatures.[633] He even states specifically that '*ophthalmia* may be cured by anointing, as it were, the eyes every morning with fasting spittle'.[634] Interestingly, considering that Pliny's work was written after the event in Alexandria occurred, although before the works of Tacitus and Suetonius, the only restriction appears to be that the saliva must come from someone who is fasting; nowhere does either Tacitus or Suetonius mention that Vespasian had been fasting. Indeed, since the requests for healing seem to have occurred without prior warning at a regular tribunal, in all likelihood he was not.

Conclusion

Eye complaints, whether in the form of infectious diseases or injuries, seem to have been prevalent throughout Roman Egypt at all levels of society. With regard to those complaints caused by an infectious disease, these were ultimately the result of certain aspects of the natural environment of Egypt such as heat, sand

---

[627] Tac. *Hist.* 4.81-82: 'One of the common people of Alexandria, well known for his loss of sight, threw himself before Vespasian's knees, praying him with groans to cure his blindness, being so directed by the god Sarapis, whom this most superstitious of nations worships before all others; and he beseeched the emperor to deign to moisten his cheeks and eyes with his spittle ... finally, he directed the physicians to give their opinion as to whether such blindness ... could be overcome by human aid ... they said that ... the power of sight had not been completely eaten away and it would return if the obstacles were removed ... such perhaps was the wish of the gods, and it might be that the emperor had been chosen for this divine service; in any case, if a cure were obtained, the glory would be Caesar's, but in the event of failure, ridicule would fall only on the poor suppliants. So Vespasian, believing that his good fortune was capable of anything and that nothing was any longer incredible, with a smiling countenance, and amid intense excitement on the part of the bystanders ... and the day again shone for the blind man. Both facts are told by eye-witnesses even now when falsehood brings no reward'.

[628] Suet. *Vesp.* 7.2-3: 'A man of the people who was blind ... came to him ... as he sat on the tribunal, begging for the help for [his] disorders which Sarapis had promised in a dream; for the god declared that Vespasian would restore the eyes, if he would spit upon them ... though he had hardly any faith that this could possibly succeed, and therefore shrank even from making the attempt, he was at last prevailed upon by his friends and ... in public before a large crowd; and with success'; these events are recounted even more briefly in Dio Cass. 66.8.1.

[629] Tac. *Hist.* 4.81.

[630] Suet. *Vesp.* 7.2.

[631] Levick (1999) 68; Levick does not regard Vespasian as responsible for cynically manipulating religion and superstition through performing these miracles, rather she sees him as 'at worst a willing dupe of stage-managers', at 69.

[632] See Henrichs (1968) for comprehensive discussion of the entire Alexandrian episode. However, with regards to the miracles, this article devotes the majority of its attention to the healing of the crippled man, dismissing the healing of the blind man in a few lines, at 71-2.

[633] *Gospel According to St Mark* 8.23; *Gospel According to St John* 9.6.

[634] Plin. *HN* 28.7.

and insect activity so no one, not even the wealthy social elite, was immune. The sheer ubiquity of eye complaints is evident both from the papyrological evidence and from the archaeological evidence; eye complaints and the healing strategies utilised are attested in documents and literature written on papyri and ostraca while glass lenses and kohl sticks and tubes of varying levels of quality and craftsmanship have been recovered from sites throughout the region. Consequently, it is not surprising to find that a wide range of treatments were available.

The examples discussed in this chapter have ranged geographically from Alexandria in the Nile Delta to Karanis in the Fayum to Oxyrhynchus in the Nile Valley to Mons Claudianus in the Eastern Desert. The status of the individuals involved has ranged from citizen landowners to weavers to quarry workers. Consequently, considering both the geographical spread and the diverse social status of the victims, it is not surprising that there were numerous different ways of dealing with eye complaints and a great deal of individual autonomy. It is clear that some individuals prepared in advance, stocking up on eye salves when the opportunity arose so that they were in a position to treat themselves while others resorted to seeing a physician or even a surgeon if the condition was more serious; eye salves were both a prophylactic measure and a cure for maladies. However, it is also clear that medicine was not necessarily the only or even the first recourse to healing. Magical spells written in both Greek and Demotic, temple oracles and accounts of divine healing prove that magical and divine help was sought too, and it is clear that these approaches were subject to uniquely Egyptian influences and belief in the power of traditional deities such as Sarapis and Isis, and even Egypt itself.

If Roman Egypt is considered in isolation, there are more references to a medical recourse to healing through eye salves than there are to magical or religious modes of healing in the documentary and literary papyri. These numerous references to salves, not only in private letters, but also in extracts from medical treatises, are supplemented by some evidence for surgical procedures. What this evidence implies is that when the inhabitants of Roman Egypt suffered problems with their eyes, they tended to treat them pharmacologically, using a salve that could be applied directly to the afflicted area. However, it is clear that such salves could be obtained from a variety of sources (physicians, apothecaries, temples, family members and friends), or even made at home; the recipes ranged from very complex and consisting of expensive ingredients such as myrrh, to very straightforward and consisting of everyday ingredients such as oil, nasturtium, or even breast milk. Surgery was also a possibility if one could find and/or afford to hire someone with the necessary ophthalmological expertise, but this might have necessitated a trip to Alexandria or one of the metropoleis, and such a journey would have been unlikely to have been undertaken on a whim.

This apparent preference for simple medical or pharmacological remedies could have been a result of the sheer frequency with which eye problems occurred; the inhabitants might well be familiar enough with the symptoms to be able to both diagnose and treat themselves or others. In addition to this, it may not necessarily have been financially viable, desirable or even physically possible to consult a medical practitioner on such a regular basis. However, it is notable that magical and religious remedies incorporated aspects of medical and pharmacological practice (such as the use and application of substances such as oil or breast milk), so two individuals afflicted with *ophthalmia* might well have been using the same substances, but for different reasons, depending on their preferences with regard to medical, magical or religious healing.

CHAPTER FOUR

FEVER IN ROMAN EGYPT

1. Introduction

Fevers were widespread throughout the ancient world.[635] As with eye diseases, the writer of the Hippocratic *Airs, Waters and Places* noted that certain types of fevers tended to occur in hot regions.[636] However, the treatise also observed that 'water contributes much towards health' and it is important to remember that while Roman Egypt was certainly a region with a hot dry climate, the Nile was also one of its most prominent features.

The term 'fever' was widely used in antiquity to denote a variety of febrile symptoms and different diseases because any disease that exhibited febrile symptoms was itself regarded as a kind of fever.[637] Consequently, there are numerous examples of outbreaks of 'fever' to be found in the documentary papyri. The words used most commonly for referring to fevers in a general sense are πυρετός in Greek and *febris* in Latin, seemingly no matter how extreme the fever happened to be, while ἀπύρετος is used to indicate that a fever has passed.[638] During the first or second century AD, Dionysios wrote to his father informing him that 'My health is as before. The night before yesterday I had a fever and would not eat, but this morning, thanks to god, I got well again'.[639] The fact that his fever was of less than two days' duration and that he was well enough to write to his father about it suggests that it was only a minor illness. The fact that indiscriminate use of the term 'fever' was recognised as being so non-specific as to be open to abuse by hypochondriacs and malingerers is attested by the fact that in AD 316 the public physicians of Oxyrhynchus, the Aurelii Heron and Didymus, were sent to examine a man claiming to be ill who turned out to be 'lying on a bed seized with a slight...fever'.[640]

However, fevers were evidently not always of such a short duration as that of Dionysios. During the first or second century AD an anonymous individual wrote 'Indeed, I have not been able during these days to write to anyone because I have been recovering from an illness and from a great ague, and with pain I have been able to write these lines, being tortured'.[641] In a list of sick and injured personnel from Mons Claudianus, dating to between 2nd and 14th June AD 137-45, an individual named Spes is described as πυρεκτικός, 'feverish'.[642] This Spes is included on a subsequent list, dated to the 6th July, and his condition is once again described as πυρεκτικός.[643] Spes is the only person to appear on both lists; assuming that they date to the same year, he could still have been suffering from the same illness almost three weeks after the initial list had been written, or he could have recovered from his original fever and subsequently suffered either a relapse or an entirely different bout of illness that was still classed as a type of fever by his superiors. Due to the brevity of the entries, the precise nature of his illness is, of course, unknown.

Galen actually opined that fever was itself a disease rather than a symptom of one.[644] However, since modern scholars recognise that fever is a symptom of illness rather than an illness in itself, it is clear that the precise cause of any instance of fever mentioned in ancient literary sources would have varied depending on the circumstances. In addition to the types of fevers that would have resulted from infected wounds, miscarriage or childbirth, a number of different conditions such as malaria, typhoid, hepatitis, influenza and brucellosis include fever amongst their symptoms and thus would have been easily confused by both the ancient medical practitioners and their patients.

The focus of this chapter will be upon the ways in which the inhabitants of Roman Egypt dealt with a range of different types of fever, including those originating from bacterial infection such as puerperal fever or those occurring in conjunction with a poorly healed wound, and those with a viral or even pestilential cause such as measles, smallpox or malaria. The fact that the cause or causes not only of specific types of fever but also of bouts of fever in general were so poorly understood naturally resulted in confusion over how one might prevent oneself most effectively from catching one in the first place, let alone treating an attack once it had begun. Thus those who wished to avoid developing or contracting a fever and those who either knew an episode was imminent or had already begun to experience one might make use of a wide range of healing strategies, drawing on a range of medical, magical and religious traditions.

2. Malarial Fever

The classification of fevers according to the length of their cycles was widely accepted in antiquity, but there

---

[635] Celsus, *Med.* 3.3.1.

[636] Hippoc. *Aer.* 7.

[637] Yeo (2005) 434.

[638] *P. Oxy.* 1582 (second century AD, Oxyrhynchus): λέγει γὰρ Σερῆνος ὁ φίλος ὅτι ἀπύρετος ἐστιν.

[639] *P. Oslo* 3.152 (first-second century AD, unprovenanced): ἐγὼ ὁ αὐτός εἰμι· τὴν νύκτα δὲ [τῆς] τὴν εἰς τὴν ἐχθὲς καὶ ἐπεπυρέχειν ἀποβαλὼν τὴν τροφήν· σύν θεῶι δὲ ... Dionysios may well have been entirely serious in attributing his recovery to his god.

[640] *P. Oxy.* 896 (AD 316, Oxyrhynchus): ὄντα πυρετίοις ἀκ[ρ]ίτοι[ς] συνεχ[όμενον].

[641] *P. Oxy. Hels.* 46 (first-second century AD, Oxyrhynchus): οὐ γὰρ ἠδυνήθην ἐπὶ τοῦ παρόντος γράψαι οὐδενὶ διὰ τὸ ἀπὸ νόσου ἀναλαμβάνειν καὶ ψυγμοῦ μεγάλου καὶ μόγις ἠδυνήθην καὶ ταῦτα γράψαι βασανιζ[ό]μενος. The word used here is ψυγμός, 'ague'.

[642] *O. Claud.* 212 (AD 137-45, Mons Claudianus).

[643] *O. Claud.* 213 (AD 137-45, Mons Claudianus).

[644] Gal. *MMG* 1.4.

was little agreement as to their actual causes.[645] Galen's theory, which appears to have been entirely original, was that different humours gave rise to fever with different cycles. Thus, phlegm was the cause of quotidian fever, yellow bile was the cause of tertian fever and black bile was the cause of quartan fever.[646] This view was accepted and repeated by later medical authors such as Oribasius, Alexander of Tralles and Pseudo-Alexander of Aphrodisias. The term 'quotidian fever' is used to refer to fevers that peak every twenty-four hours (*cotidiana* in Latin and ἀμφημερινός in Greek). Unfortunately, it is difficult to diagnose the condition responsible for causing any quotidian fever mentioned in ancient sources retrospectively because many diseases exhibit similar symptoms.[647] This confusion is reflected in Celsus' extensive description of quotidian fevers in *On Medicine*.[648] The term 'tertian fever' is used to refer to fevers that peak on the third day (*tertiana* in Latin and τριταῖος in Greek). According to Celsus, two types of tertian fever were recognised in antiquity:

> The first type commences and terminates in the same manner as quartan fever. Its distinguishing feature is that it disappears for one whole day and returns on the third day. The second type is much more pernicious. It too returns on the third day. However, out of the forty-eight hours, the paroxysm lasts for almost thirty-six hours (sometimes more or less), nor is there any cessation during the remission, but it becomes less severe.[649]

Consequently, these types are differentiated by modern scholars as benign tertian fever and malignant tertian fever respectively. The term 'quartan fever' is used to refer to fevers that peak on the fourth day (*quartana* in Latin and τεταρταῖος in Greek). According to Celsus, quartan fevers were relatively straightforward: 'Nearly always they begin with shivering, then heat breaks out, and the fever having ended, there are two days free; then on the fourth day it recurs'.[650] According to Galen, it was usual for quartan fevers contracted in the autumn to be of long duration.[651] However, although quartan fevers lasted longer than either quotidian or tertian fevers, they were rarely fatal.[652]

The terminology used to describe fevers in ancient medical writings as well as in private letters can be used

to propose retrospective diagnosis of certain medical conditions. Although, as stated previously, the causes of quotidian fevers are difficult to diagnose retrospectively because a variety of different diseases such as typhoid exhibit the same symptoms, other types of periodic fever are far more distinctive. The causes of tertian and quartan fever can be diagnosed with some degree of confidence by modern scholars as various different species of malaria; benign tertian fever is caused by *P. vivax*, malignant tertian fever is caused by *P. falciparum* and quartan fever is caused by *P. malariae*. The combination of the distinctive periodicity of the fevers with the knowledge that malaria is caused by mosquitoes that are found in marshy environments such as that of the Nile Delta and Nile Valley ensures that it is possible to state with a high degree of confidence that the inhabitants of Roman Egypt frequently suffered from malaria.[653]

The large sections devoted to what modern scholars recognise to be malarial fevers in the writings of ancient authors of all literary genres indicate that malaria was widespread in the ancient world; although certain areas such as Sardinia were known to be particularly affected by the disease. According to Walter Scheidel, even if malaria had not already been endemic in Pharaonic Egypt, it would have been introduced to the region by the Greek and Macedonian settlers of the Ptolemaic period.[654] Thus it follows logically that subsequent Roman settlers may also have contributed to this process, even before Egypt was officially annexed by the Roman Empire in 30 BC, as first Julius Caesar and then later Marcus Antonius brought large numbers of Roman soldiers with them on their military campaigns in the region. Certainly, malaria is known to have been endemic in Roman Italy and the city of Rome itself.[655]

Herodotus indicates that as early as the Late period, the inhabitants of Egypt were aware that mosquito bites caused health problems: 'Those who live upstream of the marshes have towers in which they sleep, since the mosquitoes are prevented by the winds from flying up to the towers'.[656] In the late first century BC, Vitruvius advised that architects should familiarise themselves with medicine in order to select healthy locations to site their planned buildings. He recommended that marshy areas should be avoided because the stagnant water would 'grow putrid and emit heavy and pestilent moisture'.[657] When explaining why Alexandria was such a healthy city, Strabo specifically cited its lack of stagnant marshes: 'At Alexandria, at the beginning of summer, the Nile, being full, fills the lake also, and leaves no marshy matter to corrupt the rising vapours'.[658] However, Alexandria was a comparatively new city, founded primarily because of the positive aspects of the site and comprehensively planned by Greek architects. Unfortunately, the rest of

[645] Yeo (2005) 435.
[646] Gal. *Diff. Feb.* 2.1.
[647] Sallares (2002) 11.
[648] Celsus, *Med.* 3.3.3-5.
[649] Celsus, *Med.* 3.3.2.
[650] Celsus, *Med.* 3.3.1. The most detailed account of the reality of experiencing quartan fever during the Roman period comes from Cicero's letters to his friend Atticus; both Atticus and his wife Pilia suffered from quartan fever in the period August 50 BC-May 49 BC: Cic. *Att.* 123.1; 124.1; 125.2; 128.1; 128.3; 128.5; 130.3; 131.2; 154.4; 168; 171.1; 173.3; 175.2; 200.3; 207; 208.
[651] Gal. *Cris.* 1.4.
[652] Sallares (2002) 12.

[653] Scheidel (2001) 75-91; Nerlich *et al.* (2008).
[654] Scheidel (2001) 88.
[655] On malaria in Roman Italy, see Burke (1996) and Sallares (2002); on malaria in Rome itself see Scheidel (2003).
[656] Hdt. 2.95.1.
[657] Vitr. *De arch.* 1.4.12.
[658] Strabo, *Geographica* 17.1.7.

Egypt was not so lucky. While Varro advised farmers in possession of unhealthy land in Roman Italy to either sell it or abandon it, the majority of the inhabitants of Egypt lived in either the Nile Delta or the Nile Valley, which were not only the most agriculturally fertile areas of the province, but also the only agriculturally fertile areas of a province that was primarily desert.[659]

According to Scheidel, 'geology favours the spread of malaria in the marshy areas of the Nile Delta, above all in its northern stretch that is dominated by lakes and the estuaries of the various tributaries of the Nile'.[660] Owing to the presence of a large lake, Lake Moeris, and the particular nature of its irrigation system, parts of the heavily populated Fayum were also particularly prone to outbreaks of the disease. Considering that a large number of the papyri from Roman Egypt seem to have originated in the Fayum, it is not surprising that fevers should be frequently mentioned in them. However, the disease is also attested at Oxyrhynchus, which was not actually situated on the banks of the Nile, but on those of an adjacent canal, and at Denderah, in Upper Egypt.[661]

In addition to the written references to malarial fevers found in the documentary papyri, skeletons excavated from the Kellis 2 cemetery of the Dakhleh Oasis in the Western Desert show signs of anaemic stress that could have been either caused or exacerbated by malaria. 143 skeletons from the Roman period *circa* AD100-400 exhibit *Cribra orbitalia*, bone lesions that are caused by anaemia experienced during childhood.[662] Although the Dakhleh Oasis is located in the Western Desert, far away from either the Nile or Lake Moeris, malaria is known to have been suffered by the inhabitants of the Kharga Oasis to the south east during the date season, a brief period from September to October.[663] The Kellis 2 cemetery also contains a high number of foetal skeletons; although there is no definitive evidence for women having frequently died in childbirth; only one female skeleton was buried together with a foetal skeleton.[664] The skeletons appear to have been slightly smaller than would be expected of foetuses in the third trimester.[665] Maternal malarial infection is known to reduce the weight of infants at birth, consequently increasing the incidence of stillbirths and neonatal mortality.[666] Thus it is possible that if malaria was endemic in the Dakhleh Oasis, it not only

exacerbated anaemic stress during childhood but also contributed to infant mortality.[667]

Mummies excavated from a cemetery at Dush in the Kharga Oasis, dating from the first to the fourth centuries AD, also show signs of osteological stress and poor health. Two thirds of the mummies (thirty-four out of fifty-six) exhibit Harris Lines on their femurs and tibias, indications of either severe malnutrition or illness during childhood.[668] Since mummification was practised at Dush, it was possible for conditions that affect soft tissue to be identified in addition to those that affect the bones. Ten of the individuals suffered from the internal parasite bilharzia or schistosomiasis, which, while not fatal, would certainly have contributed to other underlying health problems.[669] According to Mohamed Farid Abdel-Wahab, 'Schistosomiasis rarely exists as a sole infection or disease state in many areas of Egypt. Malnutrition, enteric diseases, viral hepatitis, malaria…and other diseases and states of ill-health more often co-exist in schistosome-infected individuals than not'.[670] Cases of typhoid fever were also identified.[671] The skeletons of the mummies from Dush certainly show evidence of malnutrition, and since malaria was known to have occurred in the Kharga Oasis, it is possible that it occurred at Dush too. Both schistosomiasis and typhoid are caused by contaminated water supplies, whether natural water sources such as rivers and lakes or artificial water sources such as canals and irrigation works.[672] Since the Kharga Oasis is located in the Western Desert, it is probable that these outbreaks were caused by irrigation works; these irrigation works could also have been infested by mosquitoes and thus responsible for the spread of malaria.

3. Fevers Caused by Bacterial Infection
A fever could be caused by a bacterial infection, and a common source of bacterial infection was a flesh wound; wounds are frequently attested in the documentary papyri, the result of both assault and accident.[673] While a wound might start off as minor or merely superficial, an infection could result in a serious illness that might leave amputation as the only means of avoiding gangrene and septicaemia. The hot, dry climate and dusty, sandy terrain of Egypt combined with the close quarter living conditions, constant proximity to livestock and laborious processes involved in washing and laundering would have made keeping a wound clean and neatly bandaged

---

[659] Varro, *Rust.* 1.12.2.
[660] Scheidel (2001) 76.
[661] For Oxyrhynchus see *P. Oxy.* 1687.11 and 20 (AD 184-5); for Denderah see Sallares (2002) 282 for an Italian translation of the original hieroglyphic text: 'Non uscire di casa dopo il tramonto del sole nelle settimane che seguono l'ingrossamento del Nilo'.
[662] Fairgrieve and Molto (2000) 319.
[663] Fairgrieve and Molto (2000) 328.
[664] Tocheri *et al.* (2005) 337, Burial 436.
[665] Tocheri *et al.* (2005) 335.
[666] Hippoc. *Epid.* 1.10: 'Most of them had difficult parturition, and after labour they were taken ill, and these most especially died, as, for example, the daughter of Telebolus died on the sixth day after delivery … But all those in the pregnant state that were attacked had abortions, as far as I observed'; see also Scheidel (2001) 75.

[667] See for example Lane (1999) 633-49 for a cemetery containing skeletons of forty seven infants thought to have died in a malaria epidemic in the fifth century AD. See Nerlich *et al.* (2008) 1318 for scientific analysis of two Egyptian mummies dating from between 1500 BC and 500 BC who suffered from both chronic anaemia and the *P. Falciparum* strain of malaria for evidence of a relationship between the two medical conditions.
[668] Lichtenburg (1998) 118.
[669] Lichtenburg (1998) 120.
[670] Abdel-Wahab (1982) 89.
[671] Lichtenburg (1998) 120.
[672] Scheidel (2001) 102.
[673] See for example *P. Tebt.* 2.304 (AD 167-8, Tebtunis); *O. Claud.* 2.212 (AD 137-45, Mons Claudianus); *P. Mert.* 2.89 (AD 300, Arsinoite nome); *P. Oxy.* 4441 (AD 315-16, Oxyrhynchus).

very difficult. Consequently, although bandages and dressings are mentioned in the documentary papyri, another popular means of treating wounds to avoid infection was the poultice or plaster.

Honey and beeswax were crucial ingredients in ancient plasters and poultices. Honey is frequently to be found as a remedy in its own right, and as a means by which other remedies can be taken or applied with ease. One such recipe dating from the second century AD calls for 'the finest honey' (μέλιτο[ς] καλλισ[του]) to be pounded and mixed with rose petals, burnt copper, red sumac and Cilician saffron in order to make a dry plaster for 'all problems in the mouth' ([π]άντα τὰ ἐν τῷ στομα[τι πάθη]).[674] Since it specified the use of high quality honey and imported saffron, this was likely a very expensive remedy and not widely used, although perhaps substitutions could have been made. By comparison, the remains of a pharmacological manual also dating from the second century AD contain fragments of a whole series of recipes for plasters, of varying levels of complexity and cost. The first recipe is very simple, indicating that a sweet raisin should be pounded and applied with honey.[675] The sweet raisin was often praised for its medicinal applications in antiquity, particularly its cleansing properties, which were specifically noted by Galen.[676] A later recipe is for 'pain and inflammation of the testicles' (ὄρχεων πόνον κα[ὶ] φλεγμονάς); it contains rue leaves and bay leaves that are ground up with honey.[677] Both rue and bay leaves were considered beneficial for inflammations in antiquity, as well as being readily available through either private cultivation or purchase.[678]

The *Michigan Medical Codex*, thought to date to the fourth century AD, is devoted to recipes for plaster and both honey and beeswax appear as an ingredient in a number of them. The first surviving recipe is for the 'Parygron' (Πάρυγρον) plaster, which contains pig fat, white beeswax, white lead and litharge.[679] The Parygron plaster was evidently a well-known and extremely popular plaster; it is promoted in treatises by medical writers such as Hippocrates, Galen, Aetius and Paul of Aegina.[680] Another recipe included is for the 'Azanites' (Ἀζανίτης) plaster.[681] It comes highly recommended for 'malignant sores', particularly those that result from infected surgical incisions and contains pitch, wax, oesypum, pig fat and bull fat, and pine resin. It also instructs that more should be used to treat ulcers, less to encourage cicatrisation. Like the Parygron plaster, the Azanites plaster is promoted by medical writers; Galen states 'the plaster of Azanites has many uses and is highly

esteemed'.[682] Another recipe included is for a plaster that 'promotes cicatrisation', which contains calamine, burnt river crabs, white lead, wax and myrtle oil.[683] This recipe is very similar to one given by Paul of Aegina and attributed to Archigenes.[684] At the very least, the sticky components of these plasters would have acted as a barrier to cover the wound while it healed; presumably it was something of this kind that an individual at Mons Claudianus wanted when he wrote his letter requesting 'Send me a plaster for the wound'.[685]

4. Puerperal Fever

The process of pregnancy and childbirth in Roman Egypt has already been discussed, but the likelihood that numerous women in Roman Egypt suffered (sometimes fatally) from puerperal fever is implied by several documentary papyri. Puerperal fever can develop at any point between the first and tenth days following childbirth, miscarriage or abortion and is caused by an infection of the placental site within the uterus. If the infection enters the bloodstream it results in puerperal sepsis, a serious form of septicaemia.

A number of documents, ranging from private letters to legal petitions, were written to inform the recipient that the wife or sister of the writer had recently given birth or miscarried and was subsequently dying or dead. On 15th October AD 64, Thaubas wrote to her father Pompeios to inform him that his daughter Herennia had died: 'Please come home as soon as you receive my letter, because your poor daughter Herennia has died. And she already came safely through a premature delivery on the 9th of Phaophi. You see, she gave birth to an eight month child, dead; she lived on for four days, but then died herself'.[686] A petition written by Thouoni to Apollonios, the *strategos* of the Arsinoite nome, in AD 47 detailed how his wife had been assaulted 'unsparingly with hard blows on every part of her body ... although she was pregnant, so that she gave birth to a dead foetus, and she herself lies in her bed and is in danger of her life'.[687] Although neither of these examples uses the term πυρετός, the fact that both women survived the process of birth only to succumb some days later implies that they were suffering from puerperal fever. Unless the living conditions in which they were labouring were highly unusual and commendably hygienic and sanitary, they would probably have been surrounded by a number of other people, not to mention animals, both of which could have contributed to septicaemia and puerperal fever.

One of the ways women sought to protect themselves from death either in childbirth or shortly afterwards was by utilising some sort of magical or religious amulet. One surviving example of a certain type of uterine amulet

[674] *SB* 14.12175 (second century AD, unprovenanced).
[675] *P. Oxy.* 4975.1-2 (second century AD, Oxyrhynchus).
[676] Gal. *Alim. Fac.* 7.10; Oribasius, *Collectiones* 3.13.10, 3.24.1.
[677] *P. Oxy.* 4975. 5-6 (second century, Oxhyrhynchus).
[678] Dioscorides, *De Materia Medica* 1.78.1, 3.45.3.
[679] *P. Mich.*17.758 (Inv. 21 A) (fourth century AD, unprovenanced).
[680] Hippocrates, *De fracturis* 3.18 B 598.10. Gal. *SMT* 11.2; *Comp. Med. Gen.* 2.6. Aët. 15. Paul of Aegina, *De Re Medica Libri Septem* 9.
[681] *P. Mich.* 17.758 (Inv. 21 B) (fourth century AD, unprovenanced).

[682] Gal. *Comp. Med. Gen.* 5.2. See also Aët. 15; Oribasius *Fr.* 90; Paul of Aegina, *De Re Medica Libri Septem* 7.19.6.
[683] *P. Mich.* 17.758 (Inv. 21 B Verso) (fourth century AD, unprovenanced).
[684] Paul of Aegina, *De Re Medica Libri Septem* 4.26.4.
[685] *O. Claud.* Inv. 1.1564 (AD 100-120, Mons Claudianus).
[686] *P. Fouad* 1.75 (AD 64, Oxyrhynchus)
[687] *P. Mich.* 5.228 (AD 47, Areos Kome).

(currently exhibited in the Kelsey Museum of Archaeology (see Figure 12)) has been carved out of a fragment of haematite, also known as 'bloodstone', and depicts a uterus with a lock at the uterine mouth to ensure that the passage only opens and closes as required, encircled by an *ouroboros* (a snake eating its own tail), a symbol of protection and containment.[688] Painted terracotta figurines depicting either women in labour or deities particularly associated with childbirth (maternal goddesses such as Isis, Hathor or Tawaret, or the protective deity of women and children, the dwarf god Bes) have been found in houses, indicating that they were present during the process of childbirth, and were perhaps family heirlooms. Another means of obtaining protection (presumably well in advance of the onset of labour) seems to have involved making some sort of ritual offering at shrines. One example of this practice (currently exhibited in the British Museum (see Figure 13)) is a sculptor's sandstone trial piece depicting a woman in labour and sitting with her feet on birthing bricks, 18 cm long, 13.6 cm wide and 4 cm thick.[689]

5. Medical Healing

Celsus states that patients suffering from fever frequently died due to their doctors treating them incorrectly.[690] It is also worth noting that the standard ancient medical treatment of bleeding a patient could have actually contributed to the spread of disease through the use of unclean medical equipment which was thus contaminated. By the middle of the first century AD, it was recognised that there was no effective medicinal cure for quartan fever, so alternative methods would have been sought for the treatment and prevention of this type of fever at least, even if physicians continued to attempt the treatment of quotidian and tertian fevers.[691]

A medical prescription dating from the late second century contains a recipe for a remedy for περίοδος, used to indicate an intermittent fever: 'Fit of fever: for eight + *drachmae* (weight) of red lead, one *drachma*; for one kotyle of oil, one *drachma* two obol; for twenty-eight *drachmae* (weight) of wax, two *drachmae*, total four *drachmae*, one obol'.[692] Considering the ingredients, it seems likely that they were mixed together into a paste which was then rubbed on the body of the sufferer.

Excavations undertaken in the village of Tebtunis in the Fayum recovered a variety of medical treatises, written in both Greek and Demotic, in addition to objects used in the preparation and administration of medicaments such as small wooden containers used for storing medicinal remedies in the form of both unguents and powders.[693] One of these medical treatises was a fragment of an extract of Herodotus Medicus' *On Remedies*, dating to the second century AD, which corresponds to a section of the same text preserved in the writings of the Emperor Julian's doctor Oribasius.[694] This extract describes treatment considered appropriate for a fever that is marked by paroxysms and thirst:

> At the times of aggravation there are many causes of increase. If during the paroxysms the patient is also attacked by severe and unbearable thirst, not because of the malignity or complication of the diseases but owing to some peculiarity of the affection, this must of necessity be taken as a mischance and relieved even if such a treatment is not required by the stage of the illness. Such will be judged to be the case if the increase of thirst is out of proportion to the height of the fever. The constitution of the patient must also be taken into consideration; for if he has general endurance but is nevertheless unable to bear the thirst [...][695]

This approach seems to be in line with Celsus' opinion that any treatments used against malaria should take care not to weaken the patient.[696]

---

[688] See Bonner (1950) 275, Hanson (1995) and Ritner (1984).

[689] If craftsmen and women were in the habit of utilising their tools for purposes other than strictly professional ones, it follows that they might also have utilised items that would otherwise have served no further professional purpose (such as trial pieces of sculpture) but were by no means considered useless and fit only to be discarded.

[690] Celsus, *Med.* 3.8.2.

[691] Plin. *HN* 30.30.98-9.

[692] *P. NYU* Inv. 468 (late second century, unprovenanced): περίοδος: σειρικοῦ (δραχμαὶ) η (δραχμὴ) α ἐλαίου κοτ(ύλη α (δραχμὴ) α (ὀβολὸς) κηροῦ (δραχμαὶ) κη (δραχμαὶ) β (δραχμαὶ) δ γί(νεται (δραχμαὶ) κα (ὀβολοὶ 2).

[693] Hanson (2005) 394.

[694] Oribasius, *Collectiones* 5.30.6-7.

[695] *P. Tebt.* 272 (late second century AD, Tebtunis).

[696] Celsus, *Med.* 3.4.8; 3.4.9.

Figure 12: Haematite uterine amulet, second-fourth century AD, Egypt
(Kelsey Museum of Archaeology Inv. 02.6067, drawn by author)

Figure 13: Sandstone trial piece with birthing scene, Graeco-Roman period, Egypt
(British Museum Inv. 1839, 0921.704, image courtesy of the British Museum)

In addition to a number of other medical treatises written in Greek, the work known as the *Crocodilopolis Medical Book*, written in Demotic and also dating from the second century AD, was recovered from the same location. It is thought to have come from one of the libraries belonging to the temple of Sobek/Suchos, and it contains a whole section taken from a treatise entitled *Treatment of Various Feverish Diseases*.[697] The content is not restricted solely to treatments for tertian and quartan fever, but ranges from fevers caused by infection to mouth disease to female complaints. The medicinal recipes include a wide variety of ingredients, both native to Egypt and from outside the region, the result of trade both within and without the Roman Empire. According to Robert Ritner, the recipes included in the *Crocodilopolis Medical Book* collectively contain around 200 ingredients, of which five minerals and sixty plants are entirely new and indicative of the fusion of traditional Egyptian pharmacology with that of Greece and Rome.[698]

The recovery of treatises such as these, in addition to a variety of other medical treatises on subjects such as ophthalmology and dentistry, all from the same location, indicates that it was entirely possible to receive medical treatment for fevers in Roman Egypt; although this medical treatment was provided by temple priests rather than physicians. Consequently, Peter van Minnen has suggested that the medical texts recovered from Tebtunis were copies owned by individual priests rather than an official part of the temple libraries.[699] However, Ann Ellis

Hanson has offered an alternative explanation, positing that the medical texts written in Greek originally belonged to privileged families who spent periods of time in Tebtunis. Her suggestion is that these members of the social elite brought the texts with them in order to enable the village priests, who were already in the habit of providing medical care to other villagers, to provide the more sophisticated medical treatment they were used to receiving from medical practitioners in the *metropoleis*.[700]

6. Magical Healing
Considering the lack of understanding of the nature and causes of fever, combined with the periodic recurrence of tertian and quartan fevers and the recognition that medical treatment was not necessarily effective and could even do more harm than good, it is not surprising that people resorted to magical remedies in an attempt to both prevent and treat fevers.

The use of amulets to protect individuals from fever is directly attested during the reigns of Caracalla (AD 198-217), Constantius (AD 337-61) and Valentinian (AD 364-75). According to the *Historia Augusta*, while Caracalla was campaigning in Raetia in AD 213 he put a number of men to death for a variety or reasons: 'Some were even condemned for wearing [garlands] around their necks as preventives of quartan or tertian fever'.[701] The emperor Constantius II is reported to have executed large numbers of people for practising this type of medical magic, along with other, more sinister, varieties.[702] Later a similar course of action seems to have been taken by

---

[697] *P. Vienna* 6257; see Reymond (1976) for translation and commentary. However, this version has been widely criticised by scholars for errors in translation and interpretation so it will not be used extensively here.
[698] Ritner (2000) 113.
[699] van Minnen (1998) 168.

[700] Hanson (2005) 401.
[701] SHA *Carac.* 5.7.4.
[702] Amm. Marc. 19.12.14.

Valentinian.[703] Although those in the immediate vicinity of certain emperors were persecuted for attempting to prevent or alleviate fevers using magical amulets, there is evidence to suggest that this practice was employed widely in Roman Egypt. One fragment of a magical spell dating to between the third and fourth centuries AD states 'Phylactery for daily fever with shivering fits: Write on a clean piece of papyrus and wear as an amulet'.[704] There are two other fragments of spells with similar content. The first, dating from the third century AD, states '[For fever with shivering fits:] Take an olive leaf and engrave [For daily] and nightly fever', while the second, dating from between the third and fourth centuries AD, states 'For daily fever and nightly fever: On the shiny side of an olive leaf write [-] and on the dark side write [-] and wear it as an amulet'.[705]

Although these spells are fragmentary, it is clear from the content that survives that all three of them were written with the express purpose of providing instructions that enabled the caster to create an amulet that either stopped the wearer from contracting fever or alleviated the symptoms once the fever had been contracted. Although papyrus is commonly recommended for making magical amulets due to the plant's ubiquity in the Nile Delta, the recommendation of olive leaves is more unusual. Pliny's *Natural History* lists fifty folk remedies for malaria, the majority of which are supposed to be used as amulets, and does not include the olive leaf amongst them; on the contrary, the majority consists of ingredients harvested from animals. According to Strabo, the only place in Egypt that olives were cultivated was the Arsinoite nome, and the only other place where olive trees were grown was in the gardens of Alexandria and although these provided olives, they were not used to produce olive oil.[706] The fact that olive trees only grew in Alexandria or the Arsinoite nome at this time rather restricts the availability of olive leaves for magical practices.

There are six other magical spells, five written in Greek and one written in Demotic that were used against fever and date to between the third and fourth centuries AD.[707] While it is possible, if not probable, that some of the pieces of papyrus that the spells were written on were themselves used as amulets, none of these spells contain instructions about making an amulet like those found in the three spells already discussed. However, one of the Greek spells and the Demotic spell both instruct the caster to recite magical words over oil before spreading the oil on the body, although the ways in which the spells do this are entirely different, and in these instances, it is

the oil that is imbued with magical power, as opposed to an amulet. The Greek spell, dating to between the third and fourth century AD, instructs, 'for fever with shivering fits: Take oil in your hands and say seven times, "SABAOTH" (add the usual, twice). And spread on oil from the sacrum to the feet'.[708] The Demotic spell, dating to the third century AD, includes a lengthy narrative:

> He said, 'Go away from me! I have no [way] to eat. My head hurts; my body hurts. A fever has taken hold of me; a south wind has seized me. Does Isis [stop] making magic? Does Nephthys stop curing? Are the sixteen those of the avenger? Is my one a divine power of a god? Are [the 365] gods sitting down to eat the produce of the fields of the Nile, my great one, until they remove the fever from the head of the son of Isis, from the head of NN, whom NN bore, being the fever of night, the fever of midday, headache, this burning, this heat of the fevers of those below the brow to his feet, [until they] remove [it] from the head of NN, whom NN bore?' [Say it] over genuine oil, seven times; anoint his hand, his body, his feet; and speak to him.[709]

It is notable that both spells instruct the caster to repeat the verbal part of the spell seven times over the oil before anointing the subject of the spell with it, although they do require different parts of the body to be anointed. During the course of the narrative of the Demotic spell, the patient suffering from the fever is identified with Horus, a common practice in Egyptian magical spells that sought to heal as it recalled the occasions on which Horus was healed of grievous conditions by his mother, Isis.

The remaining six spells, all written in Greek, include names in the body of the text; the spells were personalised, written and cast with specific people in mind. It is apparent that two of these spells were written for people that were already suffering from a fever and the aim of both spells was to cure these particular fevers. One of these spells dates to the third century AD and states its purpose quite simply: 'Get rid of Althea's daily fever with shivering fits'.[710] The other is more complicated. It dates to between the third and fourth centuries AD, specifically directs its request to 'excellent ruling angels' and includes a triangular charm with the text.[711] The folds in the papyrus indicate that it was rolled up, perhaps in order to be placed inside a small cylindrical container and worn on the body. This has led to its being classed as a Christian fever amulet.

---

[703] Amm. Marc. 29.2.26.
[704] *PGM* 7.218-221.
[705] *PGM* 119b.1-5; *PGM* 7.213-214.
[706] Strabo, *Geographica* 17.35. While this may have been the case during the early first century BC when Strabo was in Egypt, there is a significant amount of evidence to suggest that in later centuries, the Dakhleh Oasis was an important centre for the cultivation of olive groves and the production of olive oil.
[707] There is a seventh spell, *PGM* 91.1-14, written in Greek and dating to between the third and fourth century AD, that seems to be concerned with fever but it is very fragmented and reconstruction of the specifics is problematic so it will not be included here.

[708] *PGM* 7.211-212.
[709] *PDM* 14.1219-1227.
[710] *PGM* 104.1-8.
[711] *PGM* 88.1-19.

The remaining four spells seem to have been less focused; their aims seem to be a more general type of protection. One of them is concerned with a brother and sister, Dionysius and Anys, and requests that they are protected from 'each and every shivering fit and fever, whether daily or intermittent [fever] by night or day, or quartan fever'.[712] The second addresses a deity know as Kouk Kouk Koul, and requests that Tais is protected from 'every shivering fit, whether tertian or quartan or quotidian, or an every-other-day fever, or [one] by night, or [even] a mild fever'.[713] Like the Christian fever amulet discussed above, this papyrus also includes a triangular charm with the text and the folds in it indicate that it was rolled up from the top down, perhaps in order to be placed inside a small cylindrical container and worn on the body. Although it was recovered from a house in Tebtunis, it is very similar to a papyrus found at Heracleopolis that has now been lost.[714] The third addresses a deity referred to as both Adonaios and Adonai, an important figure in Gnosticism and magic with Jewish origins. It requests that Touthous be protected from 'every shivering fit and fever: tertian, quartan, quotidian, daily, or every other day [it occurs]'.[715] The fourth addresses the 'Lord Gods' and requests that Helena be protected from 'every illness and every shivering and [fever], ephemeral, quotidian, tertian, quar[tan]'.[716] It is also arranged in the shape of a triangular charm, and would likely have been worn rolled up into a cylinder. However, more peculiarly, the text is accompanied by decorative illustrations of a star and a lunar crescent. These spells are interesting because they indicate that, seemingly as far as magical practice was concerned, no matter what the origins of any given spell, fevers were grouped together, whether they occurred during the day or night and no matter what their duration.

7. Religious Healing

The cults of the fever goddesses Febris, Tertiana and Quartana were worshipped in the city of Rome, Roman Italy and other parts of the western Roman Empire. However, there is no evidence for the existence of any of these cults in Roman Egypt; the furthest east that evidence for the cult of Dea Febris has been found is on the island of Samos.[717]

A literary papyrus from Oxyrhynchus, dating to the early second century AD, contains an extensive work written in praise of the deity Imouthes-Asclepius. Imhotep (Imouthes in Greek) was an historical figure who lived and died during the reign of King Zoser, a Pharaoh of the third dynasty, and was subsequently deified.[718] Asclepius was the Graeco-Roman god of medicine. The cult of Imouthes-Asclepius is well attested in votive inscriptions from Deir el-Bahri; the writer of the literary papyrus even

states that the purpose of it, the only extract surviving from a much longer work, is to provide a votive offering to the god that will last longer than an inscription or a sacrifice. The writer first details how his mother was healed by the deity:

> For three years my mother was distracted by an ungodly quartan ague which had seized her, at length … we came as suppliants before the god, entreating him to grant recovery from the disease. He, having shown himself favourable, as he is to all, in dreams, cured her by simple remedies; and we rendered due thanks to our preserver by sacrifices.[719]

As detailed previously, a 'quartan ague' is a type of malarial fever indicative of *P. malariae* that peaks every seventy-two hours and is not generally fatal. However, while not necessarily fatal, this type of fever is still fairly debilitating and undoubtedly inconvenient, particularly when suffered over such a long period of time. The fact that the writer describes his mother as 'distracted' by her fever supports this. The sheer length of time his mother lived with the fever before seeking a cure from Asclepius through an incubation ritual makes it probable that she had exhausted all other attempts to find a cure; as discussed above, although by this point it had been recognised that there was no effective medical cure for quartan fever, numerous magical spells and amulets against the disease circulated in Egypt during this period.

It seems that the writer was so impressed his mother's cure that, when later suffering from an illness himself, he went straight to the temple of Asclepius, indicating that recommendations from trusted family members and friends could play a significant part in choosing a healing strategy and perhaps even become a tradition over time: 'When I too afterwards was suddenly seized with a pain in my right side, I quickly hastened to the helper of the human race'.[720] His account of his own illness and cure is, as might be expected, much more detailed than that of his mother's:

> It was night, when every living creature was asleep except those in pain, but divinity showed itself more effectively; a violent fever burned me, and I was convulsed with loss of breath and coughing, owing to the pain proceeding from my side. Heavy in the head with my troubles I was lapsing half-conscious into sleep, and my mother, as a mother would for her child (and she is by nature affectionate), being extremely grieved at my agonies was sitting without enjoying even a short period of slumber, when she suddenly perceived - it was no dream or sleep for her eyes were open immovably, though not

---

[712] *PGM* 18b.1-7.
[713] *PGM* 33.1-25 (third century AD, Tebtunis).
[714] *BGU* 957.
[715] *PGM* 106.1-10.
[716] *PGM* 130 /*P. Mich.* Inv. 6666 (third century AD, unprovenanced). For publication and translation, see Daniel (1983).
[717] Burke (1996) 2266.
[718] *P. Oxy.* 1381 (second century AD, Oxyrhynchus).

[719] *P. Oxy.* 1381: 64-91.
[720] *P. Oxy.* 1381: 91-4.

seeing clearly, for a divine and terrifying vision came to her, easily preventing her from observing the god himself or his servants, whichever it was. In any case there was one whose height was more than human, clothed in shining raiment and carrying in his left hand a book, who after merely regarding me two or three times from head to foot disappeared. When she recovered herself, she tried, still trembling, to wake me, and finding that the fever had left me and that much sweat was pouring off me, did reverence to the manifestation of the god, and then wiped me and made me more collected.[721]

It is clear that the writer experienced an entirely different type of fever from his mother: he expressly states that his mother suffered from a quartan fever for three years, while his fever developed rapidly as a result of pains he was experiencing on his right-hand side. However, despite these differences, an incubation ritual at the temple of Asclepius apparently cured both illnesses. In fact, the god cured the writer's fever first and it was only after a second incubation ritual that the pains in his side, the original cause of the fever in the first place, were themselves alleviated. This account is also interesting in the writer's description of his mother's actions while he is wracked with fever; he writes that she remained awake throughout the night, aggrieved 'as a mother would [be] for her child (and she is by nature affectionate)', in order to nurse him through his ordeal, clean him up and calm him down afterwards. Even though the pair went to the temple of Asclepius specifically to seek religious healing and enable the writer to undertake an incubation ritual, they maintained an element of domestic healing practice throughout.

Conclusion

Fevers were prevalent throughout Roman Egypt at all levels of society. The lack of understanding as to the true nature of fever (as a symptom of an illness rather than an illness in itself) has ensured that accurately diagnosing the cause of any fever mentioned within the documentary papyri is problematic. Ultimately, if neither a lengthy description of the fever in question nor the circumstances under which it developed/ was contracted are included, the chance of an accurate reconstruction is limited. However, certain inferences can often be made. In the case of puerperal fever, virtually every woman of childbearing age in the entire province (no matter what her social status, ethnicity or religion, or whether she was undergoing her first or fifth pregnancy) was at risk. With regard to fevers caused by bacterial infection of wounds, both men and women were at risk from injuries sustained during assaults or accidents, while for contagious diseases such as measles, smallpox or 'plague', certain settlements such as Alexandria and Berenike experienced

a great deal of seasonal migration and thus exposure to unfamiliar pathogens. Living conditions in cities, towns and even villages were close and cramped, and personal cleanliness and hygiene were often poor. In the case of diarrhoea or malarial fevers, the proximity of the majority of settlements in Egypt to the Nile, its tributaries or its canals ensured that people were surrounded by plenty of contaminated or stagnant water.

The examples discussed in this chapter have ranged geographically from the villages of the Fayum (which, it important to note, were located around Lake Moeris), to Oxyrhynchus (situated adjacent to Nile alongside the canal) to the Dakhleh and Kharga Oases in the Western Desert (which received their water by irrigation system) and Mons Claudianus in the Eastern Desert (where the rubbish dumps were situated in proximity to the living quarters). As with the victims of eye complaints in the previous chapter, the status of the individuals involved has ranged from those wealthy enough to afford elaborate funerary monuments carved from stone and plasters containing the finest imported honey and saffron, to soldiers and quarry workers and consequently the fact that people resorted to numerous different ways of dealing with fevers is not surprising. With regard to preventative measures, medical, magical and religious strategies could be utilised individually or collectively, and a certain amount of overlap between these strategies is evident. Individuals anticipating childbirth could purchase protective amulets whose quality of craftsmanship varied widely (whether carved in stone or written on papyrus) or deposit votive offerings in a shrine or temple of their choice in anticipation of the event, while at the same time tasking their family members and friends to acquire unguents, salves and oils to both ease the labour and safeguard them in the immediate aftermath when they were at risk from infection and puerperal fever. Similarly, an individual unlucky enough to suffer an open wound through assault or accident could dress or bandage the wound, or apply a plaster or poultice in an attempt to protect it from any subsequent contamination, and like the salves produced to treat *ophthalmia*, these plasters and poultices could utilise a variety of ingredients, some expensive and luxurious but most the sort of items that would already be present within the home and garden or the near vicinity.

If, however, despite these precautionary measures, a fever developed or was contracted, it is clear that there were numerous medical treatises in circulation. Such medical treatises contained treatments for a whole range of different types of fevers, whether quotidian, tertian, quatrain, with shivering fits, with extreme thirst, with paroxysms. In addition to these medical treatises, there were abundant magical spells and charms aimed specifically at treating fever, some requiring incantations, some even requiring anointing with oil and other substances. There was also the possibility of undergoing an incubation ritual at a shrine or temple and the deities that dealt with fever in Roman Egypt were not necessarily the same ones as elsewhere in the empire. Depending on the nature of the fever suffered, any number of healing

---

[721] *P. Oxy.* 1381: 95-140.

strategies might have been deemed appropriate. If a woman was suffering from puerperal fever, a midwife might have been preferable to a physician, although it is clear that families also made their own arrangements. If an individual was suffering from malaria and had experienced a sufficient number of prior attacks, any additional help might have been entirely unnecessary if he or she knew exactly what to do for themselves, but once recovered, the aid of a temple priest might be sought. If someone living in an isolated location like Mons Claudianus injured themselves and did not have access to what they needed in the way of dressings, bandages, plaster or poultices, they would write to a family member or friend for the necessary items and then presumably treat themselves using them.

If Roman Egypt is considered in isolation, it is apparent that the means by which fevers were most frequently dealt with differ significantly from the means by which eye complaints were most frequently dealt with. With respect to enumerating references to different types of healing strategy, there are far more allusions to magical healing than there are to medical or even religious healing, although some overlap is present on occasion.

Both with regard to preemptive prevention and a means of curing after the fact, magical amulets and spells appear to have been the preferred way of dealing with fever. This may well have been because, unlike a suppurating eyeball or eyelid, a fever is essentially invisible. There is no precise part of the body that the symptoms (which might include headache, rash, sweating, shivering, and being hot or cold to the touch) manifest themselves. Also unlike an eye infection, a fever could be seriously physically and mentally debilitating, not only affecting an individual's body, but also, often, their mind and with it their ability to function in normal life, albeit temporarily. The processes by which contagious diseases such as measles, smallpox, typhoid or malaria were transmitted were not entirely understood. Some means of treatment such as bleeding or sharing of instruments or medicaments might even spread the disease further. Even if the original cause of the fever was a complicated childbirth or perhaps a minor flesh wound, once the infection had progressed to septicaemia or even gangrene, the victim would exhibit symptoms elsewhere on their body, which in turn would perhaps make a holistic method such as a magical incantation seem that much more appropriate and, hopefully, effective.

CHAPTER FIVE

WILD ANIMALS IN ROMAN EGYPT

1. Introduction

According to Diodorus Siculus, writing in the middle of the first century BC, 'the upper part of [Egypt] is to this day desert and infested with wild beasts'.[722] This statement is supported by copious graffiti left at places of pilgrimage such as the remote shrine of the Egyptian god Min (equated with the Greek god Pan) at el-Kanaïs, located about fifty-five kilometres east of Edfu in the Eastern Desert along one of the major routes between the Nile Valley and the Red Sea coast.[723] These προσκύνηματα are addressed primarily to Pan Euhodos, the god of good or successful journeys (there are references to some other deities such as Arsinoe II Philadelphos and the Jewish god) and offer thanks for a safe end to what would in all likelihood have been an extremely dangerous trip. During the Pharaonic period the area was originally used for mining gold before the Red Sea trade in the Ptolemaic period led to an increase in sea travel and the hunting of wild animals, so anyone travelling in the vicinity ran the risk of encountering wild animals or even Τρωγλοδύται, Troglodytes or 'cave-dwellers'.[724]

A petition and a magical spell make it clear that little changed in Egypt over the course of the Roman period. In the petition, dating to 22nd December AD 216, Aurelia Tisais wrote to the centurion Aurelius Julius Marcellinus and stated that 'My father Kalabalis...who is a hunter, set off with my brother Neilos as long ago as the 3rd of the present month to hunt hares, and up to this time they have not returned. I therefore suspect that they have met with some accident'.[725] The magical spell, dating to either the third or fourth century AD, reiterates that people still ran the risk of encountering wild animals, marauding tribesmen or desperate criminals as they travelled: 'Against every wild animal, aquatic creature and robbers: Attach a tassel to your garment and say: "LŌMA ZATH AIŌN ACHTHASE MA...ZAL BALAMAŌN ĒIEOY, protect me, NN, in the present hour; immediately, immediately; quickly, quickly."'[726]

The exotic wildlife that permeated Egypt was a popular *topos* in both literature and art elsewhere in the Roman Empire.[727] It is clear that life in Roman Egypt was fraught with danger from the native wildlife and that certain creatures were particularly problematic. This chapter will examine the snake, the scorpion, the crocodile and the lion in turn; their presence in Roman Egypt; their interaction with the inhabitants of the province; the injuries they inflicted and the methods used to treat these injuries. This will be followed by a study of the use of the animals themselves as ingredients in *materia medica*, aphrodisiacs and cosmetics. Finally, the variety of ways in which these animals were specifically associated with ancient Egyptian, Greek and Roman deities renowned for their healing powers and the apparent contradiction of this association will be considered. More so than with eye conditions and fevers, the approaches to healing utilised to deal with the injuries inflicted by wild animals combine professional and alternative healing strategies, integrating medical, magical and religious methods of healing and specifically incorporating elements of the unique natural environment of Egypt during the Roman period.

2. Wild Animals in Roman Egypt

The spell 'against every wild animal, aquatic creature and robbers' cited above has a fairly broad remit: its purpose was to prevent attacks from happening at all by warding off the enormous variety of malign creatures or individuals that might serve as a threat to the caster.[728] However, such a spell was obviously of no use once an individual had been attacked, which meant alternative measures needed to be taken. A type of apotropaic artefact designated a 'Horus *cippus*' or 'Horus on the crocodiles' was not only a protective talisman to guard against attacks by wild animals, but also an apparatus to be employed to effect healing after the fact. The ancient Egyptians realised that animal bites and stings were responsible for injecting toxic substances, or *metut*, into the human body and it was these toxic substances that

---

[722] Diod. Sic. 1.24.6.

[723] According to an inscription left by the founder of the site, the nineteenth dynasty pharaoh Seti I, his motivation for founding it was to provide a well at which travellers in the desert could quench their thirst.

[724] For *proskynema* inscriptions to Pan Euhodos and associated gods and goddesses dating from throughout the Ptolemaic period, see Bernand (1972) and Mairs (2010). For a *proskynema* giving thanks for safe sea travel, see for example Bernand 42/*CIJ* II: 1537 (Ptolemaic period, el-Kanaïs): θεοῦ εὐλογία· Θεύδοτος Δωρίωνος Ἰουδαῖος σωθεὶς ἐκ πελ<άγ>ους. For a proskynema giving thanks for a safe hunting expedition - accompanied by a sketch of an elephant - see for example Bernand 9bis (270-64 BC, el- Kanaïs): Δωρίων τέκτων, τῶν μετ' Εὐμήδου ἀνὰ ζεύξας ἐπὶ τὴν θήραν τῶν ἐλεφάντων καὶ ἐσώθην εἰς Αἴγυπτον. For *proskynema* giving thanks for avoiding Troglodytes, see for example Bernand 43/*SB* 5.8863 (Ptolemaic period, el- Kanaïs): Πανὶ Εὐόδωι Σωτῆρι Μελανιᾶς Ἀπολλωνίου Περγάος σωθὲν [σωθεὶς] ἐκ Τρωγοδυτῶν.

[725] *P. Tebt.* 2.333 (AD 216, Tebtunis): τοῦ πατρός μου, κύριε, Καλαβάλεως κυνηγοῦ τυγχάνοντος ἀποδημήσαντος σὺν τῷ ἀδελφῷ μου Νείλῳ ἔτι ἀπὸ τῆς γ τοῦ ὄντος μηνὸς πρὸς κυνηγίαν λαγοῶν μέχρι τούτ[ο]υ οὐκ ἐπανῆλθον. ὑφορῶμαι οὖν μὴ ἔπαθον τι ἀνθρώπινον. See Alston (1995) 86-96 for the use of centurions as a common point of reference for assistance in Roman Egypt.

[726] *PGM* 7.370-373.

[727] For the portrayal of Egypt in Greek and Roman literature, see Nimis (2004). For the portrayal of Egypt in Greek and Roman art, see for example the popularity of Nilotic scenes in interior decoration of houses and temples throughout the Roman Empire, discussed in Meyboom (1995) and Versluys (2002).

[728] For a similar spell that specifically mentions scorpions and snakes (albeit from a slightly later date) see *P. Oslo* 1. 5 (fourth-fifth century AD, unprovenanced), translated and discussed in Tod (1939) 58.

subsequently caused health problems.[729] Numerous examples of Horus *cippi* survive and the majority of these can be dated definitively to the Late Period through the Ptolemaic period, although there is some disagreement amongst scholars over whether certain *cippi* actually date slightly later, to the Roman period.[730] Typically, a Horus *cippus* depicted the apotropaion of the god Horus in the form of a child, complete with sidelock, trampling upon crocodiles and holding any number of wild creatures, usually snakes and scorpions but also lions and gazelles, in his hands to prevent them from biting.[731] Around this central image magical spells were inscribed, originally in hieroglyphs but the quality of the hieroglyphic script deteriorated over time and was eventually replaced entirely by Greek. For additional protection, sometimes the head of the god Bes was included over the central image. The surviving examples make it clear that the *cippi* were available in a variety of sizes, from small enough for an individual to wear as an amulet (some even have holes drilled into them to allow for suspension from a cord) or otherwise carry around, to large enough to be set up as a monument in the courtyard of a temple or even be built into the temple itself.[732] The larger versions often incorporated channels or basins; water was poured over the *cippi* and collected in them, believed to have thus absorbed the power emanating from the inscribed magical spells, and some Horus *cippi* that have been removed from their original contexts are still attached to their basins.[733] The water would then be drunk by or poured upon an individual who had suffered at the hands of these wild animals, the most common injury likely being the bite of a snake or the sting of a scorpion. The best surviving example dates from around 350 BC and is known as the Metternich Stele; it is currently exhibited in the Metropolitan Museum of Art.[734] However, plenty of smaller, much less elaborate examples survive too and it is these specimens that would have been carried around with the inhabitants of Egypt on a daily basis as both a means of protection and as a cure.

Snakes

One of the earliest classical myths that mention Egypt includes details about its venomous snakes. On their journey back to Sparta from Troy, Menelaus and Helen visited the region and their helmsman Canopos fell asleep on the seashore where he was bitten by a viper. He died from the wound and as a consequence Menelaus founded the city of Canopus there in his memory. The event was

commemorated by Apollonius of Rhodes, a Hellenised Egyptian writing in the third century BC and best known for his *Argonautica*, who wrote a poem entitled *Canopos*. However, the only parts of the poem to survive are those detailing the wounds inflicted upon Canopos by the snake.[735]

One of the works tentatively attributed to the corpus of material written by Galen, dating to the early third century AD, relates how in Alexandria an asp was used as a method of execution. According to *On Theriac to Piso*: 'Whenever they want to put someone to death humanely and quickly - someone who has been sentenced by the law to this punishment - they throw the venomous creature against his chest and make him walk around a bit'.[736] While the lives and deaths of the criminals executed using asps in Alexandria go unrecorded, the political and historical significance of the suicide of Cleopatra VII ensured that numerous accounts of the event were circulated in antiquity, some written soon after it had occurred. The survival of a number of these accounts offers a unique opportunity to examine the consequences of snakebite in Egypt in 30 BC.

According to Florus, Cleopatra applied 'serpents to her veins [and] thus passed into death as into sleep'.[737] Velleius Paterculus offers slightly more detail by identifying the species of snake used: 'She caused an asp to be smuggled in to her, and ended her life by its venomous sting'.[738] Both Plutarch and Cassius Dio also put forward the theory that Cleopatra was killed by an asp, although they qualify this by adding that no one actually knows for certain and offer several alternative explanations.[739] The historical accounts that are the most useful for reconstructing the treatment that a victim of snakebite would, or possibly could, have received in Roman Egypt are those given by Suetonius and Cassius Dio. Suetonius recounts that Octavian 'greatly desired to save Cleopatra alive for his triumph, and even had Psylli brought to her, to suck the poison from her wound, since it was thought that she had died from the bite of an asp'.[740] Cassius Dio reiterates this: 'When Caesar heard of Cleopatra's death, he was astounded, and not only viewed her body but also made use of drugs and Psylli in

[729] Nunn (1996) 59.

[730] See Sternberg-El Hotabi (1999). The corpus comprises 433 *cippi* and approximate dates have been proposed for 300 of these.

[731] See Ritner (1989) for discussion of the iconography of the Horus *cippus* and Horus strangling these creatures in order to 'seal their mouths'. See also Collins (2002) 352 for the opinion that the crocodile, serpent, lion, scorpion and gazelle are all symbols of the 'wild realms' and represent the 'magical taming of the forces of chaos'.

[732] For examples of Horus *cippi* amulets with holes, see Musée du Louvre Inv. E.15824 (31 mm in height, 15 mm wide and 2 mm in depth) and E.15825 (27 mm in height, 11 mm wide and 1 mm in depth), both made from faience and dating to the Ptolemaic period.

[733] For Horus *cippi* with basins, see Cairo Museum Inv. 46341; and Cairo Museum Inv. 9402.

[734] Scott (1951).

[735] Apollonius of Rhodes, *Canopos Fr.3*. The event was subsequently utilised for its dramatic potential by Conon (*FGrH* 26 F I VIII) and Nicander of Colophon (Nic. *Ther.* 309), while Strabo (*Geographica* 17.1.17) reiterated that the city was named after Canopos because he died there.

[736] Gal. *Ther. Pis.* 8; this pragmatic use of a deadly breed of snake as a means of execution was mirrored in the temples of certain cults such as those of Sarapis and Asclepius, although in their case they utilised harmless ones such as *Elaph longissima* as their sacred animals.

[737] Flor. 2.21.11.11: *Admotisque ad venas serpentibus sic morte quasi somno soluta est.*

[738] Vell. Pat. 2.87.1: *Cleopatra frustratis custodibus inlata aspide in morsu et sane eius expers muliebris metus spiritum reddidit.*

[739] Plut. *Vit. Ant.* 86; Dio Cass. 51.14.1-3; in any case, asps are not native to Egypt and it has been posited that if Cleopatra was bitten by a snake, it was in all likelihood a cobra.

[740] Suet. *Aug* 17.4: *Cleopatrae, quam servatam triumpho magno opere cupiebat, etiam Psyllos admovit, qui venenum ac virus exsugerent, quod perisse morsu aspidis putabatur.*

the hope that she might revive'.[741] It is clear from these accounts that Cleopatra was thought to have been treated with a combination of medicine in the form of drugs and magic administered by the Psylli, members of a north African tribe that were reputed to be immune to snake or scorpion venom and able to cure those who had been bitten or stung by such creatures.[742]

The surviving section of the Brooklyn Museum Papyrus, which dates to the early Ptolemaic Period and is written in Middle Egyptian, is concerned entirely with snakebites. It originally contained systematic descriptions of thirty-eight snakes and their bites in addition to possible treatments, but the first thirteen of these have been lost. Its purpose seems to have been to provide a pragmatic approach to treating snakebites (such as bandaging the wound with salt) that could be used by a priest of Serket, rather than a physician: 'In the hand of the *kherep* priests of Serket ... to drive away all snakes and to seal their mouths'.[743] The inclusion of a list of snakes, complete with descriptions of them and their bites, enabled the priest to identify the snake from a description given by the patient, so that the patient could then be given the appropriate treatment and prognosis. For an idea of the kind of treatment that a victim of snakebite could have received in Ptolemaic Egypt; see for example Papyrus Brooklyn 41: 'Very good remedies to be made for those suffering from all snakebites: Onion, ground finely in beer. Eat and spit out for one day'.[744]

Celsus also states that there were specific medical treatments available for the bites of snakes in the Roman world; however, the use of these obviously depended upon identifying the type of snake responsible for any given bite and Celsus' writings do not include the kind of comprehensive list that is included in the Brooklyn Papyrus. Fortunately, there were additional measures that could be used for any bite, in the event that identification of the snake responsible was not possible:

> First the limb is to be constricted above this kind of wound, but not too tightly, lest it become numbed; next, the poison is to be drawn out. A cup does this best. But it is not amiss beforehand to make incisions with a scalpel around the wound, in order that more of the vitiated blood may be extracted. If there is no cup at hand, although this can hardly happen, use any similar vessel which can do what you want; if there is not even this, a man must be got to suck the wound.[745]

It is important to remember that in the case of Cleopatra, although later writers unanimously considered an asp to have been the type of snake responsible, Plutarch specifically states that no trace of a snake was found in Cleopatra's chamber.[746] It is possible, even probable, that the people tasked with providing immediate medical assistance to the stricken queen had no idea which species of reptile had bitten her, if indeed a snake was even responsible (Cleopatra herself would most likely have been disinclined to enlighten them, in view of the fact that this was her second suicide attempt). In this case offering a remedy that depended upon identifying the snake correctly before it could be administered would be impractical. In addition to the procedure described by Celsus, Galen also relates an example of how surgical intervention could be used to treat snakebite, without necessarily needing to identify the snake responsible:

> When I was in Alexandria, a peasant was bitten on one of his fingers by a viper not too far from the city. With a very tight, strong tourniquet he ligated the root of this finger next to the metacarpal bone. And, running to the city to his usual doctor, he presented his entire finger to be amputated from the metacarpal joint, in the hope that he would not suffer anything [fatal] as a consequence of this [snakebite]. He in fact succeeded in accordance with his hope, for his life was saved without any other treatment.[747]

The fact that Octavian was able to bring members of the Psylli to Cleopatra soon enough after the initial bite had occurred to make them saving her life a possibility implies that members of the Psylli were present in Alexandria or its environs at this time. There are several ways to explain this. It is possible that Octavian had brought them with him in his entourage, wary of the destruction of Cato's army by venomous snakes in Libya some years previously, and prepared for any eventuality

[741] Dio Cass. 51.14.3-4.
[742] On the Psylli, see Hdt. 4.173; Strabo, *Geographica* 2.5.33 and 13.1.14; and particularly Plin. *HN* 7.2: 'Varro tells us, that there are still a few individuals in that district, whose saliva effectually cures the stings of serpents. The same, too, was the case with the tribe of the Psylli, in Africa, according to the account of Agatharchides; these people received their name from Psyllus, one of their kings, whose tomb is in existence, in the district of the Greater Syrtes. In the bodies of these people there was by nature a certain kind of poison, which was fatal to serpents, and the odour of which overpowered them with torpor: with them it was a custom to expose children immediately after their birth to the fiercest serpents, and in this manner to make proof of the fidelity of their wives, the serpents not being repelled by such children as were the offspring of adultery'. See also Ael. *NA* 1.57: 'Their method is this: if one of that tribe arrive, whether summoned or by chance, before the whole body is inflamed, and if he then rinse his mouth with water and wash the bitten man's hands and give him the water from both to drink, then the victim recovers and is thereafter free from all infection'.
[743] Nunn (1996) 40; the Brooklyn Museum Papyrus is translated into French and published in Sauneron (1970). An English translation is forthcoming.
[744] The onion was (and is) frequently utilised in folk medicine as a cure for snakebite, not just in Africa but also in India and North America, and chemical analyses have found it to contain a range of therapeutic properties; see Mors *et al.* (2000). It seems that in ancient Egypt, an onion could also used as a preventative; see for example *P. Brookl.* 42: 'If one grinds it in water and one smears a man with it, the snake will not bite him. If one grinds it in beer and sprinkles it all over the house one day in the new year, no serpent male or female will penetrate therein'.
[745] Celsus, *Med* 5.27.5.3 A-B.
[746] Plut. *Vit. Ant.* 86.
[747] Galen, *De loc.aff.* 3.11.

that might arise during his campaign against Antony.[748] It is equally possible that there were members of the Psylli either permanently or, coincidentally, temporarily in residence in Egypt, thus providing a plausible alternative for those afflicted with snakebites.[749] The fact that the priests of Serket are not mentioned as a possible means of treatment is interesting and there are several potential explanations for this. It is possible that at some point during the course of the three centuries since the Brooklyn Papyrus had been written, the priests of the cult ceased to function in this way. Alternatively, perhaps the cult was unknown outside of Egypt and their treatment of snakebite was inadvertently conflated with that of the Psylli, who were themselves well known in the ancient world, although their methods differed significantly. According to Pliny, there were two ways in which a member of the Psylli could provide a patient with relief from their wound: 'Of certain men the whole bodies are beneficent, for example the members of those families that frighten serpents. These by a mere touch or by wet suction relieve the bitten victims. In this class are the Psylli, the Marsi, and the Ophiogenes, as they are called, on the island of Cyprus'.[750] Cassius Dio also describes the Psylli and the magical powers attributed to them, adding the disclaimer that they needed to treat a patient immediately.[751] Suetonius' account of Cleopatra's death includes the information that the Psylli attempted to suck the poison out of her wound, which would also have involved touching her, so it would seem that they did actively try to save her life by using both of the methods reported to be at their disposal. Unlike Pliny and Cassius Dio, and indeed Octavian, who apparently believed in the Psylli and their abilities (or was, at the very least, prepared to try anything), Celsus was more sceptical that the Psylli were needed at all:

> I declare there is no particular science in those people who are called Psylli, but a boldness confirmed by experience. For serpent's poison, like certain hunter's poisons, such as the Gauls in particular use, does no harm when swallowed, but only in a wound. Hence the snake itself may be safely eaten, whilst its stroke kills; and if one is stupefied, which frauds effect by certain medicaments, and if anyone puts his finger into its mouth and is not bitten, its saliva is harmless. Anyone, therefore, who follows the example of the Psylli and sucks out the wound, will himself be safe, and will promote the safety of the patient. He must see to it, however, beforehand that he has no sore place on his gums or palate or other parts of the mouth.[752]

When considering the treatment of snakebite in Roman Egypt, it is important to remember that both Cleopatra and the peasant in the case related by Galen were reportedly bitten either in or in close proximity to Alexandria, where there was not only a thriving medical school but also a population large enough and wealthy enough to both warrant and support numerous doctors and their specialties. The same is true, to a lesser extent, of the sizeable towns in the *chora* such as Oxyrhynchus. However, for the residents of the villages and the oases in the deserts, such help may not have been available, leaving them to fend for themselves by attempting to suck the poison out of the wound in the manner of a member of the Psylli or Marsi, or applying salt or onion juice to it.

As might be expected from a civilisation that was renowned for its medicine and medical practice throughout antiquity, Egypt had developed a comprehensive system for dealing with the bites inflicted by the country's various species of snakes. The Brooklyn Papyrus shows that at least until the Ptolemaic period, snakebites were treated pragmatically, primarily using medicinal remedies although some magical spells were also incorporated. By the Roman period, treatment for snakebite evidently also included specifically surgical intervention such as bleeding and amputation.

Scorpions

The sting of a scorpion is the injury caused by a species of wildlife native to Egypt that is most frequently attested during the Roman period, referenced in a number of letters, epitaphs and mummy labels. Perhaps justifiably, fear of the sting of a scorpion appears to have been a major preoccupation of the inhabitants of the province, as attested to by the lengths people went to in an attempt to protect themselves.

Scorpions are nocturnal creatures; during the daytime they dig themselves down into the sand and then become more active after sunset, with a tendency to crawl into clothes and shoes during the night. Two ostraca recovered from the mining communities at Mons Claudianus in the Eastern Desert attest to individuals having been stung by a scorpion. One is a list of injured personnel that states that a man named Kalpenos was out of action due to a scorpion sting, but it provides no additional details.[753] The other is a private letter in which an individual complains, 'I was hindered by a scorpion sting on my foot. I am suffering'.[754] Considering the fact that the individual was stung on his or her foot, it is reasonable to assume that in this latter case the victim either stepped on a scorpion lurking in the sandy terrain of the Eastern Desert, or inadvertently fell prey to one that had crawled into his or her shoe. Certainly, people were aware of the dangers. One letter sent from a woman to her son instructs him to take care of her grandchild by making sure that the child wears shoes: 'Put something under them and tie it...because of a scorpion'.[755] Neither the list

[748] Luc. 9.619-838.
[749] See Nutton (1985) 138 for a discussion of Galen seeking out the *Marsi* in Rome to get advice on poisons and antidotes.
[750] Plin. *HN* 28.6.30-33.
[751] Dio Cass. 51.14.3-4.
[752] Celsus, *Med* 5.27.5.3 B-C; see Nutton (1985) 139 for discussion of the Psylli tribe's abilities and whether they could be acquired by others.

[753] *O. Claud.* 212 (AD 137-45, Mons Claudianus).
[754] *O. Claud.* 223 (AD 153, Mons Claudianus).
[755] *O. Cair.* 60329, briefly discussed in Tod (1939) 61.

nor the letter from Mons Claudianus reveals whether the victims recovered from their stings, although both were alive at least long enough to report the incidents and may well have received treatment from a *marsus*, an army official that specialised in 'the antidotes and treatment in cases of snake-bite and scorpion-stings in those provinces where such precautions were necessary'.[756] However, there are examples of mummy labels and epitaphs that state a decedent's cause of death as a scorpion sting. A sandstone stele that dates to the reign of Augustus records how a woman was stung by a scorpion on 7th September AD 8 and died the following day: 'Tomb of Cleopatra, daughter of Memnon. Farewell…you who have perished ingloriously and indiscriminately by a violent death, unworthily of your goodness; for stung by a scorpion in the sanctuary of Thripis by the hill on the 10th day of Thoth in the thirty-eighth year at the fifth hour, she passed away on the 11th'.[757] In this case, the victim actually received the sting inside a religious sanctuary, possibly while she was in the middle of an act of worship or a religious ritual. Evidently worship of Thripis guaranteed no defence against the venomous stings of scorpions, even inside the goddess' own sanctuary. Perhaps she was not expected to; the fact that this Cleopatra was stung whilst in the sanctuary of Thripis could have been included in her epitaph as a warning to other devotees.

In view of how frequently scorpion stings occurred in Roman Egypt, it comes as no surprise to find a variety of remedies in circulation offering treatment, as is the case with snakebites. Since scorpion stings usually cause severe pain at the site of the sting, it makes sense that a number of treatments concentrate their attention here. One ancient remedy involved pressing malachite on the wound, but whether this was because its anti-bacterial properties were recognised (perhaps from its use as an ingredient in eye ointments) or simply because of its decorative appearance is unknown. A Greek magical spell dating to between the third and fourth centuries AD incorporates papyrus for a similar purpose: 'On a clean piece of papyrus, write the characters and place it on the part which has the sting; wrap the papyrus around it, and the sting will lose its pain immediately'.[758] There is a second magical spell, this one written in Demotic and dating slightly earlier, to the third century AD, that also concentrates its attention on the site of the sting. This second spell, however, is far longer in addition to being much more complicated:

---

[756] Davies (1989) 212; the *marsus* is attested in *CIL* VIII: 2564 column b 23 and 2618 column b 25. The *marsus* is not to be confused with the Marsi, an Italian tribe that were similar to the aforementioned Psylli, although it is possible that the title originated as a reference to their reputation as healers of venomous bites and poisonous stings. For discussion of the Marsi, see Nutton (1985) 138-9; he notes that 'they made excellent soldiers for the Roman legions', but does not elaborate upon this or cite any specific references for this being the case.
[757] Berlin Museum Inv. 2134 translated and discussed in Tod (1939) 56; discussion includes a short survey of the evidence for the goddess Thripis in Roman Egypt.
[758] *PGM* 7.193-196; see also Frembgen (2004) 113 for the use of papyrus in Coptic and early Islamic amulets to protect against scorpions, as opposed to cure a sting once it had occurred.

[Spell] to be said to the sting. 'I am the King's son, greatest and first, Anubis. My mother Sekhmet-Isis comes after me all the way to the land of Syria, to the hill of the land of Heh, to the nome of the cannibals, saying 'Hurry, hurry! Quickly, quickly, my child, King's son, greatest and first, Anubis', saying 'Arise and come to Egypt for your father Osiris is King of Egypt; he is ruler over the whole land; all the gods of Egypt are assembled to receive the crown from his hand'.

At the moment of saying these [things] she jumped at me. My strength fell from me. She coiled and she came to me with a sting; I sat down and I wept. Isis, my mother, sat near me, saying to me, 'Do not weep, do not weep, my child, King's son, greatest and first, Anubis! Lick from your tongue to your heart, and vice versa, as far as the edges of the wound! Lick from the edges of the wound up to the limits of your strength!' What you will lick up, you should swallow it. Do not spit it out on the ground, for your tongue is the tongue of the Agathodaimon, your tongue is that of Atum! You should lick it with your tongue while it is bleeding. Immediately afterwards you should speak to a little oil and you should speak to it seven times while putting it on the sting daily. You should dye a strip of linen and put it on it.

[The spell] which you should say to the oil to put it on the sting daily: 'Isis sat speaking to the oil, ABARTAT, and lamenting to the true oil, saying 'You are praised. I am going to praise you, O oil; I am going to praise you. By the Agathodaimon you are praised. By me myself you are honoured. I am going to praise you forever, O oil, O vegetable oil', 'O sweat of the Agathodaimon, amulet of Geb. Isis is the one who is speaking to the oil. O true oil, O drop of rain, O water-drawing of the planet Jupiter which comes down from the sun bark at dawn, you should do the good [deeds] of the dew of dawn which heaven cast to the ground upon every tree. You should heal the limb which is paralysed and you should act as remedy for him who lives, for I shall employ you for the sting of the King's son, greatest and first, Anubis, my child, in order that you fill it and make it well. For I shall employ you for [the] sting of [insert name], whom [insert name] bore, in order that you fill it and make it well' (seven times).[759]

It is immediately apparent that, in addition to the lengthy incantations, the spell contains three pieces of practical, possibly even purposefully medical, advice. First, the victim is required to lick the wound, conceivably either as a means of cleaning it or in an attempt to suck out the poison. Secondly, the victim is required to rub vegetable oil onto the wound on a daily basis until the wound is healed. The documentary papyri attest to the fact that different types of vegetable oil, for example radish oil, were used for a variety of purposes (including medicinal ones) in Egypt during the Roman period.[760] This is particularly interesting in view of the fact that Pliny specifically recommends radishes to treat scorpion stings.[761] Thirdly, the victim is required to bandage the wound with linen, presumably to keep it clean and dry and prevent further infection. It is important to note that these three requirements are integral to the spell and, by implication, its chances of success. However, a significant religious component is also present in addition to the medical and magical elements. The Egyptian gods Anubis, Isis, Sekhmet, Osiris, Atum and Geb are mentioned by name, as is the Greek Agathodaimon. Thus the narrative incorporates elements of Egyptian and Greek religious belief.

Just as snakebites occurred regularly in ancient Egypt, so did the stings of scorpions. The Brooklyn Papyrus originally included treatment for scorpion stings as well as snakebites, and it is tempting to speculate that, like the papyrus' treatment for snakebites, this hinged upon the identification of the type of scorpion and then proceeded to treat the sting pragmatically, using mainly medicinal remedies. Unfortunately, the accounts of scorpion stings that survive in the documentary papyri do not include details of how these injuries were treated. However, there are seven surviving magical spells that are specifically written for the treatment of scorpion stings as well as an eighth, already mentioned, that aims to ward off the creatures entirely. In view of this, it seems reasonable to assume that magical spells played a significant part in the treatment of scorpion stings in addition to medical approaches such as cleaning the wound and applying herbal remedies.

Thus, just as snakes and scorpions can be present and a threat to life and well-being not only out in their natural habitat of the wild but also in domestic and religious contexts such as homes, shrines and temples, so do the means of dealing with them integrate elements of the medical practitioner who might amputate an afflicted limb or extremity and the first aider who might apply a tourniquet or suck out the poison. This is in conjunction with so-called 'rational' medical practice such as cleaning and dressing the wound and so-called 'irrational' magical and religious practice such as anointing the wound while invoking magical and religious entities.

Crocodiles

The 'Common' or 'Nile' Crocodile (*Crocodylus niloticus*) was found throughout Egypt in antiquity, along the entire length of the river that gave the species its name as well as in the canals and pools that branched off from it. An opportunistic predator, the crocodile lies with most of its body concealed underwater before grabbing its prey and dragging it down under the water, holding it there until it drowns. It is capable of taking down almost any creature within its attacking range, including humans, and actually prefers to consume larger prey as a way of conserving its energy. Consequently, it posed a serious danger to those whose jobs or recreational activities took them onto or into the Nile: sailors, fishermen, launderers and swimmers, not to mention those who used the river less frequently as a means of transport. That this was a recognised fact well before the Roman conquest of Egypt is made clear in the *Instructions of Khety*, a satire of trades dating from the Middle Kingdom that extolled the virtues of being a scribe as opposed to any other profession: 'I mention for you also the fisherman. He is more miserable than one of any other profession, one who is at his work in a river infested with crocodiles. When the totalling of his account is made for him, then he will lament. One did not tell him that a crocodile was standing there, and fear has now blinded him'.[762] One common artistic depiction of the crocodile was of it devouring an animal, usually a donkey or a cow, while another showed crocodiles attacking boats being sailed by dwarves or pygmies. In one specific mosaic dating to the late first century BC, a boat full of passengers has run aground and is being menaced by a crocodile.[763] That these types of incident may well have occurred on a regular basis is implied by a number of documentary papyri dating from the Hellenistic period, as well as contemporaneous works of literature.[764] In Late Antiquity, the literary motif of a crocodile attacking an innocent and being repelled by a saint came to be frequently employed in early Christian writings as a means of syncretising early Christian holy men with older Egyptian religious traditions, using the crocodile to

---

[759] *PDM* 14.594-620.

[760] See for example *P Mich.* 8.508 (late second century AD, Alexandria).

[761] Plin. *HN* 20.13.

[762] *P. Sallier* 2.

[763] National Museum of Wales Cardiff Inv. 32.93, discussed in Whitehouse (1985).

[764] See for example *P. Tebt.* 3.793 (183 BC, Tebtunis): 'I sent my son Pnepheros to ... with three pairs of oxen and when he wished to cross the bridge in the road the aforesaid Ptolemaios violently seizing the boy's stick drove them into the canal and one of the three cows, worth 2000 *drachmae*, happened to be killed by a crocodile'; and *P. Cair. Zen* 3.59379 (254-1 BC): 'Amenneus the swineherd had been ordered by Zenon to fatten some pigs for the festival of Arsinoe. He did so, pawning his blanket to raise the money. But when he brought them down to a certain village, two of them were stolen; and the man who had taken them refused to give him satisfaction, pretending that the missing pigs had been eaten by a crocodile'. See also Ael. *NA* 10.21: 'And when, as often happens, their children are carried off by them, the people are overjoyed, while the mothers of the unfortunate victims are glad and go about in pride at having, I suppose, borne food and a meal for a god... a crocodile carried off the daughter of King Psammyntus, a supremely good and righteous man, and therefore in memory of that disaster even posterity abhors the whole race of crocodiles'.

symbolise the opponents of human civilisation, much as it had been used in the Pharaonic period to symbolise the forces of chaos.[765]

It would appear that crocodile bites were received regularly throughout antiquity, but in comparison to the variety of remedies offered to victims of other types of animal bites, the treatment on offer was surprisingly limited, perhaps because wounds were received so often and by people who did not necessarily have access to elaborate and expensive medical treatment, as well as generally being so extensive that no treatment would have been effective. The Ebers Papyrus, dating from 1500 BC, suggested that a crocodile bite be carefully examined and 'if you find it [with] his flesh piled up and its two sides being separated, then you should bandage it with fresh meat on the first day'.[766] Likewise, the Hearst Papyrus, dating slightly later, to 1450 BC, advises the following: 'for the bite of a crocodile in all limbs of man. You should bandage it with meat on the first day'.[767] Bandaging with fresh meat on the first day was a treatment prescribed for a variety of different types of flesh wound, not necessarily restricted to animal bites. Meat can provide blood clotting factors and there is the additional possibility that maggots would be produced as the meat decayed, consuming any flesh that became necrotic.[768] However, this treatment would in all likelihood have only affected a cure if the wound inflicted by the crocodile was relatively minor. If the wound were severe, it is doubtful that this treatment would have made much difference, one way or the other. By the Roman Period the usual treatment seems to have been based around the concept of *similia similibus*; wounds inflicted by crocodiles were treated by applying crocodile fat to them.[769]

Lions

The inhabitants of Roman Egypt were generally less likely to come face to face with a lion than a snake, scorpion or even a crocodile during the course of their daily lives simply because the lion prides of ancient Egypt tended to keep away from the more populated areas along the Nile. However, Athenaeus records that during Hadrian's visit to Egypt in AD 130, 'a huge creature had for a long time ravaged the whole of Libya, many parts of which this lion had rendered uninhabitable'.[770] This provided the Emperor and his companion Antinous with the opportunity to imitate the ancient Pharaohs of Egypt and go on a lion hunt. A short time later Pancrates, an Egyptian poet, commemorated the occasion by writing a poem about the hunt, several lines of which survive on a fragment of papyrus from Oxyrhynchus. Poetic license notwithstanding, these lines offer an insight into the dangers lions posed to the

inhabitants of Roman Egypt as well as contributing to a romanticised picture of Egypt's natural environment and mythical associations:

> The stricken beast grew ever fiercer and tore at the ground with his paws in his rage…he lunged at them both, lashing his haunches and sides with his tail…his eyes flashing dreadful fire, his ravening jaws foaming, his teeth gnashing, the hair bristling on his mighty head and shaggy neck…He charged against the glorious god and Antinous, like Typhoeus of old against Zeus the slayer of giants.[771]

The next few lines are very fragmented, but the reconstruction indicates that the lion mauled Antinous' horse before Hadrian dispatched it. Consequently, it is clear that hunting lions was hazardous not only for the hunter, but also for the horse; perhaps more so, since the horse was closer to the lion than its rider, within easy reach of claws and teeth.

While Hadrian and Antinous' encounter with the lion was clearly a special occasion, certain members of the population encountered lions on a regular basis during the activities that took place in preparation for *venationes*, or wild beast hunts. Animal spectacles were amongst the most popular spectator events held not just in Rome but also in other cities and towns throughout the Roman Empire. There is evidence to suggest that members of the Roman army were tasked with hunting and catching the animals required for these spectacles, particularly in Egypt where the native species included hippopotami, crocodiles and lions. A papyrus letter dating to the late first or early second century AD and written by a member of an auxiliary regiment makes this clear as it states 'from the month of Agrippina until now we have been hunting all species of wild animals and birds for a year under the order of the prefects'.[772]

It has been suggested that the Roman army may have had specialist lion hunters, designated as *ad leones*.[773] Although the evidence cited is for the Twentieth Palmyran Cohort serving at Dura-Europos in Syria in the period AD 219-22, there is no reason why a similar arrangement could not have operated in Egypt.[774] Julius Africanus, writing in the period AD 228-31, recommended that soldiers capture wild animals as a type of military exercise and gave detailed instructions as to how they should go about doing so, using *vestigiatores*, or specialised trackers, to first locate the animal's lair.[775] A fragment of papyrus letter, dating to the first or second century AD, attests to the presence of *vestigiatores* in Egypt as the writer and the recipient, two brothers, were evidently acting as intermediaries to a *vestigiator* and

[765] See for example *Life of John the Little Fr.* 1; and Paphnutius, *History of the Monks* 98-9. This process of syncretism is discussed in Frankfurter (2003) 373-4.
[766] *P. Ebers* 436.
[767] *P. Hearst* 239.
[768] Nunn (1996) 150.
[769] Plin. *HN* 28.28.
[770] Ath. 15.677.

[771] *P. Oxy.* 1085 (second century AD, Oxyrhynchus).
[772] For discussion of this papyrus, see Davies (1989) 193.
[773] Epplett (2001) 215.
[774] Davies (1989) 170; the assignment *ad leones* occurs seven times in AD 219 and four times in AD 222.
[775] Jul. Afr. *Cest.* 14.

shipping the animals he had captured, a group which may well have included lions.[776] While none of this material explicitly states that the soldiers and civilians involved in capturing wild animals for the *venationes* came to harm during the course of their duties, it is reasonable to assume that accidents did happen, considering the unpredictable nature of the wild animals they were hunting. Wounds caused by claws and teeth would have required medical treatment and the army was presumably well equipped to deal with these, particularly the veterinary attendants, the *veterinarii* and *pecuarii*, whose responsibilities not only included looking after the cavalry horses and beasts of burden, but also caring for the animals used for sacrifice, food or the aforementioned hunting spectacles.[777] As discussed previously, the treatment provided by the average *medicus* in the Roman army is thought to have been medical in nature, combining aspects of surgery and pharmacology, as opposed to magical or even overtly religious.

3. Wild Animals in *Materia Medica*, Aphrodisiacs and Cosmetics

So far, the assessment of snakes, scorpions, crocodiles and lions in Roman Egypt has focused primarily upon the role that individual members of these species actually played in day-to-day life. Since this was, unfortunately for the inhabitants of the province, usually a hazardous one, this has involved examining the injuries that these creatures inflicted and the ways in which such injuries were treated. These treatments evidently incorporated elements of medicine, magic and religion as deemed appropriate by the victim or the practitioner responsible for their care. However, this is only one aspect of the multi-faceted role of snakes, scorpions, crocodiles and lions in Roman Egypt and the wider Roman Empire.

In addition to causing health problems, snakes, scorpions, crocodiles and lions were thought to contribute to their treatment if employed in *materia medica*. The rationale behind this was an entrenched belief that there was a relationship between diseases and the remedies used to treat them, based around the concept of sympathy, or *concordia*, and antipathy, or *discordia*.[778] This belief in sympathetic or homeopathic magic is evident from surviving compilations of folk medicine such as Pliny's *Natural History* and receives particular attention the sections of the latter which deal specifically with remedies derived from living creatures. It was also incorporated into *physica*, a new literary genre that developed primarily in Egypt and denoted a series of writings in which the secret forces of nature were brought to light in order to make people healthy and prosperous.[779] One example of a *physica* is the *Cyranides*, a compilation dealing with the magical properties of animals, plants and stones, dating from the first or second century AD.[780]

Pliny states that 'for all injuries inflicted by serpents, and even those of an otherwise incurable nature, it is an excellent remedy to apply the entrails of the serpent itself to the wound'.[781] In addition, he recommends that 'the right eye of a serpent, worn as an amulet, is very good, it is said, for defluxions of the eyes, due care being taken to set the serpent at liberty after extracting the eye'.[782] This belief in the power of sympathetic magic extended to the employment of amulets against snakebites called snake stones, often made from serpentine and ophite because the markings present upon them resembled snakeskin.[783] These marbles originated in Egypt and were imported to the rest of the Roman Empire.

According to Celsus, 'the scorpion is itself the best remedy against itself'.[784] He gives a list of ways in which a scorpion can be used sympathetically for medicinal purposes; 'some pound up a scorpion and swallow it in wine; some pound it up in the same way and put it upon the wound; some put it upon a brazier and fumigate the wound with it, putting a cloth all round to prevent the escape of the fumes, afterwards they bandage its ash upon the wound'.[785] The ashes of a scorpion mixed with wine were also thought to cure a scorpion sting, combining aspects of two of these remedies. The belief in sympathetic magic can likewise be seen in the colloquial name given to a type of cucumber whose seeds were thought to cure scorpion stings; '*scorpionium*'.[786] In Egypt the scorpion was frequently the subject of apotropaic amulets, amulets which depicted animals that the wearer wished to avoid as well as warding off less specific malign influences such as the evil eye. Instructions on how to make one are included in the *Cyranides*: 'if you engrave in the stone hephaestites, also called pyrites, a flamingo and at its feet a scorpion, and you put a root of a small plant under the stone, you will have a good phylacterion against all venomous creatures'.[787] This apotropaic amulet merely used the image of a scorpion. The instructions regarding a second amulet go much further: 'Engrave in the stone a swallow and at its feet a scorpion staying upon the sprat, and enclose under the stone the eyes of the scorpion and of the sprat and a rootlet of the scorpion-wort, set it and wear it. For it turns away every venomous animal, reptile and quadruped…If one is hurt by a scorpion and you seal the wound with this seal, you'll put the injured person out of danger'.[788] Pliny also relates instructions on how to make an amulet against fevers, attributing the practice to magicians from Egypt, by taking four joints of a scorpion's tail, including the sting, and wrapping it in black cloth before attaching it to the body of the

[776] Epplett (2001) 218-19.
[777] Davies (1989) 212
[778] Gilhus (2006) 20.
[779] Waegeman (1987) 7.
[780] For translation (into German) of and commentary on the *Cyranides*, see Kaimakis (1976). For translation (into English) and commentary on

the first book of the *Cyranides*, see Waegeman (1987). See also Bain (1994) and (1996).
[781] Plin. *HN* 29.22.
[782] Plin. *HN* 29.38.
[783] Plin. *HN* 36.11; see discussion of the belief in snake stones of a variety of different cultures throughout history in Halliday (1921) 262-71.
[784] Celsus, *Med* 5.27.5.
[785] Celsus, *Med* 5.27.5.
[786] Plin. *HN* 11:30; 20:13.
[787] *Cyranides* 1.7.17-21.
[788] *Cyranides* 1. 24.100-15.

victim.[789] It is interesting that the sting is employed here as a remedy for fever as opposed to a scorpion sting; perhaps the scorpion's sting was where the power of the creature was thought to originate, even when a scorpion sting was not the problem that needed treatment.

In view of the abhorrence and fear with which crocodiles were viewed in antiquity, it comes as no surprise to find that, like the scorpion, the crocodile was also frequently the subject of apotropaic amulets. However, a variety of crocodile parts were sought out for medicinal purposes. The Ebers Papyrus includes crocodile fat in a recipe for greasy ointment, and this recipe or ones similar were evidently still in use in Roman times, as Pliny records that 'the Egyptians are in the habit of anointing their sick with the fat of the crocodile'.[790] In addition to the body fat, the teeth of a crocodile were employed as amulets to ward off fever, the ashes of the skin were used as a kind of rudimentary anaesthetic, the intestines were burned to fumigate the uterus and the blood and gall cured vision problems when applied to the eyes.[791]

Excrement seems to have been the most popular crocodile by-product, perhaps because, unlike body parts, it could be collected relatively easily, without requiring the collector to have to hunt, kill and dissect a crocodile first.[792] According to the Kahun Papyrus, which deals with gynaecology and dates from 1820 BC, crocodile excrement was one of the ingredients incorporated into recipes to make pessaries that were then used as methods of contraception - surprisingly effective according to modern scientists.[793] The slightly later Ebers Papyrus recommended the use of crocodile excrement in eye ointments and like the use of crocodile fat, this idea seems to have survived for centuries; Herophilos of Alexandria was prescribing an ointment made from gum, crocodile excrement, copper and hyena bile to treat nyctalopy, night or day blindness, in the third century BC.[794]

In addition to the more obvious health benefits of *materia medica*, crocodile parts were also used in products that were beneficial to an individual's health in a looser sense; aphrodisiacs and cosmetics. As an aphrodisiac, Pliny recommends attaching teeth from the right side of a crocodile's jaw to the arm.[795] This is repeated and elaborated upon in the *Cyranides*; while wearing the right molar of a small crocodile as an amulet guarantees a man an erection, the left molar ensures pleasure for a woman.[796] A perfumed substance called '*crocodilea*',

apparently taken from the intestines of a land crocodile, was applied to the face after being mixed either with oil of Cyprus to remove blemishes or water to restore the natural tint of the skin. It was also thought to remove freckles and spots.[797] Crocodile excrement was also used in an attempt to lighten the skin and make it more fashionably pale.[798]

Just as crocodiles were commonly depicted upon apotropaic amulets, lions were frequently the subject of homopoeic amulets. These homopoeic amulets differed from apotropaic amulets, however, in that they portrayed living creatures from which the wearer hoped to acquire or assimilate desirable attributes rather than creatures that the wearer wished to avoid. In view of this, it comes as no surprise to find that lion parts were highly prized for ingredients in medicine; the Ebers Papyrus includes lion fat in a recipe for greasy ointment, and at a much later date Pliny is still recommending it for several different medical reasons: 'It is remedial also for ... swellings in the joints'.[799] In point of fact, Pliny also provides evidence that the reasoning behind using the lion as a subject for a homopoeic amulet had spread to using the animal's actual body parts: 'The frivolous lies of the magicians assert that persons who are anointed with lion's fat, will more readily win favour with kings and peoples; more particularly when the fat has been used that lies between the eyebrows of the animal - a place, in fact, where there is no fat to be found!'[800] In addition to this, the fat from a lion had different medicinal effects when mixed with other substances; when mixed with gall from a lion it was apparently a cure for epilepsy, and when mixed with oil of roses, fevers. The gall, when mixed with water, was also recommended as an eye ointment.[801]

Finally, one curious example of the use of wild animal parts in a possible attempt to harness the rationale behind the use of homopoeic amulets is a suit of armour, consisting of a helmet and a cuirass, constructed entirely of crocodile skin that is currently on display in the British Museum.[802] This armour was recovered during the nineteenth century from a cave at Manfalut in the Fayum and has been radiocarbon-dated to between the third and fourth centuries AD. It has been suggested that it was made to be worn by a priest of Sobek in a religious procession in order to honour the god or perhaps even take on attributes of the crocodile such as its strength and skill at hunting. The use of crocodile skin to make armour is particularly interesting in view of the fact that certain members of the Roman army such as the *signiferi*, the *aquiliferi*, the *imaginiferi* and the *cornicines* wore uniforms decorated with lion pelts and bear skins.[803] This practice could have been where the idea for making the

[789] Plin. *HN* 30.30.
[790] *P. Ebers* 465; Plin. *HN* 28.28.
[791] Plin. *HN* 28.28.
[792] See Hanson (1998) 88-93 for discussion of excrement therapy in the ancient world.
[793] Haimov-Kochman (2005) 7 for discussion of ancient Egyptian methods of contraception.
[794] *P. Ebers* 344-370; Herophilos' *On Eyes* survives in fragments in the work of the Byzantine writer Aetius Amidenus, *Libri medicinales* 7.48 which probably dates to the late fifth or early sixth century AD; see discussion of this remedy in Plantzos (1997) 464.
[795] Plin. *HN* 28.28 and 32.50.
[796] *Cyranides* 2.29.
[797] Plin. *HN* 28.28.
[798] See Hendry (1995) for discussion as to whether Ovid is referring to crocodile excrement in the aforementioned lines.
[799] *P. Ebers* 465; Plin. *HN* 28.25.
[800] Plin. *HN* 28.25.
[801] Plin. *HN* 28.25.
[802] British Museum Inv. EA 5473.
[803] Cleland *et al.* (2007) 75-6.

suit or armour came from; during the Roman period, the Fayum was heavily populated with veteran soldiers.[804]

It is clear that the inhabitants of Egypt during the Roman period made strenuous attempts to gain control of all aspects of the natural environment of the province, from the water of the Nile to the minerals of the desert to the agricultural produce of the land, and so it is not surprising that the wild animals of the region should be included in this too. Perhaps hunting and catching scorpions, snakes, crocodiles and lions in order to utilise their parts for medicine, cosmetics and aromatics was an attempt to neutralise them and to gain power over them and the forces of chaos that they were thought to signify and represent. In any case, their incorporation into various modes of healing (both in Egypt and the Roman world at large) is a further reminder of the intimate relationship between medicine and the local natural environment, and the integration of specialised professional approaches to healing with alternative 'folk' traditions.

4. Wild Animals and Ancient Egyptian, Greek and Roman Deities

It was common knowledge amongst the diverse communities of the ancient world that Egyptian attitudes towards animals were different from those of other societies. This difference was centred upon a belief held by the Egyptians contrary to that of their contemporaries, that animals were not subordinate to humans. Rather, humans and animals were, in a sense, equals; both were created by the gods, both relied upon the gods for sustenance and both had access to life after death.[805] Since animals were not regarded as inferior or viewed with contempt, this meant that the gods of the Egyptians could be portrayed theriomorphically as well as anthropomorphically. In addition to this, the gods could also take hybrid forms, usually bearing an animal's head upon a human body. Bearing this in mind, it is no surprise to find snakes, scorpions, crocodiles and lions frequently portrayed in conjunction with the healing gods of Roman Egypt, both those originating from the beliefs of the ancient Egyptians as well as the later additions of the Greek and Roman pantheons. The ways in which these animals were portrayed varied: animals were either divine themselves, appeared as symbols of the divine, were attributes of divinities or were used as instruments.[806]

Reference has already been made to the sacred snakes that were found in the temples of Asclepius and the god was often depicted with a snake wrapped around his staff. His daughter and companion Hygieia, the personification of good health, was also often depicted with a snake, as was her Roman counterpart, Salus.[807] While Asclepius and Hygieia were both worshipped in Egypt for the purposes of healing ill health and ensuring the continuation of good health, the most popular healing deities in the province were Sarapis and Isis. While outside Egypt, there was apparently confusion over whether or not Sarapis and Asclepius were the same deity, in Egypt they were two distinct entities; Asclepius tended to be associated with Imhotep or Imouthes, the deified architect of the Great Pyramid who came to be seen as a patron of physicians.[808]

Sarapis was particularly popular in Alexandria, where there was an immense temple, the Serapeum, dedicated to him. Prayers for health, dedications and offerings to Sarapis on behalf of family and friends are a common feature of letters surviving amongst the documentary papyri that can be definitively identified as having been sent from Alexandria.[809] Demetrius of Phalerum, writing in the late fourth to the early third century BC, indicates that faith in Sarapis as a god of healing originated in the royal court during the reign of Ptolemy I.[810] There was another major centre of the cult of Sarapis at Canopus where, according to Strabo, Sarapis 'is worshipped with great reverence and brings about such cures that even the most famous people believe in them and sleep in his sanctuary, whether on their own behalf, or with others standing proxy'.[811] Like Asclepius, Sarapis was commonly depicted with a snake, although in his case the snake was the *Agathos Daimon*, the 'good spirit' of Alexandria, emphasising the special link between the god and the city in the minds of the inhabitants of Egypt during the Hellenistic and Roman periods.

Like Asclepius and Sarapis, Isis was often depicted with a snake. In addition, Isis was associated with scorpions through two of the many myths surrounding her adventures with her son Horus during their exile in the Delta, hiding from the malevolent god Seth. In the first of these, she was being protected and guarded by seven scorpions when one of the scorpions stung the son of a woman that refused the group shelter, requiring her to cure the boy. In the second, Horus was stung and Isis cured him with the help of the god Thoth.[812] This cure ensured that Isis came to be revered as a great healer, both by the ancient Egyptians and by the Greeks and Romans in turn:

> The Egyptians say that she was the discoverer of many health-giving drugs and was greatly versed in the science of healing; consequently, now that she has attained immortality, she finds her greatest delight in the healing of mankind and gives aid in their sleep to those who call upon her, plainly manifesting both her very presence and her beneficence towards men who ask for her help... For standing above the

[804] Alston (1995) 39-52.

[805] Smelik and Hemelrijk (1984) 1858.

[806] Gilhus (2006) 94-5.

[807] See *IGA I*: Cairo Museum Inv. 9265, a votive stele dedicated to Asclepius and Hygieia in AD 99.

[808] Tac. *Hist.* 4.84.5: 'Many regard the god himself as identical with Aesculapius, because he cures the sick'.

[809] See for example *P. Oxy.* 1070 (third century AD, Oxyrhynchus).

[810] Diog. Laert. 5.78; the similarities between Sarapis and Asclepius are discussed in Stambaugh (1972) 76-7.

[811] Strabo, *Geographica* 17.1.17.

[812] Scott (1951) 210-13.

sick in their sleep she gives them aid for their diseases and works remarkable cures upon such as submit themselves to her; and many who have been despaired of by their physicians because of the difficult nature of their malady are restored to health by her, while numbers who have altogether lost the use of their eyes or some other part of their body, whenever they turn for help to this goddess, are restored to their previous condition.[813]

In this description of the goddess Isis, Diodorus Siculus demonstrates precisely how integrated ancient healing strategies could be; although he is speaking of a deity, he numbers the discovery of drugs and the 'science of healing' as being among her achievements, two components of supposedly 'rational' medicine. In describing the process of undergoing an incubation ritual in the temple of Isis, he emphasises that the goddess physically manifests herself and tends to the sick, much like a family member or friend would nurse an invalid.

The ancient Egyptian goddess Serket, known by the Greeks as Selkis, was worshipped in Egypt as early as the First Dynasty of the Old Kingdom. She was specifically identified with the scorpion and usually represented in human form with a scorpion on her head, rather than in the form of the scorpion.[814] She was recognised as a major force in the protection of people from scorpions and other venomous creatures, to the point that the priests of her cult were actually sought to treat victims of scorpion stings and snakebites rather than physicians. This is clearly very different to the incubation rituals of the temples of Sarapis and Isis, where it is the god and goddess who are believed to heal the sick, rather than their priests and priestesses.

The ancient Egyptian crocodile god Sobek was worshipped both in major sanctuaries and at local temples and shrines in villages along the Nile throughout Egypt, but during the Roman Period the god was particularly popular in the Fayum, despite the fact that the area was very Hellenised.[815] Like the temples of Sarapis and Asclepius, temples precincts of Sobek contained sacred animals, although in this case the primary sacred animal was actually himself a god. In 112 BC, preparations were made for a trip to Egypt by the Roman senator Lucius Memmius and officials in the Fayum were ordered to prepare for his visit to the sacred crocodile Petesouchos at Arsinoe and provide 'the customary tit-bits for Petesouchos and the crocodiles'.[816] Strabo also visited

Petesouchos and described the process of feeding the sacred animal:

Our host, one of the officials, who was introducing us into the mysteries there, went with us to the lake, carrying from the dinner a small cake and some roasted meat and a pitcher of wine mixed with honey. We found the animal lying on the edge of the lake; and when the priests went up to it, some of them opened its mouth and another put in the cake, and again the meat, and then poured down the honey mixture. The animal then leaped into the lake and rushed across to the far side; but when another foreigner arrived, likewise carrying an offering of first-fruits, the priests took it, went around the lake in a run, took hold of the animal, and in the same manner fed it what had been brought.[817]

These entirely tame sacred crocodiles were raised by sauretai, 'crocodile keepers', near the temples, possibly even in pens inside the temple enclosure, and must have been viewed in an entirely different way to the wild crocodiles that inspired such fear in the inhabitants of Egypt, posed such a serious danger to them and caused them so many problems.[818] The god Sobek and his local variations Petesouchos and Pnepheros were viewed as benign gods, to whom people could turn if they required protection or healing.[819] A Demotic healing prayer, dating to 6th July 5 BC, and directed to Soknebtunis, 'Sobek, lord of Tebtunis', pleads for the god to intervene and heal a woman called Tshenēsi: 'I shall give you this document for you are to effect my justice [and] my judgement swiftly and not delay; you are to drive out the corruption from her bones [and] the disease from her limbs'.[820] In addition to the healing aspects of the cult of Sobek, papyrological evidence from the Fayum indicates that there were also at least three oracle temples functioning in the area from the late Pharaonic Period and through the Roman Period into the third century AD.[821] Oracle requests written in Demotic, Egyptian and Greek survive and it is possible that these oracle requests also functioned as amulets.[822]

Another interesting link between the god Sobek and healing is found in Upper Egypt, at the double temple of Sobek and Horus at Kom Ombo. The outer enclosure wall of the temple precinct dates to the late second century AD and it contains a relief depicting Roman surgical instruments, identified as such because of their similarities to actual medical instruments recovered

[813] Diod. Sic. 1.25.2-5.
[814] Smelik and Hemelrijk (1984) 1861.
[815] See Frankfurter (1998) 99-100 for discussion of Sobek worship in the Fayum; see also SEG VIII: 498, OGI 176 and 178, SB 3.6252 and 6253 for Greek inscriptions dedicated to Egyptian crocodile gods dating from the first century BC.
[816] P. Tebt. 33 (112 BC, Tebtunis); see also depictions of the sacred crocodiles being fed in a mosaic, dating to around 30 BC, and a relief, dating to around AD 250, both found in Rome.

[817] Strabo, Geographica 17.1.38.
[818] Dunand and Zivie-Coche (2004) 296.
[819] P. Amh. 2.35.32-35.
[820] P. Carlsb. 67; translated and discussed in Ray (1975).
[821] Frankfurter (1998) 159.
[822] Frankfurter (1998) 161.

through archaeological excavations.[823] These instruments are believed to be Roman rather than Egyptian because of the inclusion of weighing scales; Egyptian drugs were dispensed by volume while Roman drugs were dispensed by weight.[824]

The ancient Egyptian lion goddess Sekhmet was believed to have the ability to bring pestilence to the people of Egypt and consequently the need to appease her resulted in her having an important role in healing; her priests are believed to have functioned as both doctors and veterinarians. This is attested to by the Ebers Papyrus and later repeated in the Edwin Smith Papyrus, with regard to taking a patient's pulse: 'If any doctor, any *wab* priest of Sekhmet or any magician places his two hands or his fingers on the head, on the back of the head, on the hands, on the place of the heart, on the two arms or on each of the two legs, he measures the heart because of its vessels to all his limbs'.[825] In addition to these glosses taken from examples of ancient Egyptian medical papyri, a graffito written by a priest of Sekhmet called Hery-shef-nakht during the Middle Kingdom states, 'I am a *wab* priest of Sekhmet, capable and skilled of his brotherhood, who places a hand on a man when he knows [the illness]'.[826] There is evidence that the priests of Sekhmet continued to practise medicine and tend sacrificial animals as veterinarians at least into the second century BC and perhaps as late as the Roman Period.[827]

In the same way that real snakes, scorpions, crocodiles and lions were recognised by the inhabitants of Roman Egypt as being extremely dangerous and posing a significant risk to their health, conversely, representations of snakes, scorpions, crocodiles and lions were recognised as being benign, even beneficial, to their health. Since snakes, scorpions, crocodiles and lions were frequently represented either theriomorphically as the animal forms taken by certain ancient Egyptian gods or, as was more acceptable to the majority of the Greek and Roman immigrants, as the companions of the anthropomorphic gods and goddesses Asclepius, Hygieia, Salus, Sarapis, Isis, Selkis, Sobek and Sekhmet the inhabitants of Roman Egypt were used to associating them with healing. In a sense, this was an extension of the concept of sympathy and antipathy that led people to use certain parts of snakes, scorpions, crocodiles and lions as ingredients in antidotes and medicines; while an actual animal might have caused the injury, a version of it imbued with divine power either on its own account or through its association with another deity could cure it.

Conclusion

Dangerous fauna (insects, arachnids, reptiles, amphibians and mammals) were found throughout Egypt during the Roman period. Snakes, scorpions, crocodiles and lions

were considered particularly dangerous: scorpions not only scuttled around underfoot and amongst rocks, but could easily gain entry to houses and temples; snakes infested gardens, orchards, vineyards and fields; crocodiles were frequently sighted both on the banks of the Nile and within the tributaries and branches of the river itself; and prides of lions roamed the plains and rocky outcrops of the Eastern and Western deserts.

The examples discussed in this chapter have ranged geographically from the Brucheion in Alexandria, to Canopus in the Nile Delta and down the length of the Nile, to the quarry settlements of the Eastern Desert, and the plains of the Western Desert. Consequently, no one, no matter what their age or sex, their occupation, personal wealth or social status, or even where they lived, could avoid these creatures and the dangers they posed entirely. Nor were mythological figures (whether Egyptian such as Isis and Horus, or Greek such as Menelaus, Helen and Canopus) safe from them, as Egyptian beasts occupied a legendary status as a source of power and danger. Even the Ptolemaic queen and living goddess Cleopatra VII, and the Roman emperor Hadrian were not guaranteed immunity from harm (although admittedly, in the case of both Cleopatra and Hadrian, their encounters with a snake and a lion respectively took place by design rather than by accident).

Consequently, snakes, scorpions, crocodiles and lions were extremely significant in respect of health and healing in Roman Egypt. Not only did they pose a risk to health, in the form of the actual species of these animals that were native to Egypt, but they also had a role to play in healing, both as ingredients in remedies and as agents of a miraculous cure. This healing incorporated elements of medicine, magic and religion. Medical knowledge accrued over hundreds, if not thousands, of years of medical practice (which included pharmacology and surgery) was employed in conjunction with magical spells and religious ritual and prayer, both in public, in temples and other institutions, and in private and it is clear that medical, magical and religious approaches to healing could be employed individually or collectively. A certain amount of continuity between the Pharaonic, Ptolemaic and Roman periods is apparent, both in treatises such as the Ebers, Hearst and Brooklyn papyri, amulets such as Horus *cippi*, pharmacological remedies such as oil, meat and animal fat, and the anthropomorphic and animal deities that were invoked for protection and healing. However, it is also clear that these animals and the treatments that developed to deal with the injuries they inflicted continued to be utilised not only into Late Antiquity but also even later, when Egypt came under the control of Islam.

The injuries inflicted by wild animals (whether bites, scratches or stings) and the health problems (minor, serious or even fatal) that could result from them were caused entirely by Egypt's unique natural environment. On a daily basis, the inhabitants of Egypt during the Roman period faced dangers from Egyptian creatures that no-one else in the Roman Empire (with the exception of a

---

[823] See Jackson (1990) for a general summary of known medical instruments, complete with illustrations and photographs.
[824] Nunn (1996) 164.
[825] *P. Ebers* 854a.
[826] Nunn (1996) 135.
[827] See *Ms. Egypt.c.2* (P), a *Document of Breathing Made by Isis* translated and discussed in Coenen (2000).

small number of *bestiarii*) ever experienced. So it is not surprising that aspects of Egypt's natural environment (whether Nile mud, water, Egyptian plants or more significantly ingredients harvested from the wild animals themselves) were incorporated into the healing process to a much greater extent than in the case of eye conditions and fevers, as the link between Egypt's natural environment and the injuries inflicted by wild animals was entirely explicit. Such items were also readily accessible to those whose encounters with these creatures took place far from home, out in the desert or out on the Nile. Additionally, the focus of this chapter helps us to see just how integrated religion and ritual, and Egyptian medical practice could be, as well as offering another window onto the impact of the local natural environment upon approaches to healing within the province.

To my lady mother and my lady grandmothers, together with Kyra, Eudaimon sends greetings. I made haste right now to address you, once I found a good opportunity, praying to the divine providence that you may receive my letter in good spirits and in good health. For Heraklammon came and upset us very much, because he says 'Kyra our sister was sick'. Now, however, we thank the divine providence that helps us everywhere and in everything that she is again healthy. Let her know that the linen garments of our sister Kyrilla have been cut (from the loom). If I find a friend going, I intend to send them and the purple hooded cloak and the shoes. We now have the materials from Helen the embroideress, and I only found four books in the baggage, but you wrote 'We have sent off five'. In fact, we received all the other things, except only the container of animal fat. As a result, let our brother Theodoros be eager to search…and to know about it…He furnished in place of the container of animal fat, a jar of eye salve. Also be eager to send me the folding bronze case, so that I may make other materials, but not the same ones, and the heater in the same way, and the cupping vessels, so that I may make a …
[In the left margin] Also send three pounds of eye salve mixed from all…astringent substances and…so that I may get other attractive things…
[The address on the back] Send to the surgery. From Eudaimon.[828]

Eudaimon's letter to his mother, grandmothers and a woman named Kyra, written in the late fourth century AD and sent from wherever he was to his family home in Oxyrhynchus, illustrates the complexity of healing strategies in Egypt during the Roman period. The content of the letter strongly implies that Eudaimon and his brother Theodoros are physicians in its discussion of treatises, bronze instruments and ointments. That one or both of them could be described as being a 'professional' medical practitioner (that is with medical practice being their primary occupation, their means of earning a living, and recognised as such by individuals other than themselves) can be inferred from the fact that the address written on the verso of the papyrus is 'the surgery' (τὸ ἰατρεῖον); presumably the person tasked with delivering the letter would have known (or could at least have been

directed to) its precise location within the city of Oxyrhynchus.

However, the content of the letter also emphasises the significant role that family and kinship networks played with regard to healing strategies in Egypt during the Roman period. If both Eudaimon and Theodoros were physicians, it is not unlikely that at least one of their parents was too and that the brothers inherited the family business from him or her; it is clear that at least three generations of the family were (at the time of writing) living in one house and that house also served as a physician's surgery.[829] However, Eudaimon is not writing to his physician brother; rather he is writing to his mother, grandmothers and a woman who is possibly his sister (or sister-in-law). He enquires after the health of Kyra, who has been suffering from an illness while he has been away and (in his absence) has presumably been nursed through it by the aforementioned mother and grandmothers. He also requests that they, the female members of his family, provide him with medical apparatus, medicinal remedies and additional components and ingredients.[830]

Thus rather than 'professional' and 'amateur' healing strategies, practitioners, practices and institutions being in conflict, Eudaimon's family provides an example of just how integrated such strategies, practitioners, practices and institutions could be: 'professional' and 'amateur' healing practitioners co-exist in a location that is simultaneously a physician's surgery and a family home, containing objects that can be utilised for medicinal or non-medicinal purposes as required.[831] This is not an isolated case, as literary, documentary, and archaeological evidence from Egypt readily attests.[832] During the second century AD one man recorded how he and his mother had (on separate occasions) visited a

---

[828] *P. Oxy.* 4001 (fourth century AD, Oxyrhynchus).

[829] For families of physicians, see for example the epitaph of the child Machaon, son of Sabbataios, at *CIJ* II: 1539, dating to 14th March AD 8, as previously discussed at 20 n136. See also the dedicatory inscription of the physician brothers Horos and Papsos, at *IGRom* I: 1289, dating to 13th May AD 88. See also (from somewhat later) the will of Flavius Phoibammon, the Chief Physician of the Antinoite nome, himself the son of a physician, which entrusts his hospital to his brother John, perhaps also a physician, at *P. Cair. Masp.* 2.67151.182-95 (AD 570, Antinoopolis).
[830] The reference to Eudaimon's family having sent him animal fat is interesting in light of the frequency with which animal fat was incorporated into Egyptian medicinal remedies as well as Greek and Roman ones. See previous discussion of the use of different types of animal fat (including pig, crocodile and lion fat) for medicinal purposes, at 12 n93, 37, 45, 54, 67, 75, 88, 90 and 93.
[831] For further discussion of Eudaimon's letter with regard to the medical treatises, instruments and medicinal remedies he mentions, see 27, 29-31 and 67.
[832] For other examples of literary and documentary papyri that demonstrate the integration of different types of healing strategies, practitioners, practices and institutions, see below. For examples of archaeological artefacts and sites, see the relief at the Temple of Sobek and Horus at Kom Ombo, at 29-30; the pharmacological remedies and incubation rituals at the Temple of Sarapis and Isis at Canopus, at 34-5; the medical literature, pharmacological remedies and oracles at the Temple of Sobek at Tebtunis, at 35-6; and the grave deposit from Hawara, at 30 n248 and 37.

nearby Temple of Imouthes-Asclepius to undergo treatment for their respective ailments, and that the treatment provided there had combined aspects of religious healing (an incubation ritual and subsequent communication with Imouthes-Asclepius himself) and medical treatment consisting of simple remedies. In addition to these 'professional' religious and medical healing strategies, the writer's mother nursed him through his ailment herself, bathing him when his fever broke and helping him reorient himself when he became lucid.[833] During the fourth or fifth century, Pares wrote to his brother Papios, requesting that he send him large quantities of medicinal herbs and spices; if these herbs and spices were required for personal reasons and Pares' own personal use, then Papios was clearly contributing to and facilitating his brother's attempts to self-medicate, but if (as is more likely, considering the quantities involved) Pares was an apothecary or a pharmacist and the herbs and spices were required for professional reasons, then Pares was actively involving his brother in his business and its 'professional' healing practices.[834]

One of the innovative features of Vivian Nutton's recent study of ancient medicine was his inclusion of 'amateur', 'irrational' and 'religious' healing strategies, practitioners, practices and institutions.[835] However, despite this acknowledgement that such phenomena existed in the ancient world, the space he allotted to them was out of necessity minimal, considering the enormous amount of material he succeeded in integrating into this work. Other recent studies of ancient medicine, particularly those that focus on Egypt, have continued to downplay the role played by them.[836] In the case of Egypt during the Roman period, such an approach is particularly unfortunate because there is such a wide range of documentary, archaeological and anthropological evidence indicating their utilisation. There is a large amount of evidence for the utilisation of both 'rational' healing strategies (such as medical, surgical and pharmacological intervention) and 'irrational' healing strategies (such as magical incantations and spells, prayers and votive offerings to the gods, as well as what is commonly referred to as 'folk' medicine) throughout Egypt during the Roman period. With regard to the former, individuals in poor health were examined and treated, their wounds dressed and splinted, and medicaments prescribed and applied. With regard to the latter, oracles were consulted about maintaining good health and improving poor health, amulets were worn as both preventative and curative measures, and health-specific prayers and votive offerings were deposited at shrines and temples. In this respect, some continuity between the healing strategies utilised in Egypt during the

Pharaonic period and those utilised in the region during the Roman period is evident. These 'rational' and 'irrational' healing strategies were not necessarily (or even commonly) mutually exclusive. Works of medical literature frequently recommended a course of treatment combining both 'rational' and 'irrational' approaches. Practitioners of 'rational' medicine could be found and engaged within 'irrational' locales; there is evidence for medicine, surgery and pharmacology having taken place at a range of religious institutions including the Temple of Sarapis and Isis at Canopus, the Temple of Soknebtunis at Tebtunis and monastic communities out in the desert. While this also shows some continuity between healing practice in Egypt during the Pharaonic period and the region during the Roman period, it is important to remember that this integration of 'rational' and 'irrational' is also evident across the Greek and Roman worlds, for example in the sanctuary of Asclepius at Epidauros in Argolis and its associated institutions such as that on Tiber Island in Rome.[837]

There is considerable evidence for the presence of both so-called 'professional' and 'amateur' practitioners in Egypt during the Roman period. There seem to have been two distinct types of 'professional' medical practitioner: those who held official posts within the Roman provincial administration such as *archiatroi*, *demosioi iatroi* and army physicians and whose practice was thus restricted to a certain location such as one specific nome or military encampment; and those who operated independently and could thus choose where they wished to live and work, perhaps even relocating to an area where their skills were in greater demand and thus employment was more likely (seasonal economic migration from the *chora* to Alexandria is particularly well-attested in the documentary papyri).[838] Although medical practice was in no way standardised in the Roman world, there is evidence that attempts were made to provide appropriate training for individuals who aspired to be physicians or midwives (whether these took the form of an apprenticeship or the provision of instruction manuals, or adherence to codes of practice such as the 'Hippocratic Oath') in Egypt during the Roman period. 'Amateur' medical practice was far more flexible and consequently much less prescribed: individuals who offered healing to their family members, friends and acquaintances were under no obligation to do so on a regular basis, if at all, although some do seem to have viewed it as their familial duty.

A primary goal of this work, then, has been to demonstrate that the healing strategies utilised in the Roman world did not, as is often assumed, consist solely of 'professional' medical practitioners such as physicians, surgeons, midwives, apothecaries and even temple priests who, having received a degree of medical education and training, practised 'rational' medicine analogous to what

---

[833] See *P. Oxy.* 1381 (second century AD, Oxyrhynchus), discussed previously at 79-80.
[834] See *P. Haun.* 20 (fourth-fifth century AD, unprovenanced), discussed previously at 46-7.
[835] See Nutton (2004) Chapter 17: 'Allsorts and conditions of (mainly) men', and Chapter 18: 'Medicine and the religions of the Roman Empire'.
[836] See most recently Hirt Raj (2006) Chapter 6: 'De l'étiologie à la thérapie: le choix offert au malade', particularly 278-304.

[837] For discussion of sanctuaries dedicated to Asclepius in the ancient world, see Edelstein (1945), Burford (1969) and Meier (2003) 9-18.
[838] See Abd-el-Ghani (2004) and Adams (2007) for discussion of this phenomenon and the evidence for it.

we would expect to find in a hospital in the modern west. Rather, a range of healing strategies was utilised. What is more, individual autonomy was a key factor, and healing strategies were thoroughly integrated into all aspects of daily life, incorporating the contents of an individual's house and garden as well as their immediate surroundings. In part, this is the result of the fact that climate, geography and the natural environment had a fundamental effect on an individual's health, contributing not only to the disease environment and thus the diseases one could be exposed to and consequently suffer from, but also to environmental and work-related hazards that could be encountered, causing accidents and resulting in injuries.

It is clear that there was a range of different disease environments present within the province. A densely populated urban centre such as Alexandria (located on the Mediterranean coast as a means of utilising the area's natural harbour to facilitate international trade and travel) contained not only hundreds of thousands of permanent residents but also a sizeable transient population of seasonal economic migrants from the Egyptian *chora* and travellers from all around the Roman Empire. Ports such as Myos Hormos or Berenike, while significantly smaller than Alexandria, likewise saw large numbers of people come and go on a regular basis throughout the year. The inhabitants of such settlements were not only at risk from the sorts of diseases that any ancient urban population might experience (conditions related to overcrowding, poor sanitation and questionable hygiene) but also unfamiliar pathogens from eastern and southern Africa, India and the Orient such as bubonic plague or smallpox. Communities strongly associated with particular industries such as stone quarrying or agricultural production also had highly specific disease environments; the inhabitants of Mons Claudianus, Mons Porphyrites and the other quarry settlements in the Eastern Desert would have been far more likely to experience respiratory disorders, dehydration and sunstroke than the inhabitants of the villages of the Fayum.

The nature of the communities in which individuals lived, their geographical location and accessibility also had an impact upon the type of healing strategies that could be utilised. The inhabitants of Alexandria, the nome capitals, the cities and the larger towns seem to have had ready access to physicians, midwives and apothecaries (if they chose to patronise them) as well as to members of their families, friends and acquaintances for healing. There is evidence to suggest that 'professional' and 'amateur' practitioners coexisted; this is particularly apparent in smaller communities such as those out in the deserts. It does not appear that individuals only used alternative healing strategies when 'professional' healing practitioners were unavailable; rather there is evidence to suggest that individuals would go some way toward inconveniencing themselves and others in order to utilise these alternative means, sometimes having to send items or even travel themselves over very long distances.[839]

The nature of the communities in which individuals lived, their geographical location and accessibility also had an impact upon the type of healing strategies that could be utilised with regard to the availability of ingredients for remedies. Cities such as Alexandria and the nome capitals were large enough to support one or more apothecaries or even specialist sellers of individual drugs, but the same could not necessarily be said for smaller settlements such as towns and villages. In areas where specific commodities were produced, it stands to reason that these commodities would be more readily available and perhaps even cheaper. For example, the presence of numerous olive groves in the Dakhleh Oasis ensured a ready supply of olive oil, the beekeepers of Karanis produced honey, beeswax and propolis, and the Red Sea trade ensured that large quantities of black pepper were available at Berenike.

The crucial role that history, culture, society, climate, geography and natural environment play in the formulation both of health problems and of the healing strategies used to treat them shows that a new approach is possible in the study of health and healing in the Roman period and, by implication, other historical periods too.

This study has tackled its subject in two sections. The first examined the roles of individual healing practitioners, Chapter One focusing on so-called 'professional' healing practitioners and Chapter Two focusing on their so-called 'amateur' counterparts. Although I have attempted to distinguish the two for the sake of brevity and clarity, it is clear that there are in fact numerous ways in which these two types of healing practitioners overlap in their acquisition and use of medical literature and instruments, and their production and dissemination of medicinal prescriptions and remedies, as is evident, for example, in Eudaimon's letter to his family discussed above.

Chapter One demonstrated that not only were there numerous so-called 'professional' healing practitioners such as physicians, surgeons, midwives and apothecaries operating in Egypt during the Roman period, but that there is also a wide range of evidence for them and their activities beyond that which is most frequently cited. This frequently cited evidence is, of course, the Greek and Latin literary papyri preserving extracts from medical treatises known to have been written by famous historical figures such as Galen, and the documentary papyri preserving the reports of the public physicians of nome capitals such as Oxyrhynchus. However, using literary and documentary papyri in conjunction with epigraphy, public and private works of art, and archaeological artefacts recovered from official, military, civilian and religious site contexts, it is possible to identify where these practitioners were practising and what type of medical practice they were carrying out. What is clear is that different types of so-called 'professional' medical practitioners (whether physicians, surgeons, midwives, apothecaries or temple priests) co-existed not only in cities such as Alexandria and nome capitals such as Oxyrhynchus, but also in smaller settlements such as

---

[839] For previous discussion of this issue, see 40.

Tebtunis and Mons Claudianus. However, unlike modern professionals, they were not necessarily engaged in medical practice full time on a daily basis and receiving a salaried payment: there is evidence to suggest that expedience played a significant role in how 'professional' medical practitioners spent their time, and that in addition to practising medicine they farmed, cultivated crops, testified in legal cases and (however reluctantly and unwillingly) undertook local administrative and liturgical duties.

Having established that different types of 'professional' medical practitioners beyond those usually considered by scholars not only co-existed in Egypt during the Roman period but could operate even in small or geographically isolated communities, Chapter Two explored another contemporaneous aspect of healing: those healing strategies that were utilised as an alternative to seeking the help of a 'professional'. Such healing strategies are sometimes described as 'folk' medicine and frequently overlooked in modern scholarship. However, there is a significant amount of evidence to suggest that use of such alternative healing strategies was widespread in Egypt during the Roman period. These alternative healing strategies involved a sometimes widespread network of family members, friends and neighbours, and utilised medicinal, magical or religious remedies containing ingredients sourced from the natural environment of Roman Egypt, and in recent years scientific analysis has been used to prove that these were not necessarily ineffective. This provides evidence that the healing strategies utilised in Egypt during the Roman period were dictated by a range of historical, cultural and social factors, the most significant of which was individual autonomy, but also very important was the physical location of the individual suffering from poor health and their resultant access to practitioners (whether 'professional' or 'amateur') and treatment (whether 'rational' or 'irrational').

The second section of this study drew on the outcomes of the first (above all, that healing strategies were dictated by individual autonomy and influenced by a range of historical, cultural and social factors) in order to examine the healing strategies utilised to deal with three health problems particularly prevalent in Egypt during the Roman period: eye complaints, febrile conditions and injuries inflicted by wild animals. However, in addition to the fact that they were particularly prevalent in Egypt during the Roman period, these specific health problems were selected for study because the diverse ways in which they were dealt with offers a series of insights into how the inhabitants of Egypt in the Roman period viewed and interacted with both their own bodies and those of others in respect of the causes and effects of sickness. In the case of eye complaints, certain aspects of the architecture of the eye were reasonably well understood in antiquity, resulting in an appreciation of the fact that an eye infection (or other type of eye condition) required localised treatment, which in turn could lead to quite advanced (in a manner of speaking) ophthalmological surgical intervention. However, the fact that fever was mistakenly thought to be an illness in itself rather than a symptom of an underlying condition meant that in comparison to eye complaints, the treatment that sufferers of febrile conditions were subjected to was much less specific and, consequently, subject to much less standardisation or even regimentation. Unlike eye complaints and febrile conditions, the immediate cause of an injury inflicted by a wild animal was clear. However, the religious, ritual and symbolic significance of animals in ancient Egypt ensured that an extra dimension was present for the duration of the initial encounter with the creature, and then for healing process.

Chapter Three focused on eye complaints acquired during life, whether infectious (e.g. conjunctivitis, chlamydia trachomatis), degenerative (e.g. cataract) or the result of trauma. It appears that, although numerous different 'rational' and 'irrational' healing strategies were utilised in order to treat eye complaints, the one employed most frequently was the application of a carefully selected eye salve to the affected area, while certain conditions such as cataracts might be treated surgically. However, just as 'professional' and 'amateur' practitioners co-existed, so did 'rational' and 'irrational' healing strategies co-exist and overlap with regard to treatment of eye complaints; magical spells were cast over medicinal preparations that were then applied to the eyes, prayers and votives were offered to gods particularly associated with healing eye complaints (e.g. Sarapis) while human saliva, breast milk and colostrum were applied to the eyes, these practices incorporating a mixture of medical, magical and religious healing.

Chapter Four focused on febrile conditions, whether the result of an infected wound (e.g. septicaemia or gangrene) or an infectious disease (e.g. malaria). It appears that, in contrast to the 'rational' ways in which individuals treated their eye complaints, 'irrational' means were favoured as a treatment for fevers, whether in the form of a magical amulet or spell, or a request for divine intervention. However, once again both 'rational' and 'irrational' elements are present; wounds were cleaned, anointed and dressed, and amulets were worn or prayers were spoken in an attempt to prevent infection, or certain magical spells were cast over oil which was then spread onto the feverish patient, or those undergoing incubation rituals were nursed, kept clean, fed and hydrated.

The injuries inflicted by wild animals and the health problems that accompanied them examined in Chapter Five were caused entirely by Egypt's unique natural environment and its inherent wildlife. In this context we see the natural environment of Egypt involved in the healing process to a much greater, much more explicit extent. Although ingredients harvested from the gardens, orchards, cultivated and uncultivated land of Egypt are frequently incorporated into medicinal and magical preparations (e.g. weed flora, rose petals, honey, beeswax, olive and radish oil, Nile mud and water), treating injuries inflicted by wild animals such as snakes, scorpions, crocodiles and lions frequently involved utilising ingredients harvested from the creatures themselves (e.g. snake fangs or skin, scorpion stings, crocodile fat or excrement, lion fat or fur). Likewise, the deities associated with these dangerous animals (e.g. Serket, Sobek and Sekhmet) were not only thought to cause disease but affect cures. Such practices were unlikely to occur on a regular basis elsewhere in the Roman Empire, partly due to practical considerations such as a lack of the animals in question available (for the most part) to have the appropriate ingredients harvested from them, but also due to the other provinces of the empire not sharing Egypt's seemingly distinctive religious and magical beliefs (which of course were also influenced and shaped by the province's unique natural environment).

Thus, the approach to health and healing adopted in this study may provide a useful case study for historians of ancient, medieval and modern medicine, and also for classicists, ancient historians, archaeologists and anthropologists interested in the provincial culture of the Roman Empire. There are many possible routes for further investigation: one would be to engage in the closer study of specific communities within Egypt during the Roman period such as, for example, Karanis or Tebtunis; another potentially fruitful avenue of enquiry would be the application of this methodology to other Roman provinces with a comparable range of documentary, archaeological and anthropological evidence such as, for example, Roman Britain. Even the healing strategies employed by the inhabitants of the city of Rome and the territories of Italy during the Roman period (an aspect of life in the Roman Empire that has been much examined) would benefit from a more inclusive study that gave comparable weight to folk medicine, and magical and religious healing, alongside what passed for medical science in the ancient world.

In defence of his preference for an academic discipline that comprised a history of medical science as opposed to a history of medical practice, Plinio Prioreschi stated that 'for those who consider postmodernism a new and improved intellectual insight, science is culturally determined, that is to say, its discoveries do not reflect external reality but the prejudices, beliefs and biases of a given culture at a given time ... in general, science is not more valid that any other construct'.[840] In contrast to his dismissal of the validity of such an approach, I have argued throughout this work that, as far as the inhabitants of Egypt during the Roman period were concerned, folk medicine, and magical and religious healing strategies were indeed as valid as what passed for medical science. The purpose of this study has been to examine the healing strategies utilised by the inhabitants of Egypt during the Roman period, from the first century BC to the fourth century AD, in order to explore how Egyptian, Greek and Roman customs and traditions interacted within the province. Through the examination of a range of literary, papyrological, archaeological and anthropological sources, it is evident that the healing strategies employed

within the province of Egypt were developed in response to the interaction and integration of a range of historical, cultural and social factors, informed by the region's climate, geography and natural resources. In this respect, this work has demonstrated the importance of approaching the study of Roman medicine not as a standardised and institutionalised phenomenon but as a complex, diverse and interactive set of practices embedded in the crossroads between local traditions, provincial geography and the expansion of Roman imperial culture, but ultimately dependent upon the choices made by the patient in question.

---

[840] Prioreschi (1998) xxi-xxiv.

BIBLIOGRAPHY

Abdalla, A. (1991) 'A Graeco-Roman Statue Group of Unusual Character from Dendera' *JEg. Arch.* 77: 189-93

Abd-el-Ghani, M. (2004) 'Alexandria and Middle Egypt: Some Aspects of Social and Economic Contacts under Roman Rule' in Harris, W. V. and Ruffini, G. (eds) *Ancient Alexandria Between Egypt and Greece* (Leiden) 161-78

Abdel-Wahab, M. F. (1982) *Schistosomiasis in Egypt* (Florida)

Adams, C. E. P. (2007) *Land Transport in Roman Egypt: a Study of Economics and Administration in a Roman Province* (Oxford)

Adams, J. N. (1995) *Pelagonius and Latin Veterinary Terminology in the Roman Empire* (Leiden)

Adams, J. N. et al. (eds) (2002) *Bilingualism in Ancient Society: Language Contact and the Written Text* (Oxford)

Adams, J. N. (2003) *Bilingualism and the Latin Language* (Cambridge)

Allen, J. P. (2005) *The Art of Medicine in Ancient Egypt* (New York)

Al-Rifai, K. M. J. (1988) 'Trachoma through History' *International Ophthalmology* 12.1: 9-14

Alston, R. (1995) *Soldier and Society in Roman Egypt: a Social History* (London)

Alston, R. (2001) 'Urban Population in Late Roman Egypt and the End of the Ancient World' in Scheidel, W. (ed.) *Debating Roman Demography* (Leiden) 161-204

Alston, R. (2002) *The City in Roman and Byzantine Egypt* (London)

Alston, R. and Alston, R. D. (1997) 'Urbanism and Urban Community in Roman Egypt' *JEg. Arch.* 83: 119-216

Amundsen, D. W. (1974) 'Romanticizing the Ancient Medical Profession: The Characterization of the Physician in the Graeco-Roman Novel' *Bulletin of the History of Medicine* 48: 320-37

Amundsen, D. W. and Ferngren, G. B. (1978) 'The Forensic Role of Physicians in Ptolemaic and Roman Egypt' *Bulletin of the History of Medicine* 52.3: 336-53

Andorlini, I. (2007) 'Prescription and Practice in Greek Medical Papyri from Egypt' in Froschauer, H. and Römer, C. E. (eds) *Zwischen Magie und Wissenschaft: Ärzte und Heilkunst in den Papyri aus Ägypten* (Vienna) 23-34

Andorlini, I. (1993) 'L'appoto dei papiri alla conoscenze della scienza medica antica' *ANRW* II 37.1: 458-562

Appenzeller, O. et al. (2001) 'Neurology in Ancient Faces' *Journal of Neurological, Neurosurgery and Psychiatry* 70: 524-9

Arnst, C. B. (1990) 'Chirurgische Instrumente im Agyptischen Museum' *Forschungen und Berichte* 28: 23-33

Aufderheide, A. C. et al. (1998) *The Cambridge Encyclopedia of Human Paleopathology* (Cambridge)

Aufderheide, A. C. et al. (2003) 'Chemical Dietary Reconstruction of Greco-Roman Mummies at Egypt's Dakhleh Oasis' *Journal of the Society for the Study of Egyptian Antiquities* 30: 1-8

Aufderheide, A. C. et al. (2004) 'Mummification Practices at Kellis Site in Egypt's Dakhleh Oasis' *Journal of the Society for the Study of Egyptian Antiquities* 31: 63-86

Bagnall, R. S. (1993) *Egypt in Late Antiquity* (Princeton)

Bagnall, R. S. (ed.) (1999) *The Kellis Agricultural Account Book (P. Kell.IV Gr.96)* (Oxford)

Bagnall, R. S. (2001) 'Archaeological Work on Hellenistic and Roman Egypt, 1995-2000' *AJArch.* 105.2: 227-43

Bagnall, R. S. (ed.) (2009) *The Oxford Handbook of Papyrology* (Oxford)

Bagnall, R. S. and Cribiore, R. (2006) *Women's Letters from Ancient Egypt 300 BC- AD 800* (Ann Arbor)

Bagnall, R. S. and Davoli, P. (2011) 'Archaeological Work on Hellenistic and Roman Egypt, 2000-2009' *AJArch.* 115: 103-57

Bagnall, R. S. and Frier, B. W. (1994) *The Demography of Roman Egypt* (Cambridge)

Bagnall, R. S. and Rathbone, D. W. (2004) *Egypt: from Alexander to the Copts* (London)

Baillet, J. (1926) *Les inscriptions grecques et latines des tombeaux des rois au syringes à Thèbes* (3 volumes) (Cairo)

Bain, D. (1994) 'Some Unpublished Cyranidean Material in Marc. Gr. 512 (678): Three Addenda to Meschini' *ZPE* 104: 36-42

Bain, D. (1996) 'The Application of Leeches in the "Cyranides"' *Mnemosyne* 49.2: 182-4

Baker, P. A. (2002) 'Diagnosing Some Ills: the Archaeology, Literature and History of Roman Medicine' in Baker, P. A. and Carr, G. (eds) *Practitioners, Practices and Patients* (Oxford) 16-29

Baker, P. A. (2004a) *Medical Care for the Roman Army on the Rhine, Danube and British Frontiers from the First through Third Centuries AD* (BAR International Series 1286) (Oxford)

Baker, P. A. (2004b) 'Roman Medical Instruments: Archaeological Interpretations of their Possible "Non-functional Uses"' *Journal for the Social History of Medicine* 17: 3-21

Baker, P. A. (2009) 'Medicine, Death and Military Virtues' in Marco Simón, F., Pino Polo, F. and Remesal Rodríguez, J. (eds) *Formae Mortis: El Tránsito de la Vida a la Muerte en las Sociedades Antiguas* (Barcelona) 25-37

Baker, P. A. (2010) *Medical Practices in Roman Spain: Report on a Pilot Study of the Archaeological Remains of Medical Tools* (California)

Baker, P. A. and Carr, G. (eds) (2002) *Practitioners, Practices and Patients* (Oxford)

Balsdon, J. P. V. D. (1979) *Romans and Aliens* (London)

Barrett, J. C. (1997) 'Romanization: a Critical Comment' in Mattingly, D. J. (ed.) *Dialogues in Roman Imperialism: Power, Discourse and Discrepant*

Experience in the Roman Empire (Portsmouth) 51-66

Bartsch, S. (1989) *Decoding the Ancient Novel: The Reader and the Role of Description in Heliodorus and Achilles Tatius* (Princeton)

Bazzana, G. B. (2009) 'Early Christian Missionaries: Healing and its Cultural Value in the Greco-Roman Context' *New Testament* 51.3: 232-51

Beagon, M. (1992) *Roman Nature: the Thought of Pliny the Elder* (Oxford)

Bernal, M. (1987) *Black Athena: The Afroasiatic Roots of Classical Civilization, I: The Fabrication of Ancient Greece 1785-1985* (New Brunswick)

Bernal, M. (1992) 'Animadversions on the Origins of Western Science' *Isis* 83: 596-607

Bernal, M. (1994) 'Response to Robert Palter' *History of Science* 32: 445-68

Bernand, A. (1972) *Le Paneion d'el-Kanaïs: Les inscriptions grecques* (Leiden)

Betz, H. D. (ed.) (1992) *The Greek Magical Papyri in Translation* (Chicago)

Bingen, J. *et al.* (1992) *Mons Claudianus, Ostraca Graeca et Latina I* (*O.Claud.*1-190), (Documents de fouilles de l'Institut français d'archéologie orientale 29) (Cairo)

Bingen, J. *et al.* (1997) *Mons Claudianus, Ostraca Graeca et Latina II* (*O.Claud.* 191-414) (Documents de fouilles de l'Institut français d'archéologie orientale 32) (Cairo)

Bonafante, L. (1997) 'Nursing Mothers in Classical Art' in Koloski-Ostrow, A. O. and Lyons, C. L. (eds) *Naked Truths: Women, Sexuality and Gender in Classical Art and Archaeology* (London) 174-98

Bonneau, D. (1964) *La crue du Nil: divinité égyptienne à travers mille ans d'histoire* (Paris)

Boon, G. C. (1983) 'Potters, Oculists and Eye-Troubles' *Britannia* 14: 1-12

Bowen, G. E. *et al.* (2005) 'Reconstructing Ancient Kellis' *Buried History* 41: 51-64

Bowersock, G. W. (1984) 'Roman Senators from the Near East: Syria, Judaea, Arabia, Mesopotamia' *Epigrafia e ordine senatorio* 2.5: 651-68

Bowman, A. K. (1976) 'Papyri and Roman Imperial History 1960-75' *JRS* 66: 153-73

Bowman, A. K. (1986) *Egypt after the Pharaohs 332 BC-AD 642: From Alexander to the Arab Conquest* (Berkeley)

Bowman, A. K. and Rathbone, D. (1992) 'Cities and Administration in Roman Egypt' *JRS* 82: 107-27

Bradley, M. (2009) *Colour and Meaning in Ancient Rome* (Cambridge)

Bradley, M. (ed.) (2010) *Classics and Imperialism in the British Empire* (Cambridge)

Brashear, W. M. (1995) 'The Greek Magical Papyri: an Introduction and Survey; Annotated Bibliography (1928-1994) *ANRW* II 18.5: 3380-684

Brewster, E. H. (1927) 'A Weaver of Oxyrhynchus: Sketch of a Humble Life in Roman Egypt' *TAPA* 58: 132-154

Burford, A. (1969) *The Greek Temple Builders at Epidauros: A Social and Economic Study of the Building in the Asklepian Sanctuary during the Fourth and Early Third Centuries BC* (Liverpool)

Burke, P. F. (1996) 'Malaria in the Greco-Roman World: a Historical and Epidemiological Survey' *ANRW* II 37.3: 2252-81

Callaway, E. (2010) 'Ancient DNA Reveals Ingredients of Roman Medicines' *Nature* (http://blogs.nature.com/news/2010/09/roman_pills.html, accessed 9th September 2010)

Cappers, R. T. J. (1998) 'A Botanical Contribution to the Analysis of Subsistence and Trade at Berenike (Red Sea Coast, Egypt)' in Kaper, O. E. (ed.) *Life on the Fringe: Living in the Southern Egyptian Deserts During the Roman and Early Byzantine Periods* (Leiden) 75-86

Cappers, R. T. J. (1999) 'Trade and Subsistence at the Roman Port of Berenike, Red Sea Coast, Egypt' in van der Veen, M. (ed.) *The Exploitation of Plant Resources in Ancient Africa* (New York) 185-98

Cappers, R. T. J. (2006) *Roman Foodprints at Berenike: Archaeobotanical Evidence of Subsistence and Trade in the Eastern Desert of Egypt* (Los Angeles)

Capponi, L. (2005) *Augustan Egypt: the Creation of a Roman Province* (London)

Cassar, P. (1974) 'Surgical Instruments on a Tomb Slab in Roman Malta' *Medical History* 18.1: 89-93

Casson, L. (1989) *The Periplus Maris Erythraei* (Princeton)

Charlier, P. (2007) 'Review of Hirt Raj (2006)' *Bryn Mawr Classical Review* 2007.10.32

Ciaraldi, M. (2002) 'The Interpretation of Medicinal Plants in the Archaeological Context: Some Case Studies from Pompeii' in Arnott, R. (ed.) *The Archaeology of Medicine* (BAR International Series 1046) (Oxford) 81-5

Clarysse, W. and Thompson, D. J. (2006) *Counting the People in Hellenistic Egypt* (2 volumes) (Cambridge)

Cleland, L. *et al.* (2007) *Greek and Roman Dress from A to Z* (London)

Cockitt, J. and David, R. (2010) *Pharmacy and Medicine in Ancient Egypt* (BAR International Series 2141) (Oxford)

Coenen, M. (2000) 'The Funerary Papyri of the Bodleian Library at Oxford' *JEg. Arch.* 86: 81-98

Collins, B. J. (2002) *A History of the Animal World in the Ancient Near East* (Leiden)

Colombini, M. P. *et al.* (2005) 'Characterisation of Organic Residues in Pottery Vessels of the Roman Age from Antinoe (Egypt)' *Microchemical Journal* 79.1-2: 83-90

Cook, M. *et al.* (1989) 'Fluorochrome Labelling in Roman Period Skeletons from Dakhleh Oasis, Egypt' *American Journal of Physical Anthropology* 80.2: 137-43

Corcoran, L. H. (1995) *Portrait Mummies from Roman Egypt* (Chicago)

Crawford, D. J. (1973) 'Garlic-growing and Agricultural Specialization in Graeco-Roman Egypt' *Chron. d'É* 48.2: 350-63

Cribiore, R. (2001) *Gymnastics of the Mind: Greek Education in Hellenistic and Roman Egypt* (Princeton)

Cruse, A. (2004) *Roman Medicine* (Stroud)

Curtis, R. I. (1983) 'In Defense of Garum' *CJ* 78: 232-40

Curtis, R. I. (1984) 'Salted Fish Products in Ancient Medicine' *Journ. Hist. Med.* 39.4: 430-45

Curtis, R. I. (1991) *Garum and Salsamenta: Production and Commerce in Materia Medica* (Leiden)

Cuvigny, H. (1992) 'Morts et maladies' in Bingen, J. *et al.* (eds) *Mons Claudianus Ostraca Graeca et Latina I* (*O.Claud.*1-190), (Documents de fouilles de l'Institut français d'archéologie orientale 29) (Cairo) 75-110

Cuvigny, H. (1996) 'The Amount of Wages Paid to the Quarry-workers at Mons Claudianus' *JRS* 86: 139-45

Cuvigny, H. (1997) 'Morts et maladies' in Bingen, J. *et al.* (eds) *Mons Claudianus Ostraca Graeca et Latina II* (*O.Claud.* 191-414) (Documents de fouilles de l'Institut français d'archéologie orientale 32) (Cairo) 191-223

Cuvigny, H. (2009) 'The Finds of Papyri: the Archaeology of Papyrology' in Bagnall, R. S. (ed.) *The Oxford Handbook of Papyrology* (Oxford) 30-58

Daniel, R. W. (1983) 'P. Mich. Inv. 6666: Magic' *ZPE* 50: 147-54

Dasen, V. (2008) 'Doctors in Roman Egypt' *CR* 58.2: 554-5

David, R. (2004) 'Rationality versus Irrationality in Egyptian Medicine in the Pharaonic and Graeco-Roman Periods' in Horstmanshoff, H. F. J. and Stol, M. (eds) *Magic and Rationality in Ancient Near Eastern and Graeco-Roman Medicine* (Leiden) 133-152

David, R. (2008) 'The Art of Healing in Ancient Egypt: a Scientific Reappraisal' *Lancet* 372: 1802-3

Davies, R. W. (1989) *Service in the Roman Army* (Edinburgh)

De Carolis, S. (2009) *Ars Medica: I ferri del mestiere* (Rimini)

Delia, D. (1988) 'The Population of Roman Alexandria' *TAPA* 118: 275-92

Delia, D. (1992) 'From Romance to Rhetoric: the Alexandrian Library in Classical and Islamic Traditions' *American Historical Review* 97: 1449-67

Devijver, H. (1974) 'The Roman Army in Egypt (With Special Reference to the *Militiae Equestres*)' *ANRW* II.1: 452-492

Dillery, J. (1999) 'The First Egyptian Narrative History: Manetho and Greek Historiography' *ZPE* 127: 93-116

Dollfus, M. A. (1967) 'L'ophtalmologie dans l'ancienne Égypte' *Bulletin de la Société Française d'Egyptologie* 49: 12-23

Doxiadis, E. (1995) *The Mysterious Fayum Portraits: Faces from Ancient Egypt* (London)

Drabkin, I. E. (1943) 'On Medical Education in Greece and Rome' *Bulletin of the History of Medicine* 15: 333-51

Dueck, D. (2000) *Strabo of Amasia: a Greek Man of Letters in Augustan Rome* (London)

Dunand, F. and Zivie-Coche, C. (2004) *Gods and Men in Egypt 3000 BCE to 395 CE* (Cornell)

Duncan-Jones, R. (2002) *Structure and Scale in the Roman Economy* (Cambridge)

Dupras, T. L. *et al.* (2001) 'Infant Feeding and Weaning Practices in Roman Egypt' *American Journal of Physical Anthropology* 115: 204-12

Edelstein, L. (1945) *Asclepius: a Collection and Interpretation of Testimonies* (Baltimore)

Edwards, C. and Woolf, G. (eds) (2006) *Rome the Cosmopolis* (Cambridge)

El-Saghir, M. (1986) *Le camp romain de Louqsor: Avec une étude des graffites gréco-romains du temple d'Amon* (Paris)

Epplett, C. (2001) 'The Capture of Animals by the Roman Military' *Greece and Rome* 48.2: 210–22

Evans, J. (1961) 'A Social and Economic History of an Egyptian Temple in the Greco Roman Period' *YClS* 17: 143-283

Fagan, G. G. (2002) *Bathing in Public in the Roman World* (Michigan)

Fahmy, A. G. E. (1997) 'Evaluation of the Weed Flora of Egypt from Predynastic to Graeco-Roman Times' *Vegetation History and Archaeobotany* 6.4: 241-7

Fairgrieve, S. I. and Molto, J. E. (2000) 'Cribra Orbitalia in Two Temporally Disjunct Population Samples from the Dakhleh Oasis, Egypt' *American Journal of Physical Anthropology* 111: 319-31

Faraone, C. A. (1992) *Talismans and Trojan Horses: Guardian Statues in Ancient Greek Myth and Ritual* (Oxford)

Fearn, D. (2010) 'Imperial Fragmentation and the Discovery of Bacchylides' in Bradley, M. (ed.) *Classics and Imperialism in the British Empire* (Cambridge) 158-85

Feugère, M. *et al.* (1985) 'Les aiguilles à cataracte de Monbellet (Saône-et-Loire). Contribution à l'étude de l'ophthalmologie antique et islamique' *Jahrbuch des Römische-Germanischen Zentralmuseums* 32: 436-508

Fewster, P. (2002) 'Bilingualism in Roman Egypt' in Adams, J. N. *et al.* (eds) *Bilingualism in Ancient Society: Language Contact and the Written Text* (Oxford) 220-45

Fournet, J. L. (2009) 'The Multilingual Environment of Late Antique Egypt: Greek, Latin, Coptic and Persian Documentation' in Bagnall, R. S. (ed.) *The Oxford Handbook of Papyrology* (Oxford) 418-51

Frankfurter, D. (1998) *Religion in Roman Egypt: Assimilation and Resistance* (Princeton)

Frankfurter, D. (2003) 'Syncretism and the Holy Man in Late Antique Egypt' *Journal of Early Christian Studies* 11.3: 339-85

Frankfurter, D. (2006) 'Fetus Magic and Sorcery Fears in Roman Egypt' *GRBS* 46: 37-62

Fraser, P. M. (1972) *Ptolemaic Alexandria* (3 volumes) (Oxford)

Frembgen, J. W. (2004) 'The Scorpion in Muslim Folklore' *Asian Folklore Studies* 63: 95-123

Froschauer, H. and Römer, C. E. (eds) (2007) *Zwischen Magie und Wissenschaft : Ärzte und Heilkunst in den Papyri aus Ägypten* (Vienna)

Ghaliangui, P. (1963) *Magic and Medical Science in Ancient Egypt* (London)

Germer, R. (1993) 'Ancient Egyptian Pharmaceutical Plants and the Eastern Mediterranean' in Jacob, I. and Jacob, W. (eds) *The Healing Past: Pharmaceuticals in the Biblical and Rabbinic World* (Leiden) 69-80

Gibbins, D.J.L. (1988) 'Surgical instruments from a Roman shipwreck off Sicily' *Antiquity* 62: 294-7

Gilhus, I. S. (2006) *Animals, Gods and Humans: Changing Attitudes to Animals in Greek, Roman and Early Christian Ideas* (Oxford)

Glare, P. (1994) 'The Temple of Jupiter Capitolinus at Arsinoe and the Imperial Cult' in Bülow-Jacobsen, A. (ed.) *Proceedings of the 20th International Congress of Papyrologists* (Copenhagen) 550-5

Goddio, F. (2007) *The Topography and Excavation of Heracleion-Thonis and East Canopus (1996-2006)* (Oxford)

Gordon, R. L. (1995) 'The Healing Event in Graeco-Roman Medicine' *Clio Medica* 27: 363-76

Greenwood, D (1993) 'Wound Healing: Honey for Superficial Wounds and Ulcers' *Lancet* 341: 90-1

Grmek, M. D. and Gourevitch, D. (1998) *Les maladies dans l'art antique* (Paris)

Haimov-Kochman, R. *et al.* (2005) 'Reproduction Concepts and Practices in Ancient Egypt Mirrored by Modern Medicine' *European Journal of Obstetrics and Gynaecology and Reproductive Biology* 123: 3-8

Halliday, W. R. (1921) 'Snake Stones' *Folklore* 32.4: 262-71

Hanson, A. E. (1985) 'Papyri of Medical Content' *YClS* 28: 25-47

Hanson, A. E. (1995) 'Uterine Amulets and Greek Uterine Medicine' *Medicina nei secoli: Arte e scienza* 7: 281-99

Hanson, A. E. (1998) 'Talking Recipes in the Gynaecological Texts of the Hippocratic Corpus' in Wyke, M. (ed.) (1998) *Parchments of Gender: Deciphering the Bodies of Antiquity* (Oxford) 71-94

Hanson, A. E. (2001) 'Text and Context for the Illustrated Herbal from Tebtunis' *XXII Congresso Internazionale di Papirologia* 585-604

Hanson, A. E. (2005) 'Greek Medical Papyri from the Fayum Village of Tebtunis: Patient Involvement in a Local Healthcare System?' in van der Eijk, P. (ed.) *Hippocrates in Context* (Leiden) 387-402

Harris, W. V. and Ruffini, G. (2004) *Ancient Alexandria Between Egypt and Greece* (Leiden)

Hartog, F. (1988) *The Mirror of Herodotus* (tr. J. Lloyd) (Berkeley)

Heinrichs, A. (1968) 'Vespasian's Visit to Alexandria' *ZPE* 3: 51-80

Hendry, M. (1995) 'Rouge and Crocodile Dung: Notes on Ovid, Ars 3.199–200 and 269–70' *CQ* 45.2: 583-88

Hirt Raj, M. (2006) *Médicins et malades de l'Égypte romaine* (Leiden)

Hobson, D. W. (1983) 'Women as Property Owners in Roman Egypt' *TAPA* 113: 311-21

Hobson, D. W. (1985) 'House and Household in Roman Egypt' *YClS* 28: 211-29

Holland, B. K. (ed.) (1996) *Prospecting for Drugs in Ancient and Medieval Texts: a Scientific Approach* (Amsterdam)

Hope, C. A. (1997) 'The Dakhleh Oasis Project' in Bagnall, R. S. (ed.) *The Kellis Agricultural Account Book* (Oxford) 5-14

Hopkins, K. (1980) 'Brother-Sister Marriage in Roman Egypt' *Society for Comparative Studies in Society and History* 22: 303-54

Horsley, G. H. R. (1982) *New Documents Illustrating Early Christianity* (North Ryde)

Horstmanshoff, H. F. J. and Stol, M. (eds) (2004) *Magic and Rationality in Ancient Near Eastern and Graeco-Roman Medicine* (Leiden)

Houston, G. W. (2009) 'Papyrological Evidence for Book Collections and Libraries in the Roman Empire' in Johnson, W. A. and Parker, H. N. (eds) *Ancient Literacies: the Culture of Reading in Greece and Rome* (Oxford) 233-67

Huebner, S. R. (2007) ''Brother-Sister' Marriage in Roman Egypt: a Curiosity of Humankind or a Widespread Family Strategy?' *JRS* 97: 21-49

Ikram, S. (2003) 'Barbering the Beardless: A Possible Explanation for the Tufted. Hairstyle Depicted. in the 'Fayum' Portrait of a Young Boy (J.P. Getty 78.AP.262)' *JEg. Arch.* 89: 247-51

Isaac, B. (2004) *The Invention of Racism in Classical Antiquity* (Princeton)

Jackson, R. B. (2002) *At Empire's Edge: Exploring Rome's Egyptian Frontier* (Yale)

Jackson, R. P. J. (1988) *Doctors and Diseases in the Roman Empire* (London)

Jackson, R. P. J. (1990) 'Roman Doctors and their Instruments: Recent Research into Ancient Practice' *JRA* 3: 5-27

Jackson, R. P. J. (1993) 'Roman Medicine: the Practitioners and their Practices' *ANRW* II.37.1 79-101

Jackson, R. P. J. (1996) 'Eye Medicine in the Roman Empire' *ANRW* II.37.3 2228-51

Jackson, R. P. J. (2003) 'The Domus "del chirurgo" at Rimini: an Interim Account of the Medical Assemblage' *JRA* 16.1: 312-21

Jackson, R. P. J. (2009) 'Lo strumentario chirurgico della domus riminise' in De Carolis, S. (ed.) *Ars Medica: I ferri del mestiere* (Rimini) 73-92

Jashemski, W. F. (1995) 'Roman Gardens in Tunisia' *AJArch.* 99: 559-76

Johnson, H. M. (2005) 'Fish Bile and Cautery: Trachoma Treatment in Art' *Journal of the Royal Society of Medicine* 98: 30-2

Johnson, J. H. (ed.) (1992) *Life in a Multi-cultural Society: Egypt from Cambyses to Constantine and Beyond* (Chicago)

Johnson, W. A. and Parker, H. N. (eds) (2009) *Ancient Literacies: the Culture of Reading in Greece and Rome* (Oxford)

Kaimikis, D. (1976) *Die Kyraniden* (Meisenheim)

Kaper, O. E. (ed.) (1998) *Life on the Fringe: Living in the Southern Egyptian Deserts during the Roman and Early Byzantine Periods* (Leiden)

Kaper, O. E. (ed.) (2006) *Treasures of the Dakhleh Oasis* (Leiden)

Kayser, F. (1994) *Recueil des inscriptions grecques et latines (non funéraires) d'Alexandrie impériale* (Ier-IIIe s. apr. J. C.) (Cairo)

Knight, M. (2001) 'Curing Cut or Ritual Mutilation: Some Remarks on the Practice of Female and Male Circumcision in Graeco-Roman Egypt' *Isis* 92.2: 317-36

König, J. and Whitmarsh, T. (eds) (2007) *Ordering Knowledge in the Roman Empire* (Cambridge)

Koloski-Ostrow, A. O. and Lyons, C. L. (eds) (2000) *Naked Truths: Women, Sexuality and Gender in Classical Art and Archaeology* (London)

Krause, J. and Witschel, C. (eds) *Die Stadt in der Spätantike-Niedergang oder Wandel?* (Stuttgart)

Kudlien, F. (1976) 'Medicine as a "liberal art" and the Question of the Physician's Income' *Journ. Hist. Med.* 31.4: 448-59

Kuhrt, A. (1995) *The Ancient Near East c. 3000-330 BC* (London)

Künzl, E. (1983) 'Medizinische Instrumente aus Sepulkralfunden der Römischen Kaiserzeit' *Bonner Jahrb.* 182: 1-131

Künzl, E. (1988) 'Archaeology and the History of Medicine: Basic Questions of Methodology' in Habrich, C. and Wilmanns, J. C. (eds) *Actes du 3ème Colloque des conservateurs des musées d'histoire des sciences médicales* (Lyon) 27-34

Lane, L. D. (1999) 'Malaria: Medicine and Magic in the Roman World' in Soren, D. and Soren, N. (eds) *A Roman Villa and Late Roman Infant Cemetery: Excavation at Poggio Gramignano, Lugnano in Teverina* (Teverina) 633-49

Laskaris, J. (2008) 'Nursing Mothers in Greek and Roman Medicine' *AJArch.* 112: 459-64

Leith, D. (2006) 'The Antinoopolis Illustrated Herbal (*PJohnson* + *PAntin.* 3.214 = MP3 2095)' *ZPE* 156: 141-56

Leven, K-H. (2004) '"At Times These Ancient Facts Seem to Lie Before Me Like a Patient on a Hospital Bed" - Retrospective Diagnosis and Ancient Medical History' in Horstmanshoff, H. F. J. and Stol, M. (eds) *Magic and Rationality in Ancient Near Eastern and Graeco-Roman Medicine* (Leiden) 369-86

Levick, B. (1999) *Vespasian* (London)

Levine, M. M. (1992) 'The Use and Abuse of Black Athena' *American Historical Review* 97: 440-60

Lewis, N. (1970) '"Greco-Roman Egypt": Fact or Fiction?' *Proc. XII Int. Congr. Pap.* 3-14, reprinted in Lewis, N. (1995) On *Government and Law: Collected Essays of Naphtali Lewis* (Atlanta) 138-49

Lewis, N. (1982) *The Compulsory Public Services of Roman Egypt* (Florence)

Lewis, N. (1984) 'The Romanity of Roman Egypt: a Growing Consensus' *Atti. XVII Congr. Int. Pap.* 1077-84, reprinted in Lewis, N. (1995) On *Government and Law: Collected Essays of Naphtali Lewis* (Atlanta) 298-305

Lewis, N. (1995) On *Government and Law: Collected Essays of Naphtali Lewis* (Atlanta)

Lichtenburg, R. (1998) 'Vie, Maladies, Mort et Momification sur le Limes' in Kaper, O. E. (ed.) (1998) *Life on the Fringe: Living in the Southern Egyptian Deserts During the Roman and Early Byzantine Periods* (Leiden) 117-27

LiDonnici, L. R. (2002) 'Bears, Fleawort, and the Blood of a Hamadryas Baboon: Recipe Ingredients in Greco-Roman Magical Materials' in Mirecki, P. and Meyer, M. (eds) *Magic and Ritual in the Ancient World* (Leiden) 359-77

Littman, R. J. (1996) 'Medicine in Alexandria' *ANRW* II.37.3: 2678-708

Lloyd, A. B. (1975-88) *Herodotus Book II* (Leiden)

Lloyd, A. B. (1982) 'The Inscription of Udjahorresnet a Collaborator's Testament' *JEg. Arch.* 68: 166-80

Lloyd, A. B. (1988) 'Herodotus' Account of Pharaonic Egypt' *Historia* 37: 22-53

Longrigg, J. (1993) *Greek Rational Medicine: Philosophy and Medicine from Alcmaeon to the Alexandrians* (London)

MacKinney, L. C. (1946) 'Animal Substances in Materia Medica: a Study in the Persistence of the Primitive' *Journ. Hist. Med.* 1.1: 149-70

MacKinnon, M. (2010) 'Sick as a Dog? Zooarchaeological Evidence for Pet Dog Health and Welfare in the Roman World' *World Archaeology* 42.2: 390-409

MacLeod, R. (2000) *The Library of Alexandria: Centre of Learning in the Ancient World* (London)

Mairs, R. (2010) 'Egyptian 'Inscriptions' and Greek 'Graffiti' at El-Kanais (Egyptian Eastern Desert)' in Baird, J. and Taylor, C. (eds) *Ancient Graffiti in Context* (London) 153-64

Manniche, L. (1989) *An Ancient Egyptian Herbal* (Austin)

Marganne, M. (1981) *Inventaire analytique des papyrus grecs de medicine* (Geneva)

Marganne, M. (1987) 'Les Instruments Chirurgicaux de l'Égypt Gréco-Romain' *Archéologie et Médecine. VIIe Rencontres Internationales d'Archéologie et d'Histoire d'Antibes* 403-12

Marganne, M. (1994) *L'Ophtalmologie dans l'Egypte greco-romaine d'apres les papyrus litteraires grecs* (Leiden)

Marganne, M. (1996) 'La médicine dans l'Égypte romaine: les sources et les methodes' *ANRW* II.37.3: 2709-2740

Marganne, M. (1998) *La Chirurgie dans l'Egypte greco-romaine d'apres les papyrus grecs* (Leiden)

Marganne, M. (2002) 'L'école médicale'' d'Alexandrie et son influence sur la médecine de L'Égypte gréco-romaine' *Medicina nei secoli: Arte e scienza* 14.2: 359-82

Mattern, S. P. (1999) 'Physicians and the Roman Imperial Aristocracy: the Patronage of Therapeutics' *Bulletin of the History of Medicine* 73.1: 1-18

Mattern, S. P. (2008) *Galen and the Rhetoric of Healing* (Baltimore)

Mattingly, D. J. (1996) 'First Fruit? The Olive in the Roman World' in Shipley, G. and Salmon, J. (eds) *Human Landscapes in Classical Antiquity: Environment and Culture* (London) 213-53

Mattingly, D. J. (ed.) (1997) *Dialogues in Roman Imperialism: Power, Discourse and Discrepant Experience in the Roman Empire* (Portsmouth)

Mattingly, D. J. (1997a) 'Introduction: Dialogues of Power and Experience in the Roman Empire' in Mattingly, D. J. (ed.) *Dialogues in Roman Imperialism: Power, Discourse and Discrepant Experience in the Roman Empire* (Portsmouth) 7-26

Mattingly, D. J. (1997b) 'Africa: a Landscape of Opportunity?' in Mattingly, D. J. (ed) *Dialogues in Roman Imperialism: Power, Discourse and Discrepant Experience in the Roman Empire* (Portsmouth) 117-42

Maxfield, V. and Peacock, D. (eds) (2001) *The Roman Imperial Quarries: Survey and Excavation at Mons Porphyrites 1994-1998* (London)

McKenzie, J. S. *et al.* (2004) 'Reconstructing the Serapeum in Alexandria from the Archaeological Evidence' *JRS* 94: 73-121

McLeod, A. M. (1969)'Physiology and Medicine in a Greek Novel' *JHS* 89: 97-105

Meier, C. (2003) *Healing Dream and Ritual: Ancient Incubation and Modern Psychotherapy* (Einsiedeln)

Merkelbach, R. (1994) 'Immortality Rituals in Late Antiquity' *Diogenes* 165.42.1: 85-109

Meyboom, P. G. P. (1995) *The Nile Mosaic of Palestrina: Early Evidence of Egyptian Religion in Italy* (Leiden)

Miles, S. H. (2005) *The Hippocratic Oath and the Ethics of Medicine* (Oxford)

Millar, F. (1993) *The Roman Near East: 31 BC-AD 337* (Cambridge)

Miller, J. I. (1969) *The Spice Trade of the Roman Empire 29 BC-AD 641* (Oxford)

Mills, A. J. (1997) 'The Dakhleh Oasis Project' in Bagnall, R. S. (ed.) *The Kellis Agricultural Account Book* (Oxford) 1-3

Milne, J. S. (1907) *Surgical Instruments in Greek and Roman Times* (London)

Mors, W. B. *et al.* (2000) 'Plant Natural Products Active Against Snake Bite - the Molecular Approach' *Phytochemistry* 55: 627-42

Moss, G. A. (2002) 'The Essenes' Sister Sect in Egypt: Another Medical Site?' *Journal of the Royal Society for the Promotion of Health* 122: 256-65

Murphy, T. (2004) *Pliny the Elder's Natural History: the Empire in the Encyclopedia* (Oxford)

Murray, G. W. (1925) 'The Roman Roads and Stations in the Eastern Desert of Egypt' *JEg. Arch.* 11: 138-50

Nerlich, A. G. *et al.* (2008) 'Plasmodium Falciparum in Ancient Egypt' *Emerging Infectious Diseases* 14.8: 1317-19

Nimis, S. (2004) 'Egypt in Greco-Roman History and Fiction' *Alif: Journal of Comparative Poetics* 24: 34-67

Notis, M. R. and Shugar, A. N. (2003) 'Roman Shears: Metallography, Composition and a Historical Approach to Investigation' *Archaeometallurgy in Europe* 1: 109-18

Nunn, J. F. (1996) *Ancient Egyptian Medicine* (London)

Nutton, V. (1969) 'Medicine and the Roman Legions: a Further Reconsideration' *Medical History* 13.3: 260-70

Nutton, V. (1971a) 'L. Gellius Maximus, Physician and Procurator' *CQ* 21.1: 262-72

Nutton, V. (1971b) 'Two Notes on Immunities: *Digest* 27, 1, 6, 10, and 11' *JRS* 61: 52-63

Nutton, V. (1972) 'Ammianus and Alexandria' *Clio Medica* 7:165-176

Nutton, V. (1977) '*Archiatri* and the Medical Profession in Antiquity' *PBSR* 55: 191-226

Nutton, V. (1985a) 'The Drug Trade in Antiquity' *Journal of the Royal Society of Medicine* 78: 138-45

Nutton, V. (1985b) 'Murders and Miracles: Lay Attitudes towards Medicine in Classical Antiquity' in Porter, R. (ed.) *Patients and Practitioners: Lay Perceptions of Medicine in Pre-Industrial Society* (Cambridge) 23-54

Nutton, V. (1992) 'Healers in the Medical Market Place: Towards a Social History of Graeco-Roman Medicine' in Wear, A. (ed.) *Medicine in Society: Historical Essays* (Cambridge) 15-58

Nutton, V. (1993a) 'Galen and Egypt' in Kollesch, J. and Nickel, D. (eds) *Galen und das hellenistische Urbe* (Stuttgart) 11-31

Nutton, V. (1993b) 'Roman Medicine: Tradition, Confrontation, Assimilation' *ANRW* II.37.1 49-78

Nutton, V. (2004) *Ancient Medicine* (London)

Nutton, V. (2007) 'Greco-Roman Medicine and the Greek Papyri' in Froschauer, H. and Römer, C. E. (eds) *Zwischen Magie und Wissenschaft: Ärzte und Heilkunst in den Papyri aus Ägypten* (Vienna) 5-12

Olson, K. (2009) 'Roman Cosmetics: Substance, Remedy, Poison' *Classical World* 102.3: 291-310.

Opper, T. (2008) *Hadrian: Empire and Conflict* (Cambridge)

Palmieri, N. (ed.) (2003) *Rationnel et irrationnel dans la médecine ancienne et médiévale: aspects historiques, scientifiques et culturels* (Saint-Etienne)

Palter, R. (1993) 'Black Athena, Afro-centrism, and the History of Science' *History of Science* 31: 227-87

Panagiotakopulu, E. (2004) 'Dipterous Remains and Archaeological Interpretation' *Journal of Archaeological Science* 31.12: 1675-84

Panagiotakopulu, E. and Buckland, P. (2009) 'Environment, Insects and the Archaeology of Egypt' in Ikbram, S. and Dodson, A. (eds) *Beyond the Horizon: Studies in Egyptian Art, Archaeology and History in Honour of Barry J. Kemp* (Cairo) 347-60

Pardon, M. (2005) 'Celsus and the Hippocratic Corpus: the Originality of a "Plagiarist"' in van der Eijk, P. (ed.) *Hippocrates in Context* (Leiden) 403-12

Parker, G. (2002) 'Ex Oriente Luxuria: Indian Commodities and Roman Experience' *Journal of the Economic and Social History of the Orient* 45.1: 40-95

Peacock, D. P. S. and Maxfield, V. A. (eds) (1997) *Survey and Excavation: Mons Claudianus 1987-1993* (Cairo)

Pease, A. S. (1940) 'Some Remarks on the Diagnosis and Treatment of Tuberculosis in Antiquity' *Isis* 31.2: 380-93

Petrie, W. M. F. (1911) *Roman Portraits and Memphis IV* (London)

Plantzos, D. (1997) 'Crystals and Lenses in the Graeco-Roman World' *AJArch.* 101.3: 451-64

Plazenet, L. (1995) 'Le Nil et son delta dans les romans grecs' *Phoenix* 49: 5-22

Pleket, H. W. (1995) The Social Status of Physicians in the Graeco-Roman World' *Clio Medica* 27: 27-34

Poole, F. (2001) 'Cumin, Set Milk, Honey: An Egyptian Medicine Container (Naples 828)' *JEg. Arch.* 87:175-80

Porter, R. (ed.) (1985) *Patients and Practitioners: Lay Perceptions of Medicine in Pre-Industrial Society* (Cambridge)

Postmes, T. *et al.* (1993) 'Honey for Wounds, Ulcers, and Skin Graft Preservation' *Lancet* 341: 756-7

Prioreschi, P. (1998) *A History of Medicine Volume III: Roman Medicine* (Omaha)

Rahman, K. and Lowe, G. M. (2006) 'Garlic and Cardiovascular Disease: a Critical Review' *Journal of Nutrition* 136: 736-40

Rathbone, D. (1991) *Economic Rationalism in Rural Society and Third Century AD Egypt* (Cambridge)

Rathbone, D. (1993) 'Egypt, Augustus and Roman Taxation' *Cahiers du Centre G. Glotz* 4: 81-112

Rathbone, D. (2003) 'Review' *Population Studies* 57.1: 115-16

Rathbone, D. W. (2007) 'Roman Egypt' in Scheidel, W. *et al.* (eds) (2007) *The Cambridge Economic History of the Greco-Roman World* (Cambridge) 698-719

Ray, J. D. (1975) '*Papyrus Carlsberg* 67: a Healing Prayer from the Fayum' *JEg. Arch.* 61: 181-88

Reardon, B. P. (ed.) (1989) *Collected Ancient Greek Novels* (Berkeley)

Remijsen, S. and Clarysse, W. (2008) 'Incest or Adoption? Brother-sister Marriage in Roman Egypt Revisited' *JRS* 98: 53-61

Rémy, B. (1984) 'Les inscriptions de médecins en Gaule' *Gallia* 42: 115-52

Rémy, B. (1987a) 'Nouvelles inscriptions de médecins dans les provinces occidentales de l'empire romain (1973-1983)' *Epigraphica* 49: 261-64

Rémy, B. (1987b) 'Les inscriptions de médecins dans la province romain de Bretagne, archéologie et medecine' *Actes de VII Rencontres Internationales*

d'Archéologie et d'Histoire d'Antibes 23-25: 69-94

Reymond, E. A. E. (1976) *A Medical Book from Crocodilopolis (P. Vindob. 6257). From the contents of the Suchos temples in the Fayyum, I* (Wien)

Ribechini, E. *et al.* (2008) 'Gas Chromatographic and Mass Spectrometric Investigations of Organic Residues from Roman Glass Unguentaria' *Journal of Chromatography* 1183.1-2: 158-69

Riddle, J. M. (1984) 'Gargilius Martialis as a Medical Writer' *Journ. Hist. Med.* 39: 408-29

Riddle, J. M. (1985) *Dioscorides on Pharmacy and Medicine* (Austin)

Riddle, J. M. (1993) 'High Medicine and Low Medicine in the Roman Empire' *ANRW* II.37.1 102-20

Riddle, J. M. (1996) 'The Medicines of Greco-Roman Antiquity as a Source of Medicines for Today' in Holland, B. K. (ed.) *Prospecting for Drugs in Ancient and Medieval Texts: a Scientific Approach* (Amsterdam) 7-18

Ritner, R. K. (1984) 'A Uterine Amulet in the Oriental Institute Collection' *Journal of Near Eastern Studies* 43: 209-21

Ritner, R. K. (1989) 'Horus on the Crocodiles: A Juncture of Religion and Magic in Late Dynastic Egypt' *Religion and Philosophy in Ancient Egypt* (Yale Egyptological Studies 3) 103-16

Ritner, R. K. (1995) 'Egyptian Magical Practice under the Roman Empire: the Demotic Spells and their Religious Context' *ANRW* II.18.5: 3333-79

Ritner, R. K. (1998) 'Egypt under Roman Rule: the Legacy of Ancient Egypt' in Petry, C. F. (ed.) *The Cambridge History of Egypt: Volume One: Islamic Egypt 640-1517* (Cambridge) 1-33

Ritner, R. K. (2000) 'Innovations and Adaptations in Ancient Egyptian Medicine' *Journal of Near Eastern Studies* 59.2: 107-17

Roberts, C. (2002) 'Palaeopathology and archaeology: the current state of play' in Arnott, R. (ed.) *The Archaeology of Medicine* (Oxford) 1-20

Roberts, C. H. (1950) 'An Army Doctor in Alexandria' in *Festschrift W. Schubart* (Leipzig) 112-5

Roesch, P. (1982) 'Médecins publics dans l'Egypte impériale' in Sabbah, G. (ed.) *Mémoires III: Médecins et Médecine dans l'Antiquité* (Saint-Étienne) 119-28

Römer, C. (1990) 'Ehrung für den Arzt Themison' *ZPE* 84: 81-8.

Rondot, V. (2004) *Tebtynis II: Le Temple de Soknebtynis et son Dromos* (Cairo)

Rowlandson, J. (1998) *Women and Society in Greek and Roman Egypt* (Cambridge)

Rowlandson, J. and Takahashi, R. (2009) 'Brother-Sister Marriage and Inheritance Strategies in Greco-Roman Egypt' *JRS* 99: 104-39

Sallares, R. (2002) *Malaria and Rome: a History of Malaria in Ancient Italy* (Oxford)

Samama, E. (2003) *Les médecins dans le monde grec: sources épigraphiques sur la naissance d'un corps médical* (Geneva)

Sauneron, S. (1970) *Le papyrus magique illustré de Brooklyn* (Brooklyn)

Scarborough, J. (1968) 'Roman Medicine and the Legions: a Reconsideration' *Medical History* 12.3: 254-61

Scarborough, J. (1969) *Roman Medicine* (London)

Scarborough, J. (1993) 'Roman Medicine to Galen' *ANRW* II.37.1: 3-48

Scheidel, W. (1995) 'Incest Revisited: Three Notes on the Demography of Sibling Marriage in Roman Egypt' *BASP* 32: 143-155

Scheidel, W. (1996a) 'Brother-Sister and Parent-Child Marriage outside Royal Families in Ancient Egypt and Iran: a Challenge to the Sociobiological View of Incest Avoidance?' *Ethology and Sociobiology* 17: 319-40

Scheidel, W. (1996b) *Measuring Age, Sex and Death in the Roman Empire: Explorations in Ancient Demography* (Michigan)

Scheidel, W. (2001a) *Death on the Nile: Disease and the Demography of Roman Egypt* (Leiden)

Scheidel, W. (2001b) *Debating Roman Demography* (Leiden)

Scheidel, W. (2003) 'Germs for Rome' in Edwards, C. and Woolf, G. (eds) *Rome the Cosmopolis* (Cambridge) 158-76

Scheidel, W. *et al.* (eds) (2007) *The Cambridge Economic History of the Greco-Roman World* (Cambridge)

Scott, N. E. (1951) 'The Metternich Stele' *The Metropolitan Museum of Art Bulletin* 9.8: 201-17

Shaw, B. D. (1992) 'Explaining Incest: Brother-sister Marriage in Graeco-Roman Egypt' *Man* 27.2: 267-99

Sherwin-White, A. N. (1966) *The Letters of Pliny: a Historical and Social Commentary* (Oxford)

Shipley, G. and Salmon, J. (eds) (1996) *Human Landscapes in Classical Antiquity: Environment and Culture* (London)

Sidebotham, S. E, (2011) *Berenike and the Ancient Maritime Spice Route* (Berkeley)

Sines, G. and Sakellarakis, Y. A. (1987) 'Lenses in Antiquity' *AJArch.* 91.2: 191-6

Smelik, K. A. D. and Hemelrijk, E. A. (1984) ''Who Knows What Monsters Demented Egypt Worships?' Opinions on Egyptian Animal Worship in Antiquity as Part of the Ancient Conception of Egypt' *ANRW* II.17.4: 1852-2000

Smith, D. E. (1977) 'The Egyptian Cults at Corinth' *Harv. Theol. Rev.* 70.3-4: 201-31

Smith, E. M. (1927) 'The Egypt of the Greek Romance' *CJ* 23: 531-7

Smith, W. (2003) *Archaeobotanical Investigations of Agriculture at late Antique Kom el-Nana (Tell el-Amarna)* (London)

Soren, D. and Soren, N. (eds) (1999) *A Roman Villa and Late Roman Infant Cemetery: Excavation at Poggio Gramignano, Lugnano in Teverina* (Teverina)

Southern, P. (2006) *The Roman Army: a Social and Institutional History* (California)

Stambaugh, J. E. (1972) *Sarapis Under the Early Ptolemies* (Leiden)

Stephens, S. A. and Winkler, J. J. (1995) *Ancient Greek Novels: The Fragments* (Princeton)

Sternberg-El Hotabi, H. (1999) *Untersuchungen zur Überlieferungsgeschichte der Horusstelen: Ein Beitrag zur Religionsgeschichte Agyptens* (Wiesbaden)

Stettler, A. (1982) 'Der Instrumentenschrank von Kom Ombo' *Antike Welt* 13.3: 48-53

Strouhal, E. and Jungwirth, J. (1980) 'Paleopathology of the Late Roman-Early Byzantine Cemeteries at Sayala, Egyptian Nubia' *Journal of Human Evolution* 9.1: 61-70

Sullivan, R. D. (1973) 'A Petition of Beekeepers at Oxyrhynchus' *BASP* 10.1-4: 5-13

Taubenschlag, R. (1944) *The Law of Greco-Roman Egypt in the Light of the Papyri 332 BC-640 AD* (New York)

Taylor, J. E. and Davies, P. R. (1998) 'The So-called Therapeutae of "De Vita Contemplativa": Identity and Character' *Harv. Theol. Rev.* 91.1: 3-24

Thompson, D. J. (1990) 'The High Priests of Memphis under Ptolemaic Rule' in Beard, M. and North, J. (eds) *Pagan Priests: Religion and Power in the Ancient World* (Ithaca) 95-116

Thompson, D. J. (2009) 'The Multilingual Environment of Persian and Ptolemaic Egypt: Egyptian, Aramaic, and Greek Documentation' in Bagnall, R. S. (ed.) *The Oxford Handbook of Papyrology* (Oxford) 395-417

Tower, P. (1963) 'The History of Trachoma: Military and Sociological Implications' *Archives of Ophthalmology* 69.1: 123-30

Toynbee, J. M. C. (1973) *Animals in Roman Life and Art* (London)

Tocheri, M. W. *et al.* (2005) 'Roman Period Fetal Skeletons from the East Cemetery (Kellis 2) of Kellis, Egypt' *International Journal of Osteology* 15: 326-41

Tod, M. N. (1939) 'The Scorpion in Graeco-Roman Egypt' *JEg. Arch.* 25.1: 55-61

Toynbee, J. M. C. (1973) *Animals in Roman Life and Art* (London)

Trinquier, J. (2002) '*Confusis Oculis Prosunt Uirentia* (Sénèque, *De ira*, 3, 9, 2): Les vertus magiques et hygiéniques du vert dans l'antiquité' in Villard, L. (ed.) *Couleurs et vision dans l'Antiquité classique* (Rouen) 97-128.

True, R. H. (1901) 'Folk Materia Medica', *Journal of American Folklore* 14.53: 105-14

Turner, E. G. (1952) 'Roman Oxyrhynchus' *JEg. Arch.* 38: 78-93

Vallance, J. (2000) 'Doctors in the Library: the Strange Tale of Apollonius the Bookworm and Other Stories' in MacLeod, R. (ed.) *The Library of Alexandria: Centre of Learning in the Ancient World* (London) 95-114

van der Eijk, P. J. (2004) 'Introduction' in Horstmanshoff, H. F. J. and Stol, M. (eds) *Magic and Rationality in Ancient Near Eastern and Graeco-Roman Medicine* (Leiden) 1-10 van der Eijk, P. J. (2005) *Medicine and Philosophy in Classical Antiquity: Doctors and Philosophers on Nature, Soul, Health and Disease* (Cambridge)

van der Veen, M. (1998a) 'A Life of Luxury in the Desert? The Food and Fodder Supply to Mons Claudianus' *JRA* 11: 101-16

van der Veen, M. (1998b) 'Gardens in the Desert' in Kaper, O. E. (ed.) *Life on the Fringe: Living in the Southern Egyptian Deserts During the Roman and Early Byzantine Periods* (Leiden) 221-42

van der Veen, M. (ed.) (1999) *The Exploitation of Plant Resources in Ancient Africa* (New York)

van Minnen, P. (1998) 'Boorish or Bookish? Literature in Egyptian Villages in the Fayum in the Graeco-Roman Period' *JJP* 28: 99-184

van Minnen (2000) 'Euergetism in Graeco-Roman Egypt' Mooren, L. (ed.) *Politics, Administration and Society in the Hellenistic and Roman World* (Leuven) 437-70

van Minnen, P. (2006) 'The Changing World of the Cities of Later Roman Egypt' in Krause, J. and Witschel, C. (eds) *Die Stadt in der Spätantike-Niedergang oder Wandel?* (Stuttgart) 153-80

Vassilika, E. (1994) 'Museum Acquisitions 1992: Egyptian Antiquities Accessioned in 1992 by Museums in the United Kingdom' *JEg. Arch.* 80: 179-81

Versluys, M. J. (2002) *Aegyptiaca Romana: Nilotic Scenes and the Roman Views of Egypt* (Leiden)

Visavadia, B. G. *et al.* (2008) 'Manuka Honey Dressing: an effective treatment for chronic wound infections' *British Journal of Oral Maxillofacial Surgery* 46.1: 55-6

von Staden, H. (1983) 'Hairesis and Heresy: the Case of the Hareseis Iatrikai' in Meyer, B. F. and Sanders, E. P. (eds) *Jewish and Christian Self-Definition III* (3 volumes) (Philadelphia) 76-100

von Staden, H. (1989) *Herophilus: The Art of Medicine in Early Alexandria* (Cambridge)

von Staden, H. (2003) 'Galen's Daimon: Reflections on irrational and rational' in Palmieri, N. (ed.) *Rationnel et irrationnel dans la médecine ancienne et médiévale: aspects historiques, scientifiques et culturels* (Saint-Etienne) 15-44

von Staden, H. (2004) 'Galen's Alexandria' in Harris, W. V. and Ruffini, G. (eds) *Ancient Alexandria Between Egypt and Greece* (Leiden) 179-216

Vout, C. (2006) 'Embracing Egypt' in Edwards, C. and Woolf, G. (eds) *Rome the Cosmopolis* (Cambridge) 177-203

Waegeman, M. (1987) *Amulet and Alphabet: Magical Amulets in the First Book of Cyranides* (Amsterdam)

Walker, S. (2000) 'Mummy Portraits and Roman Portraiture' in Walker, S. and Bierbrier, M. (eds) *Ancient Faces: Mummy Portraits from Roman Egypt* (London) 23-5

Walker, S. and Bierbrier, M. (eds) (2000) *Ancient Faces: Mummy Portraits from Roman Egypt* (London)

Webster, G. (1998) *The Roman Imperial Army of the First and Second Centuries AD* (London)

Wendrich, W. Z. *et al.* (2003) 'Berenike Crossroads: the Integration of Information' *Journal of the Economic and Social History of the Orient* 46.1: 46-87

Westermann, W. L. (1914) 'Apprentice Contracts and the Apprentice System in Roman Egypt' *CP* 9.3: 295-315

Whitehorne, J. E. G. (1980) 'New Light on Temple and State in Roman Egypt' *Journal of Religious History* 11: 218-26

Whitehouse, H. (1985) 'Shipwreck on the Nile: A Greek Novel on a 'Lost' Roman Mosaic?' *AJArch.* 89: 129-134

Wild, R. A. (1981) *Water in the Cultic Worship of Isis and Sarapis* (Leiden)

Winkler, J. J. (1989) 'Achilles Tatius: Leucippe and Clitophon' in Reardon, B. P. (ed.) (1989) *Collected. Ancient Greek Novels* (Berkeley) 170-284

Wyke, M. (ed.) (1998) *Parchments of Gender: Deciphering the Bodies of Antiquity* (Oxford)

Yeo, I. (2005) 'Hippocrates in the Context of Galen: Galen's Commentary on the Clarification of Fevers in Epidemics VI' in van der Eijk, P. (ed.) *Hippocrates in Context* (Leiden) 433-43

Young, G. K. (2001) *Rome's Eastern Trade: International Commerce and Imperial Policy 31 BC-AD 305* (London)

Youtie, L. C. (1976) 'A Medical Prescription for an Eye Salve' *ZPE* 23: 121-9

Youtie, L. C. (1977) '*O. Bodl.* 2.8182 and 2185' *BASP* 14.1: 39-43

Youtie, L. C. (1979) '*P. Grenf.* 1.52' *BASP* 16.1-2: 149-51

www.ingramcontent.com/pod-product-compliance
Lightning Source LLC
Chambersburg PA
CBHW061007030426
42334CB00033B/3395